HUMAN DEVELOPMENT
AND EDUCATION

HUMAN DEVELOPMENT
AND EDUCATION

by

Robert J. Havighurst

PROFESSOR OF EDUCATION
AND CHAIRMAN,
COMMITTEE ON HUMAN DEVELOPMENT
THE UNIVERSITY OF CHICAGO

DAVID McKAY COMPANY, INC.
NEW YORK

HUMAN DEVELOPMENT AND EDUCATION

Preface

THIS BOOK COMPLETES THE PROJECT that started with the plano-graphing of the writer's pamphlet on developmental tasks in 1948. Added to the material of that pamphlet are several practical and theoretical sections, which explain further the meaning of the developmental task concept for education.

In its present form the book should be most useful to advanced students as a basic reference for courses in Education, Educational Psychology, and Human Development.

Students in elementary courses in Education or Educational Psychology may get an overview of the developmental tasks of childhood and adolescence by reading Chapters 1, 2, 4, 9, 10, and 11, which can be read with understanding without reference to the rest of the book. To complete a view of the developmental tasks of the life cycle one should read Chapters 16, 17, and 18.

For readers interested in the school curriculum and in the evaluation of educational outcomes, Parts Two, Three, and Five will be especially useful. Parts Two and Three treat the developmental tasks as objectives of education, and give behavioral descriptions of success and failure in the developmental tasks of middle childhood and adolescence. Part Five describes an empirical test of some of the hypotheses about developmental tasks, and contains, in Chapter 19, a set of rating scales for estimating the achievement of developmental tasks at ages 10, 13, and 16, which will be useful to research workers.

For readers interested in child development and adolescent development, Parts One, Two, and Three will be most useful.

Chicago, Illinois   ROBERT J. HAVIGHURST
January, 1953

Contents

vii

Tables

HUMAN DEVELOPMENT
AND EDUCATION

CHAPTER 1

Life and Learning:
Introduction to the Developmental Task Concept

LIVING IS LEARNING, and growing is learning. One learns to walk, talk, and throw a ball; to read, bake a cake, and get along with agemates of the opposite sex; to hold down a job, to raise children; to retire gracefully when too old to work effectively, and to get along without a husband or wife who has been at one's side for forty years. These are all learning tasks. To understand human development, one must understand learning. The human individual learns his way through life.

The lower animals rely more than human beings do on maturation, or "doing what comes naturally," to meet the problems of growing up. Apparently, playing with a mouse comes naturally to a kitten, without learning, and so does the salmon's long journey back to the waters of his birth, and the ways of the ant to the young graduate from the larval stage to adult anthood. Human beings are not built this way, with almost fully developed action patterns emerging as their nerves and glands and muscles grow. Very little of human behavior is such a crude product of maturation unformed by learning.

Nature lays down wide possibilities in the developing of the human body, and which possibilities shall be realized depends on what the individual learns. This is true even of such crude biological realities as feeding habits and sexual relations, while the more highly social realities of language, economic behavior, and religion are almost completely the product of learning at the hands of society.

The path of learning is not one long slow uphill climb with something to learn every new day, but consists of steep places, where the learning effort is severe, interspersed with plateaus where one can speed along almost without effort. For instance, the little boy works hard to learn how to throw and catch a ball, but once he has mastered this skill he may coast along on it for years without further improvement. The little girl works hard to learn to form her letters into a neat feminine script. She learns this during the years from age five to ten, and then has mastered the task. In simple unchanging societies, the young adult has mastered most of the learning tasks of his life. He knows the solutions to most of life's problems. For him, learning is just about over. Not so in the modern changing society where social life changes so rapidly that the individual must continually learn to adapt himself to changed conditions.

Living in a modern society such as that of the U.S.A. is a long series of tasks to learn, where learning well brings satisfaction and reward, while learning poorly brings unhappiness and social disapproval.

The tasks the individual must learn—*the developmental tasks* of life—are those things that constitute healthy and satisfactory growth in our society. They are the things a person must learn if he is to be judged and to judge himself to be a reasonably happy and successful person. *A developmental task is a task which arises at or about a certain period in the life of the individual, successful achievement of which leads to his happiness and to success with later tasks, while failure leads to unhappiness in the individual, disapproval by the society, and difficulty with later tasks.*

The prototype of the developmental task is the purely biological formation of organs in the embryo. "In this development each organ has its time of origin and this time factor is as important as the place of origin. If the eye, for example, does not arise at the appointed time 'it will never be able to express itself fully, since the moment for the rapid outgrowth of some other part will have arrived, and this will tend to dominate the less active region, and suppress the belated tendency for eye expression.'

"After the organ has begun to arise at the right time, still another time factor determines the most critical stage of its development: 'A given organ must be interrupted during the early stage of its development in order to be completely suppressed or grossly modified. . . . After an organ has arisen successfully from the anlage, it may be lamed or runted, but its nature and actual existence can no longer be destroyed by interrupting the growth.'

"The organ which misses its time of ascendancy is doomed not only as an individual, it endangers at the same time the whole hierarchy of organs. 'Not only does the arrest of a rapidly budding part, therefore, tend to suppress its development temporarily, but the premature loss of supremacy to some other organ renders it impossible for the suppressed part to come again into dominance, so that it is permanently modified. . . .' The result of normal development is proper relationship of size and function among the body organs: The liver adjusted in size to the stomach and intestine, the heart and lungs properly balanced, and the capacity of the vascular system accurately proportioned to the body as a whole. Through developmental arrest one or more organs may become disproportionately small; this upsets functional harmony and produces a defective person." [1]

These purely biological developmental tasks of the body illustrate the essentials of the bio-socio-psychological tasks with which we are concerned. If the task is not achieved at the proper time it will not be achieved well, and failure in this task will cause partial or complete failure in the achievement of other tasks yet to come.

Consider the task of learning to talk, for example. Sometime between the ages of one and two most children master the essentials of human speech and language. They still have much to learn at the end of the second year, but they are well started. *They have learned to talk.* There is some evidence, from the few cases on record of children who were denied human companionship during their first few years of life and therefore did not learn to talk, that the task of learning to talk is extremely difficult and may never be accomplished well if it is not achieved in the second year of life. This is the crucial period for this particular task. And, if the task is

[1] Quoted from Erik Erikson, *Childhood and Society* (New York: W. W. Norton, 1950), pp. 61–62. Inner quotations taken by Erikson from C. H. Stockard, *The Physical Basis of Personality* (New York: W. W. Norton, 1931).

not learned, the failure will stand in the way of learning a series of later tasks which depend greatly upon language.

The Origin of Developmental Tasks

As the individual grows, he finds himself possessed of new physical and psychological resources. The infant's legs grow larger and stronger, enabling him to walk. The child's nervous system grows more complex, enabling him to reason more subtly and to understand the complexities of subjects such as arithmetic. The individual also finds himself facing new demands and expectations from the society around him. The infant is expected to learn to talk, the child to learn to subtract and divide.

These inner and outer forces contrive to set for the individual a series of developmental tasks which must be mastered if he is to be a successful human being.

Some tasks arise mainly from physical maturation, such as learning to walk, learning to behave acceptably to the opposite sex in adolescence, and (for women) adjusting to the menopause in middle life. Other tasks, arising primarily from the cultural pressure of society, are learning to read, and learning to participate as a socially responsible citizen in society.

There is a third source of developmental tasks—namely, the personal values and aspirations of the individual, which are part of his personality, or self. The personality, or self, emerges from the interaction of organic and environmental forces. As the self evolves, it becomes increasingly a force in its own right in the subsequent development of the individual. Already by the age of three or four the individual's self is effective in the defining and accomplishing of his developmental tasks.

Examples of tasks arising primarily from the personal motives and values of the individual are: choosing and preparing for an occupation, and achieving a scale of values and a philosophy of life.

Thus developmental tasks may arise from physical maturation, from the pressure of cultural processes upon the individual, from the desires, aspirations, and values of the emerging personality, and they arise in most cases from combinations of these factors acting together.

The Teachable Moment

There are two reasons why the concept of developmental tasks is useful to educators. First, it helps in discovering and stating the purposes of education in the schools. Education may be conceived as the effort of the society, through the school, to help the individual achieve certain of his developmental tasks.

The second use of the concept is in the timing of educational efforts. When the body is ripe, and society requires, and the self is ready to achieve a certain task, the teachable moment has come. Efforts at teaching which would have been largely wasted if they had come earlier, give gratifying results when they come at the *teachable moment,* when the task should be learned. For example, the best times to teach reading, the care of children, and adjustment to retirement from one's job can be discovered by studying human development, and finding out when conditions are most favorable for learning these tasks.

PART ONE

Infancy and Early Childhood

CHAPTER 2

Developmental Tasks of Infancy and Early Childhood

THIS CHAPTER will summarize and discuss the principal developmental tasks of infancy and early childhood. The number of developmental tasks is somewhat arbitrary, since it depends both upon the biosocial realities out of which the tasks arise and upon the refinement of analysis made by the writer. For example, the task of learning independent locomotion may be considered as one single complex task or as a group of smaller tasks, including creeping, standing, walking, running, jumping, and skipping.

For application of the concept to problems of education a coarse-grained analysis is desirable, resulting in some six to ten developmental tasks for a given age period.

Accordingly, the following series of developmental tasks of infancy and early childhood is presented as a list of broadly defined units, each of which could be broken down into smaller tasks.

1. LEARNING TO WALK

Sometime between the ages of nine and fifteeen months most children become biologically ready to walk. The bones, muscles, and nerves of their legs and trunk have developed to the point where they are equal to the task. The child then learns to walk, with varying amounts of stimulation and assistance from other people. Once the basic skills are mastered, he learns during later years to run, jump, and skip.

2. LEARNING TO TAKE SOLID FOODS

The baby's digestive system gradually grows ready to digest and assimilate a variety of foods, and his chewing apparatus develops to the point where he can handle solid foods during the second year of life. As his diet changes to include semisolid and solid food, he gradually ceases to use the earlier and profoundly important mechanism of sucking and nursing. The way the child is treated during the weaning period, the schedule on which he is fed, and the age and suddenness of weaning, all have profound effects upon his personality. There are great variations in the weaning and feeding development of children in different cultures, and these probably account in some degree for the characteristic personality differences of people of different cultures.

3. LEARNING TO TALK

Nature of the Task. To learn to make meaningful sounds and to communicate with other people through the use of these sounds.

Biological Basis. The nerves and muscles of the speaking apparatus are already fairly well developed at birth. The newborn child makes the vowel sounds *ă* (as in *add*) and *ĕ* (as in *eh*), the "back-consonants," *g, k, x,* and guttural sounds such as the German *ch* and the French *r*. Probably there is a further maturation of the equipment for speaking, but the limiting factor in learning to talk is not biological. The child is biologically ready well before he actually learns to talk.

Psychological Basis. There are two possible explanations of how babies acquire the ability to talk, in the human sense.[1] "One explanation is that the infant begins by accidentally uttering a variety of meaningless sounds. From these, *the people around him select* certain ones to repeat regularly in certain situations, until the child learns to 'associate' certain sounds with certain *situations.* To illustrate: the sound *ma-ma,* made accidentally by the child, is repeated by people when his *mother* is present. Furthermore,

[1] The following quotations are taken from Allison Davis and Robert J. Havighurst, *Father of the Man* (Boston: Houghton Mifflin, 1947), Chapter 11.

whenever he happens to utter this sound in the presence of his *mother,* she smiles and pays attention to him. Thus he learns to say *mama* when his mother is present, and also when he wants his mother.

"The rival explanation of the first stage of speech development is based on the theory that the infant's earliest utterances are *not* accidental, but have meaning to him, because they express *his feelings.* There are 'pleasure-sounds,' made when he is contented and well-fed; 'pain-sounds,' made when he is hungry, cold, wet, or has a stomachache. Charles Darwin developed this theory. He observed that the sounds made by his own infant son were expressive of pain and pleasure. According to this theory, the most frequent pain-sounds are *ma-ma* and *na-na;* these are made most frequently when the baby is hungry. Since the mother or the nurse usually feeds the child when he utters these cries, he comes to 'associate' them with these sounds.

"The two theories agree to this extent, namely (1) that the human infant develops a repertory of speech-*sounds* without having to learn them, and (2) that the people around him teach him to attach certain *meanings* to these sounds. At first the baby learns language by responding to his own sounds, as spoken by himself and repeated by others. At later stages, the child learns new sounds by imitating the people around him.

"From the age of about six months (when he uses and responds to sounds much as a puppy does), the child requires another six months or so before he makes a really human use of speech. Between the ages of twelve and eighteen months, the great moment of speech arrives. The child begins consistently to utter a specific sound in a specific situation, and this sound is taken from adult language or influenced by its forms. He says *mama* consistently to refer to his mother, or perhaps he says *didda* (tick-tock) to refer to a watch, or *ba* to refer to a ball. The 'single-word sentence' next appears (at about eighteen months); the baby uses a single word, such as *mook,* to convey a complete thought ('I want a drink of milk').

"At this stage, the child has got (1) the central idea of language —that a word stands for something—and also (2) his own repertory of *sounds* to draw from in fashioning words. His repertory of sounds is far from complete, however. It lacks some that adults use, especially the consonants.

"The time from eighteen months to four or five years is the period of 'baby-talk,' when the child tries, with the aid of his own repertory, to say everything he hears, and slowly adds new sounds under the pressure of social reward and social punishment. 'Baby-talk' is distinguished chiefly by the omission of certain consonants, and by the substitution of one consonant for another—*keem* for *cream*, and *didda* for *tick-tock*. The child makes a sketchy effort at saying the word, omitting the harder details. He omits the *r* in *cream* because it requires considerable effort to pronounce two successive consonants. But if he is pressed a bit by his environment, he soon learns to add the *r*.

"In 'baby-talk,' children cling to the consonants which were learned first. A three-year-old may say *woll* for *roll*. He can say *r,* but he has a stronger habit of saying *w,* and this habit prevails. Incidentally, one reason 'baby-talk' is not the same for all children seems to be that children vary considerably in the *order* in which they learn the consonants.

"From the third year on, the child rapidly expands his vocabulary. He tightens his hold on grammar more slowly. Yet, in his efforts to learn grammar, he shows remarkable reasoning power. Unfortunately, this developing reasoning ability is largely wasted on the English language, because it has little reason to its structure. Adhering to the most logical and praiseworthy generalizations, the child rationally makes many errors in English grammar. He notices that the way to show that the action is past is to add an 'ed' to the verb, and so he says, 'I rided the street-car.' His mother corrects him and he learns to say 'I rode.' Reasoning on this basis, he says, 'I gode to the store,' and is reproached for his mistake and told to say 'went.' The next time he tries logic once more, and says, 'I wented to the store.' When he is told that this is wrong, it is a wonder that he does not lose faith in his power of generalization altogether. The English language, by its many exceptions to its few rules, seems calculated to defeat the child's attempts at logical generalizations and to destroy his confidence in his reason!

"The growth of vocabulary occurs very much like the growth of some physical aspect of the human being. In fact, when the number of words understood by children is plotted on a graph against the age of the individuals, the resulting curve is very similar to a graph for the growth of children in height or weight. After a slow start during his first two years, when he is just getting the hang of language, the young child accumulates words rapidly. By the time he is six he understands about twenty thousand words, which are about six per cent of the words in a standard unabridged dictionary. Then, vocabulary growth shoots up rapidly for eight or ten years. The average high school senior knows the meanings of eighty thousand words, or about twenty-two per cent of the words in the English language. Girls move faster than boys, on the average, in the development of language. Nobody knows why this is, nor whether it is a phenomenon limited to our own culture." [2]

There is evidence of a period of "speech readiness" at the onset of which and for some months following, spoken language may be most readily acquired by the young child. This period is age twelve to eighteen months.[3] If speech is not learned during this period, the child is apt to become emotionally disturbed. Speech becomes increasingly a means of expressing feelings, and a child with delayed or inadequate means of expressing his feelings may become maladjusted for this reason.

Cultural Basis. The age at which language is learned by children is approximately the same in all societies, although it may be slightly earlier in modern than in primitive societies. If children do learn to talk earlier in some societies than in others, this is probably due to the greater emphasis on language in the more verbal societies, and to their training the child early to talk.

Within the American society there are social class differences in the learning of language. The middle-class child is taught very early that language is important. His father may talk or write for a living. In all cases he learns that his language is a mark of his station in life. For the lower-class child, however, language does not

---

[2] Davis and Havighurst, *loc. cit.*
[3] Sara M. Stinchfield, *Children with Delayed or Defective Speech* (Stanford, Calif.: Stanford University Press, 1937).

count so much. His father handles *things* rather than *symbols* in order to make a living. His family does not train him as carefully in the correct use of language.

4. LEARNING TO CONTROL THE ELIMINATION OF BODY WASTES

Nature of the Task. To learn to urinate and defecate at socially acceptable times and places.

Biological Basis. The development of the nerves that govern voluntary urination is not complete until somewhere between the ages of two and four years. We do not know at what age the nerves that control the anal muscles and regulate defecation are fully able to function.

Psychological Basis. The child can be regarded as trained for toilet habits when he (1) recognizes the need to urinate or defecate and has voluntary control over these acts, and (2) accepts responsibility for keeping himself clean and dry. The evidence is that these conditions are seldom met before the age of two or two and a half years, and that bladder control at night is not achieved by the average child until his fourth birthday.

Attempts to train children earlier than these ages occasionally succeed through the establishment of conditioned responses (to the toilet seat, soap stick, etc.). But these attempts fail to teach the child the meaning of toilet training, as a social habit. Early training requires great effort on the part of parents and a good deal of systematic training, including punishment, before the child can grasp the meaning and social significance of what is being done to him.

Toilet training is the first *moral* training that the child receives. The stamp of this first moral training probably persists in the child's later character.

Cultural Basis. Societies vary in their timing and methods of toilet training. The American society tends to be early and severe, as compared with other societies. Within the American society there is a difference between middle-class and lower-class training. The average middle-class mother starts to train her baby earlier and punishes the child more severely in the process of this training than the average working-class mother.[4] This is a part of the complex

[4] Cf. Davis and Havighurst, *op. cit.,* Chapter 10.

of training practices by which middle-class parents attempt to make their children careful, self-controlled, foresightful, and self-dependent.

5. LEARNING SEX DIFFERENCES AND SEXUAL MODESTY

The child is early made aware of the sexual polarity of the human species. He observes behavior differences between the sexes and very early is taught to behave like a boy or a girl, as the case may be. Very soon he learns that there are anatomical differences between boys and girls, and in some societies he must learn to cover his genital organs. Since the genital organs are areas of pleasure, even to the young child, and since the older people are so much interested in sexual differences and sexual behavior, the child learns to fix a great deal of attention on his own and other people's sexual organs. The kinds of sexual behavior he learns and the attitudes and feelings he develops about sex in these early years probably have an abiding effect upon his sexuality throughout his life.

6. ACHIEVING PHYSIOLOGICAL STABILITY

The human organism at birth is much more *labile,* much more variable in its physiological state than at adulthood. The body temperature fluctuates widely under slight stimuli. Most of the homeostatic mechanisms that keep the adult body stable are not yet functioning effectively.

Such things as the salt and sugar content of the blood, the water content of the body, the basal metabolic rate, and the heart rate are changed by relatively small variations in diet and in external conditions for the young child. It takes as many as five years for the child's body to settle down to something like the physiological stability of the adult. This developmental task is the only purely biological one of the series. As far as we know, its accomplishment is not noticeably affected by social demands and by cultural variations in the environment, although it is certainly not improbable that social learning and emotional experience may affect the achievement of physiological stability to a limited extent.

7. FORMING SIMPLE CONCEPTS OF SOCIAL AND PHYSICAL REALITY

Out of the initial buzzing confusion of the world the child discovers regularities and makes generalizations. He learns that certain images and sounds are people, who look after him and meet his needs. He learns that many particular perceptions can be grouped together and called by one name—such as *round*, or *animal*, or *man*, or *good*. His nervous system must have developed to a certain level of physical-chemical complexity before he can form concepts such as these. And, when his nervous system is ready, he must have the experience and the teachers to enable him to form a stock of concepts and learn the names for them. On this basis his later mental development is built.

8. LEARNING TO RELATE ONESELF EMOTIONALLY TO PARENTS, SIBLINGS, AND OTHER PEOPLE

Through gestures of various kinds culminating in language the young child learns to share some of his experience with other people. With the aid of language he puts himself in the place of others. "I'm daddy," he says, or "I'm the doctor." He learns the habit of unconscious imitation of parents and older brothers and sisters and of others in positions of prestige. He learns the process of identifying himself with other people, especially his parents. The way he achieves this task of relating himself emotionally to other people will have a large part in determining whether he will be friendly or cold, outgoing or introversive, in his social relations in later life.

9. LEARNING TO DISTINGUISH RIGHT AND WRONG AND DEVELOPING A CONSCIENCE

Departing from the naïve hedonism of infancy, when pleasure is good and pain is evil, the child must learn the concepts of good and bad and he must give content to these concepts. During the later years of early childhood he takes into himself the warning and punishing voices of his parents, in ways that depend upon their peculiar displays of affection and punishment toward him. Thus he develops the bases of his conscience, upon which a later structure of values and moral character will be built.

Outline for Analysis of a Developmental Task

In this chapter we have given an expanded treatment of two of the developmental tasks of infancy. We have done this according to the following scheme, which will be followed in the analysis of developmental tasks of middle childhood and adolescence.

TITLE OF THE TASK

The Nature of the Task. A brief definition.

Biological Basis. What the biological sciences can tell us about this task. How is the physical maturation of the individual related to its accomplishment? How do individual physical differences affect accomplishment of the task?

Psychological Basis. What can psychology tell us about this task? How is the mental development of the individual related to it? How do the values and aspirations of the individual affect accomplishment of this task? How is the task related to individual differences of mind and personality? How do success and failure in this task influence personality?

Cultural Basis. What can sociology and social anthropology tell us about this task? How does the task vary from one culture to another? How is the task defined in the upper, middle, and lower classes in America?

Educational Implications. What are the responsibilities of general education for helping youth accomplish this task? How well are these responsibilities now met? How might the educational system do better in relation to this task?

CHAPTER 3

Biosocial Development in Early Childhood

IN THIS CHAPTER we shall take a searching look at the young child, to see how the developmental tasks of infancy and early childhood arise, and what they signify for the later life and happiness of the child.

Characteristic of most of the developmental tasks of infancy is that they are biosocial in nature. They have a biological basis in that they are based on the successive maturation of zones and organs in the body. They have a social basis in that success or failure or any combination of the two depends largely on the social (family) environment. They lack the basis that later developmental tasks have in the self, with its values and aspirations. But the self is actually being formed in the experience of the child with these early developmental tasks.[1]

Learning a Basic Attitude of Trust

In the first few months the crucial developmental area for the baby is his mouth. This is his source of contact with what is essential in the world about him. Not only does he meet his hunger-needs by sucking, he also gets positive pleasure from the contact of the mucous membranes of lips, tongue, and mouth with the nipple and with the other things he puts in his mouth. Later in these first months his eyes, ears, and hands become able to take in the world immediately around him. The child's first basic attitude toward life

[1] The essentials of the discussion in this chapter are taken from Freudian theory, by way of Erik Erikson, Ch. 7, *Childhood and Society* (New York: W. W. Norton, 1950).

is thus learned through his experience in "taking in" the outer world through his mouth and other senses.

If he is comfortable and his wants are satisfied, he comes to feel "at home" in his world. Not only does he enjoy the presence and the loving attention of his mother and others who tend him, he also becomes sure enough of the goodness of his world to let his mother go out of sight, confident that she will return to him. Thus, he acquires a basic optimism, or confidence in the goodness of the world, taught to him by the familiar and the predictable and the affectionate qualities of his relations with people.

While the very young child centers his feelings in his mouth, and while his outlook on life depends on his oral experience, other aspects of his experience support or hinder the development of his personality. Consequently, it is not enough for the mother to feed the child amply. How she *holds* the child when feeding him will affect his oral development. Somehow, by the quality of her relationship with the baby she conveys to him her own sense of the rightness or wrongness of things, her own conviction of the stability of the culture in which the child will grow.

The mother's love is important because she is the most potent person whom the child sees. It is not that she is the child's biological mother—that is not important. The important thing is that the baby shall have an affectionate, trustworthy mother-person, who may be an older sister, or a grandmother, or a foster mother, or the true mother.

If the combination of social environment and biological maturation fails the child in these months, he learns to mistrust the world, to expect unpleasantness, and to be emotionally insecure.

Learning a Sense of Autonomy

During the second year the baby meets the task of becoming autonomous or self-determining with the alternative of remaining a dependent creature, and solves the problem in ways decisively contributing to his later character and personality. He acquires a sense of his own individual existence and the power of decision.

Biologically speaking, this is the period of acquiring conscious control of his comings and goings about the house and, above all, of acquiring control of the muscles that govern his eliminative organs. In these organs, and especially in the process of emptying the bowels, the child of one to three years finds his principal sources of pleasure and of discomfort.

In the biological task of learning when to *let go* and when to *hold on*, when to crawl or toddle and when to sit still, when to grasp things and when to throw them, the child learns the first lessons of self-control and self-decision, or autonomy.

For the parents, this is the period when they must cope with the problems of toilet training, of penning up the baby so that he can't get into trouble, of teaching him not to touch certain valuable or dangerous objects, and teaching him to control his aggressive feelings. All the time they are really working with or against the child on his task of developing autonomy.

The child in his second and third year is ready gradually to control his bowels and his explorations. If he is not started too early by his parents, before his nerves and muscles have matured to the point where he can consciously control them and before he can understand that he is being asked to control himself, he acquires the sense of autonomy or of self-decision that will stand him in good stead as he grows up. What he needs is firm, consistent handling by his parents, which protects him from the chaos of his own undiscriminating impulses, and at the same time gives him opportunity, when he is biologically ready, to make his own decisions.

This is the beginning of moral responsibility and the dawn of conscience. The child is now learning the simple concepts of right and wrong and relating them to his sense of responsibility for self-control.

If the child is not handled well in this period, he will become either overdependent and unable to make decisions for himself, or he will become a hostile, willful person. He will have insufficient autonomy, or he will overdo his autonomy without self-control. In the end he will make a poor citizen of a democracy. Erikson says, "I would like to suggest in all seriousness that early bowel training and other arrangements invented to condition the child in advance of his ability to regulate himself may be a very questionable practice in the upbringing of individuals who later on are supposed to exert vigorous and free choice as citizens." [2]

Learning Initiative and Developing Conscience

Having acquired a basic sense of trust and having laid the foundations for becoming an autonomous and self-directing person in the first three years of life, the child is ready in his fourth and fifth years for the next steps toward a mature personality, the learning of initiative and development of conscience as an inner moral guide.

During these two years he accomplishes the tasks of locomotion; he will run and jump and walk all over the neighborhood, and has lost all fear of being out of sight of his parents. He gets pleasure from sheer locomotion.

At this time, too, he discovers pleasure in his genital organs. He fixes a good deal of his attention on these and on his ability to get around.

At the same time, his mind develops and his vocabulary expands to the point where he can think of new and often strange and terrifying things. Thus he is equipped in body and mind for the development of initiative.

Initiative means motion into the future. It means doing new things, asking new questions, looking into new situations. There is a large element of curiosity in initiative, as well as the idea of making things.

As the child projects himself into the future, he takes his parent of the opposite sex along with him. The little boy plans to marry his mother, and the little girl her father. Having become aware of his sexuality, it is natural for him to think of a sexual partner for himself. But here his childish initiative meets an insuperable obstacle. It becomes obvious to the boy that he cannot win his mother away from his father, and the girl realizes that she cannot take her father away from her mother.

In this crisis the child discovers a way out which aids him greatly in the development of initiative. He *identifies* with the parent whose

[2] Erikson, *op. cit.*, p. 270.

place he would like to take. Coming now to think of himself as his father, the little boy has a safe guide in his trying-out of new roles. Thus, the boy becomes aggressive, masterful, attacking in his approach to life. The girl, following her mother's example, becomes endearing, attractive, and indirect in her mode of catching what she wants.

But there must be a control over the child's initiative, or it may go so far as to get him in trouble, and to hurt other people. And so the parents supply the control, in our society, by aiding the child to install in himself a governor of initiative—the conscience. They do this by a combination of love and punishment. If they have loved the child enough so that he wants to identify himself with them, and if they have shamed and scolded and punished him at times, he takes into himself the controlling and punishing voice of his parents. He then can feel guilty for thoughts and deeds which nobody has seen but which he knows to be wrong.

Both the quality of the child's initiative and the quality of his conscience depend mainly upon his parents—the kinds of people they are, the examples they set him, and the ways they deal with him. Parents can encourage curiosity, open-mindedness, willingness to try new things, readiness to see new solutions to problems. They can instill in the child a positive conscience that assures him that within limits his impulses are to be trusted and followed. On the other hand, parents can stifle curiosity and kill initiative, while they instill in the child a punitive, rigid conscience that prevents him from trusting any of his impulses.

Finally, after five years, the child is a person, and his own self will take a hand in defining future developmental tasks. He is ready to live in an expanding world which carries him out of the family into the school and neighborhood and society, and out of the present in time and space into the widest reaches of space and time, mentally. He is ready for the developmental tasks of middle childhood.

PART TWO

Middle Childhood

CHAPTER 4

Developmental Tasks of Middle Childhood

MIDDLE CHILDHOOD—or the period from about six to about twelve years of age—is characterized by three great outward pushes. There is the thrust of the child out of the home and into the peer group, the physical thrust into the world of games and work requiring neuromuscular skills, and the mental thrust into the world of adult concepts, logic, symbolism, and communication. By the end of middle childhood the individual has worked out his particular style and his level in all three areas. At the beginning of this period he is all possibilities, waiting to be realized through the unfolding powers of his body and mind and through the lessons his society will teach him.

The developmental tasks of middle childhood grow out of these three thrusts of growth in the child.

Developmental Tasks and the School

Formal education may be defined as a procedure set up by society to help children achieve certain of their developmental tasks. The tasks in which the school specializes are those involving the learning of mental skills—the three R's.

The school has primary responsibility for supplying the books and the training that are necessary for the development of reading and writing and calculating abilities.

In some societies the school goes far beyond this minimal program. The middle-class part of American society uses the school for a wider variety of purposes than any other society. Since American boys and girls are thrown together in the school by age-groups, the school becomes a place where they may learn the tasks of social development, and American educators consider the teaching of these tasks an important part of the school's responsibility. Also the American school is expected to help out other training institutions of society—the family, church, industry, youth-serving organizations—in the teaching of such diverse tasks as learning physical skills, selecting and preparing for an occupation, preparation for marriage, and learning a scale of values.

There is no developmental task of children or adolescents which the school can completely ignore, for the reason that the tasks are so closely interrelated that difficulty in one task, which may show in the school, is often tied up with difficulty in another task for which the school has little direct responsibility. For instance, failure in academic work may be due to failure in some other developmental task.

Cultural Relativity of Developmental Tasks

Some developmental tasks are practically universal and invariable from one culture to another. But other tasks are found only in certain societies, or they are peculiarly defined by the culture of the society. The tasks that are most completely based upon biological maturation, such as learning to walk, show the smallest cultural variation. Others, and especially those that grow principally out of social demands on the individual, show great variation among various cultures. The task of selecting and preparing for an occupation, for example, is a very simple one in a primitive society where there is little or no division of labor and everyone has practically the same occupation, whereas it is one of the most complex and worrisome tasks of middle-class adolescents in America. The task of learning toilet habits is very different even between middle and lower socioeconomic groups in the United States, while it varies greatly in its timing and the means used to teach it among the many human societies.

Therefore, lists and descriptions of developmental tasks will vary from one culture to another, and will depend upon the cultural values of the person who states them. This particular statement is based on American democratic values seen from a middle-class point of view, with some attempt at pointing out the variations for lower-class and upper-class Americans.

The American middle class is thought of as a group comprising about 40 to 50 per cent of the population, with occupations ranging from skilled labor and clerical work to the professions and managerial positions, and with the middle-class ideology of thrift, self-improvement, and foresight for the future. The lower class is about the same size as the middle class, and has low social status, low income, little education, and variations of respectability, from the hard-working "respectable poor" to the shiftlessness and immorality of the "people that live like animals." The upper class comprises about 3 per cent of the population, characterized by high social prestige, wealth in the past or present, and long-time ownership of property.

Recurrent and Nonrecurrent Tasks

One of the characteristics of most developmental tasks, it has been pointed out, is that there are special times in life for their achievement—teachable moments when the individual is ripe to learn them. But we have already begun to see that this is not true of certain tasks.

It is true of learning to walk and to talk, of learning elimination habits, and of selecting a vocation. But there are other tasks that never end; they recur over a long period of time, in varying but closely related aspects.

Learning to get along with one's age-mates is a good example of the recurrent task. It begins in earnest for most people about the time they start to school, and in its first phase it is pretty well mastered by the age of nine or ten. But the coming of puberty changes the nature of the task and it has to be carried on into a new phase, that of learning to get along with age-mates of the opposite sex. Soon another phase of the task develops—that of learning to get along with age-mates of both sexes in a socially mature way, where one cooperates with others not because of friendship alone, but because of some impersonal purpose. And even then the task is not completed. The old person often faces

it in a new guise when he has to learn to accept the fact of his age
and to associate happily with the "elders" of the society.

Success with a recurring task in its earliest phases probably
augurs well for success in the later phases. Consequently, the
crucial period for the learning of the task is when it first appears.
But new learning must be added as the task changes during later
life.

Learning a masculine or feminine social role is another recurrent task. It starts with infancy, and becomes most central and
perhaps most difficult in our society at adolescence. But even then
it is not finally finished. Learning to be a man or a woman is a
lifelong task.

Learning to participate responsibly as a citizen is also a recurrent task, which is most important and most demanding in early
and middle adulthood, but has its beginnings earlier and has a
final phase in old age.

It will be useful to keep this distinction between recurrent and
nonrecurrent tasks in mind during the analyses to come.

1. LEARNING PHYSICAL SKILLS NECESSARY FOR ORDINARY GAMES

Nature of the Task. To learn the physical skills that are necessary for the games and physical activities that are highly valued
in childhood—such skills as throwing and catching, kicking, tum-
bling, swimming, and handling simple tools.

Biological Basis. This is a period of general growth of muscle
and bone, with possibly some neural maturation to make muscular
coordination easier. In general, large muscle coordination precedes
that of the small muscles, and therefore the refinements of neuromuscular skill come at the end rather than at the beginning of
this period.

Psychological Basis. The peer group rewards a child for success
and punishes him by indifference or disdain for failure in this task.

Cultural Basis. Boys are expected to learn these skills to a higher
degree than girls. A girl can do rather poorly on them and still
hold status in the peer group, while a boy who does poorly is
called a "sissy" and loses status. Boys of all social classes are
expected to acquire physical skills.

Educational Implications. The peer culture teaches these skills so successfully to most boys and girls that the school can be content with trying to help the ones who have special difficulty with the task. This special help may take the form of arranging play-groups of the more awkward youngsters, so that they can learn at their own rates without being punished by faster-moving age-mates.

2. BUILDING WHOLESOME ATTITUDES TOWARD ONESELF AS A GROW-
ING ORGANISM

Nature of the Task. To develop habits of care of the body, of cleanliness and safety, consistent with a wholesome, realistic attitude which includes a sense of physical normality and adequacy, the ability to enjoy using the body, and a wholesome attitude toward sex.

Biological Basis. Physical growth is taking place, muscles developing rapidly. Permanent teeth are coming in. Postural habits are becoming established. Genital glands are quiescent until age nine or ten.

Psychological Basis. The immediate rewards for healthy habits of diet, sleep, etc., are scanty. Learning in this area must rely on something other than direct immediate rewards.

Children are approved and disapproved by age-mates and adults on account of their physique and physical skills.

Active games are a source of great enjoyment in this period.

During the latency period, there is relatively little physiologically instigated sexual behavior, though sexual curiosity and experimentation are present.

Cultural Basis. There is a considerable stress on the "physical" in the American culture, as compared with other cultures. The body is regarded as a source of pleasure and of value. Children are rated on their physique by other children and adults.

There is a great stress on health habits and practices in American culture, compared with other cultures. "Correct" diet, cleanliness, and regular health habits are highly valued.

There is relatively great parental sense of guilt and embarrassment over sex, especially among middle-class parents. Also there is severe punishment by parents for sexual curiosity and experimentation in childhood—more among middle-class than lower-class parents. But this does not deter children from sexual experimentation and talk about sex.

Educational Implications. Success in this task leads to a well-balanced personality, with a reasonable degree of physical neatness and orderliness, and a set of attitudes about sex which permit sex to become a source of pleasure in later life without causing either guilt feelings on the one hand or complete servitude to the sex impulse on the other.

Health habits should be taught routinely, using the prestige of glamorous figures in athletics and the movies to impress them favorably upon children. Sex education should be a matter of agreement between school and parents, with the school doing what the parents feel they cannot do so well. The facts about animal and human reproduction should be taught before puberty. The school should be on the watch for troubled and confused children, and should arrange to give them individual counseling.

3. LEARNING TO GET ALONG WITH AGE-MATES

Nature of the Task. To learn the give-and-take of social life among peers. To learn to make friends and to get along with enemies. To develop a "social personality."

Biological Basis. Acceptable physique and physical skills are important as a basis for good relations with peers.

Psychological Basis. The child moves out from the family circle into the world of his age-mates at the beginning of middle childhood. This is a move from a situation in which the child gets emotional security by his close relations with his mother and other family members into a new world where he must make a place for himself among a group of age-mates or "peers," all more or less competing for the attention of one "mother person" or "father person"—the teacher or adult supervisor. The child must learn to get more and more satisfaction from his social life with age-mates.

The process of learning to get along with age-mates is really the process of learning a "social personality" or acquiring social stimulus value. The child learns ways of approaching strangers, shy or bold, stand-offish or friendly. He learns how to treat friends. He learns what it means to "play fair" in games. Once he has learned these social habits, he tends to continue them throughout life. Consequently, the nine- or ten-year-old already shows what he will be like, socially, at fifty.

During middle childhood the need for social approval, which has been acquired during infancy, is met increasingly by approval from the peer group and decreasingly by approval from the family.

Cultural Basis. In the American society the child usually learns this task in a mixed-sex group, with a female teacher in general charge of the situation. He is limited in his social contacts by his family's scrutiny of his playmates and by their place of residence, which usually determines the school he will attend and the neighborhood in which he must find his closest friends.

Lower-class children have more freedom of choice and of social contact than middle-class children, as far as parental controls are concerned. But lower-class children are often systematically shunned and barred from participation with middle-class children by the latter, who, as early as the age of ten, discriminate quite clearly against them.[1]

Educational Implications. School is the place where most children work out the task of learning to get along with age-mates. Whether the teacher pays any attention to it or not, the child's chief concern is with this task. Often the key to understanding a child's difficulties with his school subjects, or to understanding a discipline problem in class, is given by a knowledge of his difficulties in achieving this particular developmental task.

The skillful teacher studies and understands the peer culture of her school and community. She uses sociometric devices to learn the social structure of her particular class. She learns both to cooperate with the peer group in some of its activities, and to direct and control it at places where it may do harm to individual children.

[1] Bernice Neugarten, "Social Class and Friendships among School Children," *Amer. J. Sociology,* 51 (January, 1946), 305–13.

4. LEARNING AN APPROPRIATE MASCULINE OR FEMININE SOCIAL
   ROLE

Nature of the Task. To learn to be a boy or a girl—to act the
role that is expected and rewarded.

Biological Basis. The actual anatomical differences between boys
and girls do not require a difference in sex role during middle
childhood. Girls' bodies are as well built for physical activities as
are boys' bodies, and girls are nearly as large and strong as boys.
It is not until adolescence that the anatomical differences between
the sexes make girls actually inferior to boys in certain physical
activities. Toward the end of middle childhood, about age nine or
ten, the body chemistry of boys and girls becomes differentiated.

Psychological Basis. The psychological basis for this task is laid
in the family, where boy babies are taught to behave like boys, and
girl babies like girls. These teachings are re-enforced by the psychological identification which the child usually makes with the
parent of the same sex in early childhood.

Cultural Basis. The American culture expects differences in the
behavior of boys and girls, and lays these expectations on the child
early, through the agency of the family. Through the peer culture
these same expectations are enforced during middle childhood.

There are differences in the acceptable sex role in different
social classes. For instance, the lower-class boy is expected to be a
good fighter, while the middle-class boy is not expected to be
openly aggressive, though he is taught to fight "in self-defense."

Educational Implications. The sex role is taught so vigorously
by so many agencies that the school probably has little more than
a remedial function, which is to assist boys and girls who are having
difficulty with the task. However, there have been some criticisms
of American manhood, coming from representatives of other societies, to the effect that the American male grows up too much
under the domination of women to learn most successfully a male
role. In any case, it is generally conceded that increasing the proportion of male teachers for children in middle childhood would
have a good influence on boys, by giving them a closer relationship
with male models at a time when they are engaged in learning
how to behave like men.

5. DEVELOPING FUNDAMENTAL SKILLS IN READING, WRITING, AND CALCULATING

Nature of the Task. To learn to read, write, and calculate well enough to get along in American society.

Biological Basis. The nervous system becomes mature enough and complex enough to permit the learning of reading, writing, and arithmetic during the early years of this period. There is some evidence that the body is not biologically "ready" for handwriting before the sixth year. That is, the nerves and muscles of the fingers, hand, and arm have not developed to the degree that permits the learning of handwriting before this age. The eyes are not biologically "ready" for reading in most cases before the sixth year. That is, the fine coordination required of the eye muscles for moving rapidly over a page of print is achieved partly as a result of nerve and muscle growth. Furthermore, most children are naturally far-sighted in early childhood, and their eyes naturally become normal-sighted and best adapted to reading at about eight years of age.

Psychological Basis. Psychological studies have shown that reading is learned by most people, as well as they will ever learn it, by the age of twelve or thirteen. Their speed of silent reading and their oral reading ability seldom improve after that age. However, their ability to get meaning from what they read develops indefinitely, provided they go on learning. Thus the more mechanical aspects of the reading task are completed by the end of middle childhood. Similarly with handwriting and spelling. These skills rarely improve after age twelve.

Arithmetic skills improve up to the age of twelve or thirteen and then seldom improve unless they are used in high-school and college courses or on the job.

In general, the basic mental skills are acquired well enough by the age of twelve or thirteen to enable a person to get through life at the working-class and perhaps the lower-middle-class level.

Cultural Basis. The level of mental skills demanded by everyday life and by the largest occupations has been raised by industrialization and technological change. Thus the minimum level required for success in American life is probably higher than it was a cen-

tury ago. (Yet studies of "morons" or slow-learning people with
IQ's of 50 to 75 show that many of them succeed quite well in
working-class occupations, with what is no better than a ten- or
twelve-year mental level.)

Social class differences in the basic mental skills are considerable,
with upper-middle-class position requiring a relatively high development of mental skills. Middle-class adults stimulate their
children to a higher level of development of mental skills than do
lower-class adults, whose level is usually reached by their children
when the latter reach the age of eleven or twelve.

Educational Implications. The findings concerning the importance of biological maturation in the processes of reading and
writing indicate that children are sometimes taught these skills
before they are "ready" for them. As a result of these findings,
schools now put less pressure on children to learn to read and
write at the age of six. Often it turns out that children learn these
skills very rapidly and easily if they are allowed to wait until seven
or eight before starting.

6. DEVELOPING CONCEPTS NECESSARY FOR EVERYDAY LIVING

Nature of the Task. A concept is an idea which stands for a
large number of particular sense perceptions, or which stands for
a number of ideas of lesser degrees of abstraction. The task is to
acquire a store of concepts sufficient for thinking effectively about
ordinary occupational, civic, and social matters.

Biological Basis. Probably a certain level of complexity in organization must be achieved by the brain before it can acquire a
concept of a given level of abstraction.

Psychological Basis. By the time a child is ready for school he
already has a store of several hundred concepts—mainly simple
ones such as roundness, sweetness, redness, animal, dog, food,
anger, and love. Concepts are tools to think with. As William
James put it, "Without abstract concepts to handle our perceptual
particulars by, we are like men hopping on one foot. Using concepts along with particulars, we become bipedal. We throw our
concept forward, get a foothold on the consequence, hitch our line

to this, and draw our percept up, traveling along with a hop, skip, and jump over the surface of life at a vastly rapider rate than if we merely waded through the thickness of particulars as accident rained them down upon our heads. Animals do this but men raise their heads higher and breathe fully in the upper conceptual air."

During the period of middle childhood the individual forms several thousand concepts. If these concepts are true to reality, a good share of them must have grown out of his concrete experience. Then, as he grows older and stores up concepts, he becomes able to form new concepts on the vicarious experiences afforded by reading, or hearing lectures, or seeing movies. For instance, after a child has already formed an accurate concept of a camel by actually seeing a number of camels, he can form a fairly accurate concept of a llama by seeing pictures of it and hearing it described as "a South American animal something like a camel."

Cultural Basis. There are certain concepts common to all Americans—such as time, space, number, hot, high, and fast. These concepts are usually learned during middle childhood or earlier, and they may be modified by later experience. The school is the place where these are mainly learned.

Other concepts are limited by social class. Their meaning depends largely upon the social class of the person holding them, as they are learned mainly in the home and in class-limited play groups. Such concepts are—maid, nurse, laundry, park, grandma, work, travel.

Educational Implications. The greatest peril in the school learning of concepts is that they may lack sufficient concrete basis in experience to make them trustworthy. A fifth-grade mountain child in Tennessee reading about life in Holland may form quite erroneous concepts of Holland, while at the same time he fails to form certain useful concepts about diet, disease, and agriculture which the school could easily teach him by direct, first-hand experience in connection with school lunch, garden, and local health programs.

In general, it may be urged that the school curriculum be as full of concrete experience as possible in the early years, so as to help the child build concepts on a realistic basis; then more and more concept formation may be encouraged through reading in the later school years.

Grade placement of such subjects as history and geography and arithmetic would be made more sure if we knew more about the child's formation of concepts of time, space, and number.

7. DEVELOPING CONSCIENCE, MORALITY, AND A SCALE OF VALUES

Nature of the Task. To develop an inner moral control, respect for moral rules, and the beginning of a rational scale of values.

Biological Basis. ?

Psychological Basis. The child at birth has no conscience and no scale of values. The principal values for him are food and warmth. Gradually he learns values and is taught to distinguish "good" from "bad."

The basis of conscience is probably the punishing acts of the parents combined with their love and reward for the child and the child's love and dependence on them. Through the process of *identification* with parents or *taking the role* of the parents, the child develops within himself the warning and punishing voice of conscience. From this time on he carries with him a moral controlling force wherever he goes.

Morality, or respect for rules of behavior, is imposed on the child first by the parents. Later, according to Piaget, the child learns that rules are necessary and useful to the conduct of any social enterprise, from games to government, and thus learns a "morality of cooperation or agreement" which is a true moral autonomy and necessary in a modern democratic society. Piaget believes that middle childhood is the crucial period for learning the morality of cooperation.

Since living requires choosing between values, which are more or less desirable objects or modes of action, and since many important life situations require a choice between two or more values, the growing child must develop a scale of values which will enable him to make stable choices and to hold himself to these choices. For instance, his choice of working at a job to earn money rather than going to a movie and spending money must be one that he can justify to himself and to others and stand by in spite of temptation to go to the movie for the sake of immediate enjoyment. Such a scale of values develops very slowly during middle childhood, but by the age of twelve the child is expected to be something more stable than a creature who is dominated at every moment by urgent but temporary whims.

Cultural Basis. The moral rules of various societies differ, and so a highly "moral" person in one society might transgress many moral rules if he were transplanted to another society. Moral rules differ even between social classes in American society, as Kinsey has demonstrated in the sexual area of behavior, which is more thoroughly permeated by moral considerations than any other one. Consequently, children of lower socioeconomic status often seem highly immoral to middle-class teachers when they are really following the mores of their own social group.

There are also cultural differences in the strength of conscience between various social groups. In many societies there is very little of the punishing "Puritan" conscience that we know so well in America. Even in lower-class American society there is probably a less severe conscience, on the average, than in middle-class Americans.

Educational Implications.[2] The school affects the child's conscience and his morality

    (a) through its teachings about morality,
    (b) through the teachers' punishments and rewards,
    (c) through the teachers' examples,
    (d) through the child's experience in the peer group.

From very early in middle childhood the school can teach democratic values, by precept and by example of the teachers and the peer group.

[2] Cf. Robert J. Havighurst, "The Children's World and the School Program," *Bulletin of the Menninger Clinic*, 5 (1941), 214–22.

Jean Piaget, *The Moral Judgment of the Child* (New York: Harcourt, Brace and Co., 1932).

8. ACHIEVING PERSONAL INDEPENDENCE

Nature of the Task. To become an autonomous person, able to make plans and to act in the present and immediate future independently of one's parents and other adults.

Biological Basis. ?

Psychological Basis. The young child has become physically independent of his parents but remains emotionally dependent on them. They are all-wise in his eyes, and all-powerful. He does not question their authority. What "Daddy said" and later what "Teacher said" is the truth and that is the end of it.

Then, gradually, during middle childhood, it dawns on the child that his parents and his teachers are not infallible. They can be wrong, or they can be ignorant. The child himself may know some facts better than they do. He begins to develop his own independent store of knowledge, and with knowledge comes a certain degree of authority to make choices for himself.

Success in the world of his peers also helps the child to become independent of adults. The peer world supports him and gives him an opportunity to make plans and decisions that do not concern his parents. He must be an independent person if he is to be successful with his age-mates. This means that he must free himself to some extent from his close identification with his parents. Whereas the child of seven or eight can only think of himself in the future as an adult like his father or mother or some parent-surrogate, the child of ten thinks of himself as being a movie star, a professional athlete, an airplane pilot, or some other kind of glamorous person.

Independence from adults grows slowly and is by no means complete at the end of middle childhood. It comes first in the choice of things to do around the home—of games to play, radio or television programs to hear, books to read. Then it extends to choice of friends and places to play. The child gains some geographical space-freedom. He becomes able to stay away from home for longer periods of time, and eventually to sleep away from home.

Cultural Basis. In all societies there is a growth of personal independence during middle childhood. Children take increasing responsibility for their own personal safety, for planning the use of their time, and for choosing their friends. Most societies allow boys more freedom than girls in these respects. Boys spend much time away from home, in the company of other boys the same age; while girls are kept closer to home, more dependent on the mother, and more responsible for work around the house, baby-tending, and the like.

In general, the simpler societies allow the individual adult less autonomy and personal independence than do the complex, modern, democratic societies. But every society recognizes the growth of personal independence and initiative as desirable during middle childhood. The American society sets greater store than most by personal independence and starts training for independence at a relatively early age.

There is some evidence that American middle-class families encourage personal independence at an earlier age than American working-class families do.[3] Middle-class parents, on the average, teach their girls to cook, to sew, and to wash dishes earlier than working-class parents do, and they expect their boys to get around the city earlier, to museums, dentists' offices, and libraries. This is part of the American middle-class emphasis on growing up rapidly, getting ahead, being alert, and taking the initiative.

Educational Implications. The school and the peer group are laboratories for the working-through of this task. Much of the success or failure of children on this task depends on the relationship between the teacher and the pupils. If the teacher is a despot, even a benevolent one, children will get very little practice in the achievement of personal independence. On the other hand, if the teacher can play the roles both of umpire and of committee chairman, the children will get abundant opportunity to take responsibility for their own studies, to organize school activities, and to discover for themselves a true and adult basis of authority—namely, knowledge and experience with the subject under consideration.

If the elementary school aims to promote the personal inde-

---

[3] Allison Davis and Robert J. Havighurst, "Social Class and Color Differences in Child-rearing," *Amer. Sociol. Review*, 11 (1946), 698–710.

pendence of its pupils, it will teach them how to study and learn independently; it will give them opportunity to plan a part of the school program and to discuss and criticize the results of their planning; all under a kind of supervision that supports children when they make mistakes, and sets limits for their growing independence to protect them from going too far.

9. DEVELOPING ATTITUDES TOWARD SOCIAL GROUPS AND
INSTITUTIONS

Nature of the Task. To develop social attitudes that are basically democratic.

Biological Basis.   ?

Psychological Basis. Attitudes, or emotionalized dispositions to act, are learned mainly in three ways:

(1) by imitation of people with prestige in the eyes of the learner;

(2) by collection and combination of pleasant or unpleasant experiences associated with a given object or situation;

(3) by a single deeply emotional experience—pleasant or unpleasant—associated with a given object or situation.

Middle childhood is the period when the basic social attitudes are learned, such as attitudes toward religion, toward social groups, toward political and economic groups. These attitudes may be changed by later experience, but they do not change easily.

As he emerges from the family into the broad world at about the age of six, the ordinary child has little or no stock of social attitudes. He has no disposition to favor or disfavor one religion or another, one race or color, one political party. He has no attitude toward the economic system, toward social classes or occupational groups. Yet, by the end of elementary school, this same child has a full complement of social attitudes, picked up or absorbed from his family, his teachers, his peer group, and his contact with the community and the wide world through movies, radio, television, books, and lectures. Once he has a store of social attitudes, there is little reason for him to change them. He knows how to act, what discriminations to make, what people to favor, and whom to disfavor. Unless he finds these attitudes to be grossly unpopular as he grows older, or to get him into difficulties, he is likely to retain them through life.

Cultural Basis. Social attitudes make up a good part of what we call the "culture" of a people. Every society inculcates its most important and significant social attitudes into its children during middle childhood. In America there are some social attitudes which are characteristic of almost all Americans, such as a favorable set toward freedom of expression, a kind of optimistic belief in a better and ever-better future, and a favorable attitude toward a democratic form of government.

However, there are differences in attitudes between the social classes in America, which show up very clearly in school. The various socioeconomic groups have different attitudes toward education, for example, and different attitudes toward belonging to civic organizations. Thus the teacher of a heterogeneous group of children of various social orgins must expect to meet a varied and often contradictory set of social attitudes among the children.

Educational Implications. The school should work explicitly to inculcate certain basic democratic social attitudes which are generally agreed upon as desirable for all Americans. For example, attitudes of religious and racial tolerance, respect for freedom of of speech and other civil rights, political democracy, international cooperation.

CHAPTER 5

The Role of the Peer Group in Helping Children Achieve Developmental Tasks in Middle Childhood[1]

MOVING FROM EARLY CHILDHOOD into middle childhood is more of a change than we usually recognize. It is more of a change than moving from childhood into adolescence, if we look at only the psychological changes. The period from four or five to six or seven includes psychological changes as profound as the physiological and physical changes that signal the transition from childhood to adolescence.

The great change from age four to seven is a change in the child's social world, from a single small world centered in the family to an expanding world with a second center in the peer group. And the child's experiences in the peer group are crucial to the principal developmental tasks of middle childhood.

It has been said by keen observers that during the period from seven to ten children behave as if they were being propelled into group activity by some inner force or drive. It has also been said that in its prevalence and force the push into the peer group resembles a biological drive. One writer speaks of this desire for the company of one's age-mates at this period as "social hunger."

---

[1] It is a pleasure to acknowledge the assistance of Ruth Nedelsky in the preparation of this chapter. The writer has drawn freely from papers which she prepared and which have been published elsewhere. See Ruth Nedelsky. "The Teacher's Role in the Peer Group during Middle Childhood," *Elementary School Journal,* 52 (1952), 325–34.

The Young Child Approaches the Peer Group

Let us look at the child of six or seven as he enters this period called middle childhood and see what kind of a world he is living in, and how it differs from the world of the nursery-school or pre-school child.

School

He has started school. He is now a part of a social community that is an entity in itself, a community apart from the family. Unlike a good nursery school, it is not and does not try to be an extension of the family in its relation to the child.

The school is also a much larger social group than any the child has had experience with before. The child now comes into daily contact with a great number of children and has to establish some kind of relationship with many of them.

Increased Freedom in His Goings and Comings

By seven (frequently even by six) the child goes to school and comes home by himself. He is no longer entirely dependent on his family for his explorations of his neighborhood or for his social contacts.

Learns To Read

Learning to read opens up a whole new world, or series of worlds, which can be explored vicariously. Here the child has complete control (within the limit set by the books he has access to) over his own exploration of these worlds.

Three significant learnings that have contributed to his increased maturity are:

1. As the young child comes to learn what is expected of him by his family, as he gradually learns the kinds of things he can do and cannot do, he evolves a code of behavior. By seven this code will be an integral part of him, though still incomplete; he will modify and expand it as he has new experiences and as he experiments with new behaviors. He is not likely, as yet, to be able to control his be-

havior to the end that he will always act in accordance with his own code, but he is at least able to accept responsibility for his own actions. He knows when he has done wrong (within limits, of course, but these limits will expand with new experiences). It is this learning that accounts for his being able to come and go on his own without adult supervision. It constitutes a measure of real independence.

2. He has learned to accept reality, even unpleasant reality. This is an important factor in his being able to accept responsibility for his own actions.

3. He has arrived at a conception of himself in relation to the other members of his family. He has worked through some idea of what his own particular role is as a part of his family. He has come a long way from feeling himself to be the only reality, as he did in infancy, to becoming aware of himself as a child of seven, with his own particular ways of feeling and behaving, living with other persons each with a reality of his own. Another way of putting it is that he is approaching a more objective or realistic understanding of himself as a person.

As he sees himself more clearly for the child he is, so is he able to perceive the adult world and adult roles more clearly. He has a more objective view of his relationship to the adult world.

With this measure of inner independence and this new awareness of himself as a person, the child must find a place for himself in his rapidly expanding world. He must relate himself to his larger world, just as in his early days he had to work out his relationships within the family circle. He has to find his role in the larger world just as he had to find his role in the family. In a sense, he has two problems to cope with simultaneously. He has to deal with the problems growing out of his changed status and his increasingly objective understanding of his status on the one hand, and the problems growing out of living in a new world with expanding horizons on the other. He cannot accept the same kind of support from his family that it gave him earlier; his world now extends far beyond the family, and, even more important, he has grown out of his old relationships.

So it is to his peers that a child turns for help and support as he tries to make sense out of his new world, as he tries to establish new relationships with the adult world. Children are able to turn to each other now for support because the initiative they have achieved permits them to act for themselves, even if in a limited sense. They are able to recognize each other as equals now because of their ability to accept the reality of the existence of others besides themselves to a degree not possible for the four-year-old.

Perhaps the peer group plays the same psychological role in middle childhood that the family did in early childhood. This does not mean that adults are no longer necessary. They are as necessary as ever. In middle childhood, without an adult to structure the group, to set the limits within which it is to function, children are unable to work out a constructive or cohesive group. The interpretations of experiences that children have must come from the adult world; one of the main tasks of adults is to interpret reality to the child. This is as true in middle childhood as in the earlier years. But now it is through the peer group that many children are able to make use of the adult interpretations most effectively.

We have spoken earlier of the child's strong push out into the peer group. But to balance the picture we should recognize the child's conflicting feelings about growing up. No child is undividedly desirous of growing away from his family toward the peer group.

There was a boy in the third grade who found it especially difficult to move out from the haven of loving care that his home offered. He did not succeed in making his way into the peer group. He did not find his teacher sufficiently attentive to him, and he was upset by her urging him to work faster than his ordinary rather deliberate tempo. One day he came home crying and told his mother that he just could not stand the grating sound of his teacher's voice as she told him, over and over again, to "hurry up." His mother gave him a hot bath and put him to bed. In other words, she treated him like a baby, and gave him the satisfactions of being a baby again, when he found the journey into independent childhood too rough. His mother took him out of school and taught him herself the rest of the semester.

Without trying to assess blame, we can point out several important things about this situation. First, the boy found it easier and more pleasant to go back into babyhood than to go ahead into middle childhood. Second, the mother found it pleasant to have her baby back again. (She had no younger children.) Although she undoubtedly wanted her boy to grow up, she also wanted him as a baby. Third, the school missed an opportunity to counsel with the parents of this boy on the all-important matter of his growing up. At a crisis in his development, when he needed special help on a crucial developmental task, his school as well as his parents failed him.

Another third grade boy had a more fortunate experience. He, too, was the youngest in the family, and his mother and father unconsciously desired him to be their baby as long as possible. Yet he made several good friends in school and got along well enough in a quiet way with his developing peer group. Still, he always spent his after-school and Saturday hours playing around the house, within sight or call of his mother. He still was happiest when he was securely at home.

One day a friend of his, who had joined the Y.M.C.A., invited him to go along as a guest and see what it was like. The friend had an older brother in the Y.M.C.A. who had helped him to get into things there. Our boy spoke to his mother and father that evening, saying, "Richard wants me to go to the Y.M.C.A. next Saturday morning as his guest. Shall I go?" His father thought this was a fine thing to do, and said so. The boy stood there silently, in front of his parents, and big tears came welling out of his eyes. His father and mother were surprised, and at first could not understand why the boy was crying. They thought he had wanted to go to the Y.M.C.A., and was merely asking their permission.

Then they realized that this was a crisis for their boy. It symbolized for him the real break from the family into the peer group, which he had been unable to make up to now. The Y.M.C.A. was a big, strange place, with a lot of rough, strange boys. There would be no mother-person there. His Saturday morning would be a threat to him, or at best an uncertainty, instead of the sure pleasure of playing around home. He had really hoped that his parents would think he was too young to go to the Y.M.C.A. Now it seemed that perhaps they did not love him enough to want him at home with them.

The father then said, "I'll tell you, I've got time on Saturday morning, and I'll go with you to the Y.M.C.A. We'll see what kind of place it is." Thus reassured that his parents were not going to desert him, the boy began to enjoy thinking about going to the Y.M.C.A., and he and his father went cheerfully off together the next Saturday morning. The father went into the locker room where the boys were undressing, and went up to the gymnasium with them. There the boy found that he could run as fast, turn somersaults as well, and play games as well as most of the other boys. He found several boys he knew on the playground at school. Back to the locker room, his father with him; then he got ready for a swim, and found that he could swim a little better than most of the boys, for they were all beginners. At this point the father left. An hour later the boy came home, full of the pleasure of the morning. He had stayed to see a movie cartoon in the Boys' Room, and, all in all, it had been a great experience. He asked his parents whether he could join the Y.M.C.A., and go there two or three times a week; and this time his eyes danced when they gave him permission.

Thus we see that both the child and his parents are ambivalent about his growing up and out into the peer group. There are advantages in remaining a young child. There are perils and uncertainties in growing up. But the peer group usually wins out.

What the Peer Group Does for the Child

A peer group is an aggregation of people of approximately the same age *who feel and act together.* Practically every neighborhood play group is a peer group, but not all adult-led groups of a given age are peer groups. A school class may or may not be a peer group, depending largely on how the teacher treats the class, but also on the cultural and religious backgrounds of the children. If they are very diverse in background, it will be difficult for them to become a peer group. On the playground, peer groups form more freely, as they do in recreation centers.

The peer group provides the setting, and the means, by which a boy or girl achieves several of the developmental tasks of middle childhood. Specifically, it can help him in four ways.

1. *To Get Along with Age-Mates* [2]

Let us observe a group of second graders in a relatively free situation, and one in which they are completely at ease—the lunch period—to see how children establish common bonds, feelings of group solidarity. The following observations come from *Child Life in School* [3] and were made over a six-week period in the spring of the year in the Little Red School House. Small groups of children are at the several tables. There are adults in attendance. Except for a few simple rules, the children determine their own conduct. Conversation is free-flowing and varied, accompanied by all kinds of gestures and games. The children seem to thoroughly enjoy eating together.

P. 147: Pat: "Whoever likes milk, raise their hands!" Amy smiled but continued eating. . . . There is more raising of hands and voting and Dick exclaims, "Chocolate ice cream," adding, "I like Lima beans this much" raising two, then three, fingers. Christopher picks up the idea of evaluating the degree to which they like foods by raising a certain number of fingers.

P. 148: "Who likes mice?" They all got down on the floor to express extreme dislike.

Sylvia: "Who likes parsnips?" Down again on the floor. "Who likes beets?" Allison says, "Fair," with hands midway, at about shoulder level.

Sylvia: "Ice cream?" They all raise hands enthusiastically, except Allison, who says again, "Fair."

P. 149: They discuss ice creams for a while and at last Carol says to Dick, "Do you like Borden's MeloRol?" They discuss kinds of ice creams and pickles, saying "Yum" and rubbing their tummies until they are reminded to eat.

Christopher says, "Like salt pickles?" and Carol puts her hand up. Carol, talking of sweet pickles, points to the window and says dramatically, "There's the window—here's sweet pickles— BOOM!" with a full-arm gesture of throwing. Walter takes it up and says the same thing. Then Carol calls, "Dick—there's the window—Here's the baseball bat—I use sweet pickles for the baseball—BOOM!"

[2] See Developmental Task #3, pp. 30–31.
[3] Barbara Biber, *et al., Child Life in School* (New York: Dutton, 1942).

They all lean back in their chairs and giggle about pickles. Carol now is very much a member of the group.

P. 138: Hitler is being discussed at the next table and Christopher's table took up the topic enthusiastically. Demonstrations were given of various kinds of salutes. Christopher said, "Here is General Franco," and showed a Fascist salute. . . .

At this point Leon picks up the theme from the neighboring table and says emphatically: "I hate Hitler." Mark turns to the recorder, asking if she would like to know how he would get rid of Mussolini if he knew where his house was. "I would get under his window with one of those toy guns and shoot him."

Christopher says, "Whoever likes Hitler, raise their hands." Virginia joins them in slumping down low and then holding her hands down below the table in voting. . . . Then they all go down again for Hitler and up for Russia.

Pat: "Whoever likes Hitler here, don't raise your hands." This confuses them. Amy keeps on eating, except when they raise hands for not liking Hitler, when she joins them.

Here in the voting episodes we see the children experimenting with an adult role, with an adult pattern of acting. Because it is a pattern of behaving that is familiar to all the children and one within their mastery, all the children can participate. As they express their feelings, their preferences, a common store of feelings emerges, a common sense of identity. Voting against Hitler was acted out again and again with variations because it expressed a homogeneous reaction which the children felt strongly. The voting also permitted individual children to make points of contact with the group. Carol, as she pretended to throw a pickle out of the window, struck a responsive chord in the others and momentarily built up a sense of common identity as the others giggled over the thoughts of doing the same.

In this same lunch group we see also the use of stock phrases, games, tricks, as a means of augmenting a feeling of social communion. Children at about the same level of development enjoy many of the same kinds of things, react to many situations with somewhat similar feelings. It is the sharing of these common pleasures and fears that makes possible a sense of group identity.

We find children of seven and eight enjoying puns, plays on the meanings of words. We find them enjoying certain newly developed skills. The patterns they develop, both action and verbal patterns, are sufficiently formalized so that they become almost another language. By building up a repertoire of game patterns they secure for themselves a means of checking their feelings of familiarity with each other. To illustrate:

P. 152:   Douglas heard a game going on at the next large table across the room, each child poking the next and saying, "Pass it on." He rose from his chair to look over at these children, but he did not initiate the game at his own table.

Here the pleasure is derived in part, at least, from the fact that a child can poke another child without recrimination. It is unlikely that a child could poke an adult without evoking displeasure or annoyance. Nursery-school children are likely to look upon a poke as an unfriendly gesture. Now, however, children have reached a stage of development where they are able to formalize such expressions of aggression to a degree, and, accepting one another as equals, are able to make a game out of them.

P. 152:   Peter says, "Silence in the courtroom, the monkey . . ." etc. Christopher speaks first and Dick fills his mouth and makes ape motions.
"We're all monkeys." How they decide I don't know, but they giggle and seem pleased.
They start the same game again, all covering their mouths with their hands.
They point at each other as they make inarticulate sounds.
P. 153:   Geoffrey says, "Who can do this?" holding his hand so that the first and second, and the third and fourth fingers are joined with a wide space between the pairs.
Allison responds, "Who can do this?" crossing two sets of fingers—the second over the first and the third over the fourth. She tells how she used to try and try to do it before she learned how. She illustrates with both hands. Then Geoffrey began the old hand play with palms together and one big finger extending out each way.

P. 154: Douglas: "Hey, let's play. . . ." (I cannot hear the game but it sounds like "lock-up.") They all close their mouths tightly. Allison talks first. "Douglas, you've got to eat the rotten potato."
They all hum lightly through closed lips. Sylvia yells suddenly. "You've got to eat the rotten potato," says Douglas. They discuss who talked and who didn't.
Sylvia: "Let's start a game."
Douglas: "Okay. You're excused. We're all excused once." He refers to the talking after a game is started.
Allison talks again.
Douglas says, "That's all."
They try the game but all talk. Apparently it is too much for them to keep quiet.
. . . Allison starts talking and crosses her fingers.
Douglas: "You've got to eat the rotten potato."
Then they decide that they can talk if fingers are crossed.
They cross braids—Margaret, Sylvia, and Clara.
Douglas crosses his tie-ends, calling them "fins."

Here a group is being structured around a communal bag of tricks. Thus we see these children working out a feeling of belonging together as they express their common feelings of hatred of Hitler, dislike of mice, enjoyment of ice cream. We see them establish patterns of behaving, of expressing their feelings that all can participate in and that give them a feeling of acting in concert in a group.

Clearly, the peer group here was giving children practice in learning a social personality—learning how to express themselves in socially acceptable ways with their peers. They were learning a set of skills for casual social relations—how to enjoy life with people whom one does not know intimately. How to start something interesting, and how to go along with the group on something they are doing.

Another example of learning to get along with people through the peer group is trading. For trading there must be a medium of exchange, something that both persons value and because of which they get together. Take trading cards, which are popular with boys and girls of nine and ten during the current years. Playing cards are

collected in terms of the decorations on their backs, such as geo-
metrical designs, landscapes, pictures of animals, etc. There are
common, familiar varieties that anybody can get, and there are rare
varieties that may be worth five or ten of the common kinds. A child
trades in order to get a wider variety, or to extend a certain set, such
as cards with animals on their backs.

The act of trading is impersonal enough to be fairly easy for a
shy child to initiate. He can approach a stranger with his cards in
his hand, and engage in a conversation without any claim to friendship or prior acquaintance. Many children who are much too shy
to approach other children with overtures of friendship find it fairly
easy to initiate the relatively impersonal relationship of trading.
Thus they gain skill and assurance in dealing with other people.

Perhaps the popularity of trading among children in middle
childhood is due in part to the assistance this act gives them on the
task of learning to get along with age-mates. Any kind of trading
will do—trading of marbles, postage stamps, baseball cards,
coins, etc.

2. *To Develop a Rational Conscience and a Scale of Values* [4]

Normally, in our society, the six-year-old has acquired a moral
conscience which can properly be called *authoritarian*. He has taken
into himself the moral voice of his parents. Just as they have punished him for doing what was wrong and rewarded him for doing
what was right, now his conscience punishes and rewards him.
Since to him they appeared omniscient and the final authority, now
his conscience is the final authority. He is now prepared to go
through life *making moral choices*.

But his authoritarian conscience will not serve him adequately,
because it does not equip him to get what he and his parents want
him to get from the peer group. His parents teach him that he must
get along with his age-mates, do as well or better than they do, and
measure himself in part at least by their standards. In other words,
his parents tell him that, in addition to obeying their moral teachings, he must adapt himself to the code of the crowd to which he
belongs. But allegiance to the peer group usually demands of the

[4] See Developmental Task #7, pp. 36–37.

child that he depart from the parental moral code in some respects. For example, if the peer group uses slang expressions such as "stinker," "bitch," and "queer," when the startled parents hear these words they are caught in the conflict of wanting to apply their own moral code and at the same time wanting their child to be successful in the peer group. In any case, it is their child and not they who must resolve the conflict between his authoritarian conscience and the peer-group standards. But the parents have shown him in many ways that they want him to come to terms with peer-group standards.

Furthermore, the child lives in a changing society, which almost immediately confronts him with moral choices for which he has no ready answer from his parents' teachings. The movies and television he sees are not seen by his parents, and they have put no specific rules into his conscience which tell him what is right or what is wrong in this domain. When he gets along toward adolescence, he finds that the prevailing code of boy-girl relations is different from what his parents are accustomed to, and, while they express some concern about the morality of the peer group's standards, they nevertheless make it clear to him that they expect him to retain his popularity in the peer group somehow. His parents have given him moral principles but he finds that answers to specific questions about moral behavior must be worked out anew.

The task for the child is to change from an *authoritarian* to a *rational* conscience. By the term rational conscience we mean a conscience that chooses means appropriate to the ends it holds most valuable. The ends are the moral principles that the parents have taught the child and continue to teach him by example and by precept: honesty, loyalty, responsibility, the Golden Rule, and so on. The means are for the child to discover with help from parents, teachers, and age-mates. The difference between a rational and an authoritarian conscience is that in the latter the means are laid down authoritatively and rigidly by the parents and become a part of the content of his conscience—"you must not use certain bad words, you must not smoke, you must go to Sunday School, you must do just what your teacher tells you, you must never play with Jewish children, you must not go to the movies on Sunday," etc. In the rational conscience, on the other hand, the means are kept flexible, to be adapted to serve the ends in a changing society.

The rational conscience does not require the child to submit to the peer-group code. It enables him to come to terms with the peer code, if that is possible without sacrificing the basic moral values of his conscience as he acquired it from his parents. It enables him usually to solve the problem of obeying his conscience, at the same time gaining and keeping the approval of his peers.

How the Peer Group Helps. The most important effect of the peer group on conscience in middle childhood is exerted through games. The child's attitude toward rules of games is really his attitude toward moral rules in general, for rules of games are rules for conducting what the child regards as his most important business. In the attitudes of the six- or seven-year-old child to rules of games the authoritarian conscience is well illustrated. He thinks they are unchangeable. He believes they come from some unchallengeable authority. When asked who made the rules he often says, "God," or "father," or "the government." When asked whether children can change the rules, he thinks not.

During the years of middle childhood boys and girls gradually learn that rules of games are made for the satisfaction of the players, and that the players can change the rules by mutual agreement. They learn that "the Sabbath was made for man, not man for the Sabbath." By the end of middle childhood there is much experimentation with rules of games. New games are invented. New "ground rules" are invented for games like baseball and basketball.

Piaget has called the transition in attitudes toward rules of games a growth from a "morality of constraint" to a "morality of coopera-- tion." We can also call it a growth from the authoritarian to the rational conscience. Undoubtedly, this experience of children helps to prepare them for the law-making and law-changing activities of citizens in a democracy.

Can a Child Achieve a Rational Conscience without a Peer Group? What about the children who seem to be poised, sure of themselves, able to get along well with adults, who know how to win praise and approval from adults, yet are disliked by their peers and are not included in the little groups that grow up? Every teacher has had experience with such children and she may often have enjoyed these children and may even have silently condemned the other children for not accepting such a child. Can such children develop a rational conscience?

It is our guess that in our society, at one time or another, a child must find some group of his peers that he can identify himself with, whose standards he can accept, before he is able to achieve a rational conscience. Our society is highly diversified, it has few rituals to govern our actions, it poses for the adult a great number of choices. Although an individual cannot make wise or mature choices except within a framework that is his own, that framework must extend beyond himself. If an individual is truly isolated, it is likely that he is adrift and cannot make wise choices; that is, choices that are in keeping with his individual, personal conscience and in keeping with the demands, goals, aspirations of his society. In a society that was itself more rigidly structured and in which the roles were more clearly defined by sex and by station, the codes of behavior would be inherent in one's role; in such a society, the freely formed peer groups probably would not be so necessary. But in our society, where so few roles are any longer clearly defined by society, where a man is free to make choices (and indeed cannot escape from this freedom), it is only as he identifies himself with some section of society, only as he accepts their values, their beliefs, that he is able to interpret his own conscience in any kind of a mature fashion. So long as a child continues to identify solely with adults, so long as he uses as his standard of behavior those actions that give him status with adults, he is not developing a set of standards that are his own. He continues to judge worth, goodness, desirability, in terms of the reactions they elicit from adults. So long as this process is prolonged, the child's conscience cannot develop. Some people manage to go through life in this manner, but this is not the behavior that is termed "mature" in our society.

But can the child retain any conscience at all if he adapts himself to a peer group that has standards that conflict with those of his parents? To use Riesman's distinction between the "inner-directed" and the "other-directed" child,[5] will not the child become mainly

[5] David Riesman and others, *The Lonely Crowd: A Study of the Changing American Character* (New Haven, Conn.: Yale University Press, 1950).

other-directed and lose his inner direction? Must not the child who adapts himself to the peer group surrender his claim to independence of judgment and value?

By transferring allegiance from parental standards of dress and language and reading material to peer standards he has not necessarily become either more independent or more dependent. In the course of this transfer he may free himself somewhat from dependence upon his parents and discover a way of mutual interdependence with age-mates; or, he may learn to take the lead in the peer group, or to be a follower. There are a number of social roles available in the peer group, which can be described by such names as *clarifier, maintainer, supporter, complier, disruptor, stranger, permission giver,* and *scapegoat.* In our studies of boys and girls moving through middle childhood and adolescence, some of the most popular and successful children in the peer group created for themselves positions of independence, both of parents and peers.

The reason this is possible seems to lie in the fact that adults and children remain in basic agreement on the moral values of the society. They all favor certain fundamental moral principles and the behavior that results from applying these principles. For example, adults and children alike believe in fair play, honesty, loyalty, responsibility, and friendliness. Believing in these basic values, they also agree quite well on the kinds of behavior that exemplify these values.

Hence the child can live up to the values of his parents and still adapt himself to the fashions and the fads of his peer group. To a considerable extent this is what the rational conscience is about. By developing a rational conscience the child is able to distinguish the ends from the means. The ends or basic moral principles and values that his parents have given to him are preserved in his conscience. But some of the means that his parents have taught him are dropped or modified under the influence of the peer group. This child does not become a slave to the peer group. He becomes a discriminating and participating and responsible member of it.

When parents give a child a good conscience and stand by him while he adapts himself to the peer group, the child wins a rational conscience and a rational scale of values.

3. *To Learn Appropriate Social Attitudes* [6]

Only the most unfortunate children fail to learn to enjoy and love their families. The family is certainly the most-loved social institution in our society, and this is due to the fact that the individual finds so many of his needs satisfied by it.

But a pleasant experience in one's family does not insure enjoyment of all the social groups with whom one comes into contact. A pleasant family experience probably predisposes a person to find happiness in other social groups also, but still each new group is a new experience, and the quality of this experience will determine his attitude toward this and other social groups.

The peer group, which is the first social group the child meets outside his family, tends to condition his attitude toward social groups in general. If he enjoys the peer group, he is likely to approach all groups with the expectation of liking them. The experience of building loyalty to the peer group, if it is a rewarding experience, helps a person to become a loyal member of a church, a community, a nation.

If the peer group is to serve this purpose, it must be a place in which casual social contacts are easy and rewarding, where one child can approach other children casually and enjoyably. The trading of cards is an example of the easy and impersonal kind of social contact that can be fostered in the peer group.

Another example is that of spontaneous conversation between children during work periods at school. During a period of writing drill, quiet conversation with one's neighbors can be permitted without interfering with the work. Similarly with work in the art or science rooms. In the school there may be a variety of these casual social contacts. A child will comment on a drawing of another child, telling what it reminds him of; one child may stop by the desk of another to chat about something he has just thought of; a group of friends may be working and talking together over a project.

In addition to the general attitude of pleasure in group activities, the peer group may also teach attitudes about specific social groups. If the group is mixed in racial or religious or economic background,

[6] See Developmental Task #9, pp. 40–41.

and if the peer-group experience is pleasurable, the children will learn to appreciate and to enjoy being with people of other social groups.

4. *To Achieve Personal Independence* [7]

It is certainly not a mere coincidence that a child is searching for ways of identifying himself with his peers at the very time that he has gained a real measure of independence in his relations to his family. As he becomes more aware of himself as a person in his own right, as he accepts increased responsibility for his own actions, his need grows for identifying himself with his peers in order to gain some sense of who he is, what he can do, how he is to behave. Identity with adults cannot fill this particular gap because he is only too aware that he is *not* an adult. Rather, as he now experiments with adult roles, with adults behaviors, he turns to the company of his peers to practice these new roles.

Children help one another to achieve personal independence by giving a basic emotional support and by accepting one another in attempts at playing adult roles. Children can offer comfort and support to their peers, and can in turn accept it, because they share a world in common, because they are in the same boat and are aware of it. As other children react to his telling about his doubts and fears, the child can get some sense of proportion, some more objective insight into troubles. As he finds that other children have similar fears and have learned to work them through, he may be better able to handle his feelings.

Below are some anecdotal recordings of situations in which one child was sensitive to the troubles of another child and helped the child in one way or another to overcome his fears, to face a situation more objectively, or to handle his feelings in a more acceptable manner. They were made at the Sonia Shankman Orthogenic School, a residential institution for severely emotionally disturbed children of normal or better than normal intelligence, ranging in age from six to fourteen years. The excerpts are from *Love Is Not Enough*,[8] by Bruno Bettelheim, the principal of the school.

---

[7] See Developmental Task #8, pp. 38–40.

[8] Bruno Bettelheim, *Love Is Not Enough* (Glencoe, Illinois: The Free Press, 1950).

Although these are illustrations of the behaviors of emotionally disturbed children, we see no reason to believe that a child who was not disturbed would in virtue of his greater health have less empathy for other children or would be less sensitive either to his own needs or to the needs of others. However, the kinds of situations or the kinds of problems to which a healthy child will react with empathy are likely to be different from those to which a disturbed child will react. In the following illustration a normal child may be insensitive to or bored with the problems these children face in waking up, and consequently will not respond to the situation.

Many a child needs the invitation to play from another child before he is able to leave his bed. Then he feels sure he is accepted. Some of our children, particularly those who have been at the School for some time and have made real progress, behave as if they knew exactly what the fearful child needs in the morning. And they act accordingly, usually with much greater success than an adult might have had with the same tactic. They take some of their toys over to the timid child's bed and start to play with him, sitting on or right next to his bed. They put the dolls or toy cars or airplanes right on the sleepy child's bedcover and slowly involve him in the game.

The child who dreads meeting the day cannot help becoming interested in the play that another child spreads right on his blanket. Soon he has said something, one word has led to another, and he has joined the game. The instigator, as if he knew how to proceed, then extends the limits of the game beyond the bed, then takes it onto the floor just in front of the bed, then farther out into the room, and soon the child who was hesitant to get up finds himself sitting on the floor or at the table, wrapped up in the game, not quite knowing how he got so awake and out of bed. But the ban has been broken; he has stepped out towards reality and nothing bad has happened. . . .

How children do these things will naturally depend upon their interests, their age, intelligence, and maturity, and that of the child they are trying to involve in their game.

Mitchell, aged eleven, would bring his chess board to the bed of another boy, quietly and deliberately setting the board and the men up on the blanket. First, he moves both the black and white figures, as though only playing by himself. Soon the sleepy child becomes interested and tells Mitchell how to move his figures, and finally he moves his figures himself, becomes wider and wider awake. (P. 103 f.)

Since our classes are arranged neither by grade nor by age, children who have just successfully outgrown one emotional or learning difficulty are sometimes the best persons to help others with theirs. In this way they can test their own newly acquired gains and also fight the temptation to submit to their former behavior in the way it is easiest to do that—namely, by fighting it in others instead of themselves.

For example, Harry's teacher found it impossible at first to keep him in the classroom. (Harry was then a seven-year-old delinquent.) But when Joe, aged twelve, offered to help, she had a valuable ally. Joe had barely outgrown his own delinquency, and valued his newly acquired status as a citizen of the classroom. Because of his recent past he had more of the necessary empathy with Harry than the teacher; but because of his still shaky controls, Harry's truancy was unbearable to him. At any rate, he volunteered his help and it was agreed that his desk and chair should be placed beside Harry's.

Whenever Harry got restless, Joe sensed it much sooner than the teacher could have done. He would put his arm around the younger child consolingly and Harry was reassured by it, though he would never have permitted the teacher to touch him. Harry trusted Joe as a former delinquent, but was still suspicious of his teacher. If she came near him he became jittery, while Joe had an easy time quieting him down. Joe himself enjoyed this very much, which was helpful both to him and to Harry. (P. 163 f.)

Here are examples of the insight children often have into others' behavior, and their ability to communicate their understanding. It should again be pointed out that children are free to behave in this fashion only when they live in an accepting, nonthreatening milieu.

George got very angry one day because some of the children were being critical of his nasty remarks. By way of reply he announced that he was going for a walk by himself. In general we do not stop children from isolating themselves when they feel uncomfortable in the group, but in this case the counselor felt it was not to George's advantage to let him annoy the other children and run off to dodge the consequences of his hostility. She felt that by now he was well enough ahead in development to learn to give up discharging random hostility against others without any connection to their attitude toward him, which in this case had been very friendly. But George insisted, saying in a grandiose way that he was going off and that he didn't wish to be bothered by what other children felt about his remarks. He added that he didn't care how the counselor felt about them either, at which she shrugged her shoulders.

But now Paul, one of the other boys, took over and said: "Your wanting to take a walk is just like a man who drinks. You know some people go and get drunk when they have lots of troubles, and they think they'll forget them that way. And then they go and sleep it off, but after they wake up they find that they have the same troubles and didn't get rid of them. It's just like that when you want to take a walk."

Paul's reasonable approach changed the situation for George. It gave him something to think about and he began to wonder if his efforts to evade issues by just going away by himself was really such a successful way of dealing with reality. (P. 275)

Jack was present when another child was pretending to be a bear. The counselor looked askance at the game in view of the other child's tendencies to avoid reality, and told him he wasn't a bear at all or even an animal, but a human being. Jack, who had never admitted that he, too, imagined himself to be an animal, became very incensed and said, "Aw, that's another of your damn rules. That rule is so filthy it needs a bath." His angry explosions continued for some time until another boy finally told him, "Now shut up. You're not an animal, you're a human being," at which Jack complained, "I always made believe I was an animal, but you and these damn rules around here won't let me."

Thus for the first time, and due to group pressure, Jack not only admitted to phantasies he had previously hidden, but also conceded the possibility of having to give them up. The argument was concluded when the other boy announced with an air of finality, "Well, you are a human being, and if that's a rule, it's a damn good one." (P. 275)

Bert, a relative newcomer, was testing out counselor and group one day by trying to annoy Hank. First, he put his foot up on the table where Hank was trying to play, until Hank moved away. But Bert followed him and again put his foot on the table so as to prevent the other child from going ahead with what he was doing. At that time the counselor took hold of Bert's foot and put it gently but firmly on the floor.

Bert sat there quietly for several minutes and then began to cry. He hid his head under the table as if he hoped no one could see he was crying and tried to separate himself from the group. The counselor asked him if she had hurt his foot, but Bert shook his head and went on crying hopelessly. At this point Ralph spoke up and said, "Of course, you didn't hurt his foot, Gayle. You hurt his feelings." And then Bert, who had been crying to himself, began to cry openly, raising his head and looking around the group whose understanding and support he now seemed to sense.

While previous efforts by the counselor to console him had had to be rejected he could see for himself now that the group understood and accepted his feelings (although he had been the aggressor), and he was ready to accept her consolation. Pretty soon he stopped crying and curled up in her lap—shortly afterward, entered play with the children. (P. 273)

Middle childhood is an age of activity, of exploration and investigation. The activity now is rarely random activity; it is usually directed to a purpose, such as playing within the rules of a game or understanding some phenomenon in the physical world. To an increasing extent, a child's conception of himself is tied up with the skills he has. It is as though his acceptance of himself comes in part from his ability to master different forms of the world outside himself. We think that this affects his relations with his peers. As a child becomes part of an activity group that grows up around a common interest or a common project, he contributes certain skills, certain knowledge. He has the opportunity to test his skills against those of his peers. He adds to his conception of himself as his peers react to his skills, as he helps get a job done. The role that he is assigned by the group is determined largely by the relationship between the requirements of the job and his assets. His sense of adequacy, his feelings about his skills, his feelings about his ability to master his world, all these will be affected by the contribution he makes, the role he plays within an activity group. That is, the child gets a feeling about who he is, what he can do, how effectively he can perform a task by being a part of a group of other children who are doing similar things or contributing to the same goal. He adds to his conception of himself in a way that he could not do if he completed the same job in isolation.

In addition to the broad base of emotional support which the peer group can give to a child, there is also another kind of assistance. This assistance consists of supporting children in their efforts to play adult roles. During the latter part of middle childhood a boy or girl spends a great deal of time practicing roles of adults. A girl likes to think of herself as a dancer, a singer, a movie actress, a secretary, or a nurse. A boy takes the roles of cowboy, airplane pilot, ballplayer, farmer, truck driver.

Success in these roles strengthens the feeling of independence and of assurance that one can be an effective adult. What are the evidences of success or failure? The child experiences success if the people around him accept his performance, if they play up to him by taking similar roles, and by seeming to respect his roles. This is easy for the peer group to do. All the members of the group being in the same need of mutual reassurance, they can play at adult roles and support one another. On the other hand, adults are often too busy to pay attention to what children are doing, or to take these games seriously enough to give children a feeling of success in them.

CHAPTER 6

The Teacher's Relations with the Peer Group in Middle Childhood [1]

THE KINDS OF GROUPS children form, and the kinds of relationships they establish within the groups, will depend very much upon the kinds of situations in which children come together. A child spends a great deal of his time in school in these years; consequently, the school is an important setting in which children relate to one another. If one accepts the theory that it is as a member of a peer group that a child is able to do the most effective job of working through the developmental tasks he faces in these years, then the question of the teacher's role in this process becomes an important one.

The school class becomes a group as the children react to one another (and to the teacher) in the course of doing the assignments, living under the rules and regulations, and sharing the penalties and rewards assigned by the teacher. It is, in other words, the teacher's presence that makes it possible for some thirty or forty children to arrive at common feelings about themselves as Miss Smith's Third Graders or Miss Jones' Fourth Graders.

Much as children may want to have a sense of belonging together, much as they may need the support that comes from identifying with other children in a group, they are unable at this period to function constructively for any length of time as a group unless there are clearly defined limits within which they are to operate. Sometimes, as in games, the limits are inherent in the activity.

[1] This chapter was originally written by Ruth Nedelsky and is taken with minor modifications from "The Teacher's Role in the Peer Group during Middle Childhood," *Elementary School Journal, loc. cit.*

Usually, however, the children need the help of an adult in establishing the limits.[2] This dependence on adults to structure a group decreases as the children grow older. One finds that the seven-year-olds, even at play, are unable to sustain group activities for any length of time by themselves. The ten-year-olds can and do.

Defining Limits in the Classroom
Inherent in the Role of the Teacher

Thus, in the classroom, it is the teacher who must assume responsibility for outlining the activities, for providing appropriate materials, for defining the goals, the penalties, and the rewards. This is true regardless of the philosophy of education under which the school system and the teacher operate. It is inherent in her role as teacher and at the same time is required by the needs of the children.

As she chooses certain activities in preference to others, as she sets up certain standards and not others by which to judge the behavior and the achievements of the children, the teacher is structuring the group. The feelings the children have about themselves as a group, the kinds of situations in which they are likely to feel and act as a group, the extent to which everyone in the class feels a part of the class group, all these follow from the choices the teacher makes.

When the teacher makes her choices of the kinds of activities and materials, the kinds of procedures, rewards, and punishments, she makes them with reference to her conceptions of what children are like, how they ought to behave, what they ought to learn. The extent to which her conceptions are based on a sympathetic and objective understanding of the nature of the children she teaches is one of the most important factors affecting the peer relations in the classroom. If the activities a teacher plans and the kinds of be-

[2] In *Child Life in School* there is a verbatim report of a spontaneous sit-down strike initiated by some of the seven-year-olds against a too-long rest period. The strike had a large popular support. But without an adult to channel the discussion and proceedings the children soon lost sight of the purpose of the strike. The group rapidly disintegrated, becoming noisy and somewhat rowdy, discharging its energy at random without any particular focus. It was only upon the insistence of the teacher, and with her help, that the group was able to formulate its grievance and work through an acceptable solution.

haviors she expects from the children are in harmony with the kinds of behaviors normal for children of that age, then the children are likely to feel at home in the classroom. They are likely to feel accepted by the teacher and this feeling of acceptance will carry over into their relationships with one another and with the teacher.

How the Teacher Affects the Peer Group

The conceptions that children have of themselves in the classroom stem mainly from their feelings about their work and from the way the teacher reacts to their behavior. Let us look at two different classroom situations and see how the difference in the ways the teacher conducts the class affects the child's feelings about himself and in turn the relations within the peer group.

In a number of public-school systems a teacher's rating depends, to a large extent, on the academic achievements of her class. Thus a teacher must get her pupils through so many readers, must have them make a satisfactory showing on a spelling test, etc. Consequently, the activities she plans for the children may fall within a narrow range of academic work—perhaps drill in spelling and arithmetic, learning to pronounce the words correctly in the reader, finding the proper answers in the geography or history books. Within this range, many of the children may not be able to find experiences in the classroom that give them an inherent sense of worth, an adequate sense of achievement. There are two reasons for this:

First: There will be a range of ability in the group. The level of intellectual maturity and the rate at which children can handle materials and learn new skills will vary. Yet the children will all be judged in terms of their ability to achieve certain fixed standards. To varying degrees the children will feel that their worth is being appraised by their success in these subjects. It is unlikely that the children who consistently fall below the level of achievement that is acceptable to the teacher will have any real sense of security or adequacy as a result of being in the class.

Second: The tasks may have little real significance for the children. Consequently, if a child does such a task, he does it either because he wants the praise of the teacher or to escape punishment. The mastery of a task that is not accepted as valid by the child cannot in itself lead to an increased sense of adequacy. On the other hand, if the task is one that the child accepts as valid, then he makes it his own. Thus he gets a feeling about himself in relation to the job independent of the teacher's praise.

Thus, if the activities are of such a nature that the children are dependent on the teacher for their sense of worth, and if the standards by which the teacher judges the children are such that some of the children will frequently have to face failure (in the sense of falling below the acceptable standard) few of the children will feel sure of their worth. There will be an endless struggle to achieve status, either with the teacher or within a peer group. Not being sure of their worth, children will compete with one another for whatever marks of status they evolve. In such a situation it is unlikely that they will be able to move freely from group to group. It is in such a climate that cliques, or closed friendship groups, are most likely to occur. Efforts of the teacher to separate the group, by changing seats, reprimands, etc., only increase the insecurity of the children and usually result in making the clique a tighter knit group than before.

Many children are likely to be deprived of any group status at all. Some children will just give up the struggle entirely. In a West Coast school system it was found that where the ability grouping plan was in effect grade after grade many of the children who were in the slowest group year after year finally lost all sense of their own worth. When given a sociometric test these children were unable or unwilling to express any choice of a child to work with or sit next to.

Yet even within a school system where emphasis is placed on mastery of the three R's, such a situation can be modified. There are probably few if any classrooms today where the children spend all their time in drill. The children are permitted to draw and color, to cut and paste. There is always time for children to tell of interesting things that have happened to them, for the class to write a story of something the children have done together. What matters is the teacher's attitude toward these activities. The children will welcome them, whatever value the teacher assigns to them. But if the teacher looks upon these activities only as something to keep the children busy in their spare moments, if the children are made to feel that the only achievements the teacher values, the only accomplishments by which they are judged, are those connected with their drill work and the subjects listed on their report cards, then for many children these other activities can contribute little to their feelings about themselves as a part of that particular class. On the other hand, if the teacher herself believes that there are many important learnings beyond the mastery of the "basic skills," if she values and enjoys these extra activities, then for the children they become a bona fide part of the school day.

Let us look now at a classroom where the teacher provides (1) a range of activities in keeping with the interests, concerns, and abilities of the children in her group; (2) materials that the children enjoy working with and can learn to manipulate; and (3), and perhaps most important of all, an atmosphere in which she respects the different kinds of achievements that grow out of the different activities. In such a situation it is likely that each child will find one or more areas in which he can achieve mastery. Then, with each task he completes, he will feel greater confidence in himself as a person and in his ability to master the tasks that are a necessary part of growing up in this culture.

As he finds projects in which he can achieve success, he will also have the satisfaction that comes from making a contribution to the group. The very fact that the teacher feels respect for whatever tasks a child does, whether they are washing the blackboard, keeping charge of supplies, helping paint a mural for the classroom, dramatizing a favorite story, making a fine map drawing, makes the child feel that he is contributing to the whole group. He feels that he *is* a part of the group. To the extent that he takes for granted that he is a part of the group, he has no need to fight for status.

In such a climate children will freely join one another in different activities. The children are likely to choose those groups to work with which best meet their needs. It may be a group in which the child can make an important contribution, it may be a group in which he can handle apparatus or material that he enjoys, it may be a group in which he can practice a skill he is working on, or it may be a group in which he can be with a child whose company he prefers. In the course of a day he is likely to join in a number of different groups, each time getting different satisfactions and making different kinds of contributions.

Standards of Conduct

A group of children can live and work together only if there is a common understanding among the children about the kinds of things they may do, about the ways of expressing themselves that are permitted. This means that the children must express their feelings within certain modes, must channel their energies in certain directions and not others. In the classroom, it is the teacher who has the responsibility for defining the behaviors that are expected, those that are permitted, and those that are frowned upon or forbidden. It is important for the children to know clearly the areas within which they may experiment as well as to understand just what is expected of them. Having the boundaries sharply defined is a source of security for the child. He knows then what is expected of him and what to expect of the teacher.[3]

But the mere existence of sharply defined boundaries is not enough to give the child a sense of security. The behaviors that are expected of him must be within his ability to accomplish, and the field in which he can experiment should be broad enough to give him genuine satisfaction. Perhaps most important, though, are the feelings that the teacher has about the children and their ways of behaving. If she is able to accept the children as they are, with whatever their particular shortcomings, they will feel at home in the classroom.

To the extent that the children feel secure and accepted, they will

[3] The defining of boundaries and the structuring of peer-group activities that we have advocated as proper functions of the teacher are appropriate for middle childhood, but not for adolescence. As children move into adolescence they should get less and less direct control from the teacher. Their peer group becomes increasingly able to rule its own affairs, and should itself take more responsibility for defining boundaries and setting limits.

be able to accept one another, and these feelings will carry over into the relationships within the peer groups.

However, in many classrooms behavior is expected of children that runs counter to what can be called normal behavior patterns for children of this age. Children are expected to sit still for long periods of time. They may be required to stay at a task until it is completed. The day may be organized in such a way that many of the children feel the constant pressure of finishing one job after another. The natural desires of children to talk together, to help one another with the work, to share secrets, are frowned upon. Besides that, the teacher may really expect the children to be quiet, polite, and obedient. She may be able to accept warmly and without reservation only those children who fall into this category.

If the children come to feel that they really are expected to be extraordinarily quiet, industrious, polite, and obedient in order to have status with the teacher, then their doubts about their abilities to grow up to the expectations of the adult world are intensified. The effect on children of being expected to exercise controls they are unable to master at the time is to increase their anxieties about being able to conform to the standards of the adult world.

Children express their anxieties in different ways, but whatever form it takes it has its repercussions in the peer-group relationships. Some children may become more passive, more (rather than less) dependent on the praise and blame of adults for their own sense of worth. Others may retreat into a pleasanter world, a world of fantasy. These children are likely to find it difficult to face the tasks necessary to being part of a group; either they will be too preoccupied with trying to maintain a relationship with the teacher, or they will be lost in their own fantasies.

Other children may act out their anxieties by rebelling against the standards that cause them. They may become erratic in their behavior, challenging the authority of the teacher, behaving defiantly, and at times deliberately violating the codes the teacher has set up. It may be feelings of hostility against the teacher, gripes against the activities in the classroom, that are the feelings that begin to bind together either a small group or the whole class. If the codes the teacher establishes make the children feel anxious about being able to achieve adult status, then it is likely that the codes the peer groups build up will be at variance with those of the teacher.

Children become tense and irritable in situations where they are able to achieve adult approval only by struggling for controls that are beyond their ability to manage easily, where they can feel no certainty of being accepted by the adult. These tensions and resentments are often expressed against each other. Children may pick on the "teacher's pet" or they may gang up on some child who is particularly vulnerable. What groups do spring up are likely to be closely knit, with strong loyalties within each group and little movement of individuals from group to group.

In a classroom where the children feel that the teacher does not accept the kinds of feelings and behaviors that are a very real part of them, they are likely to have very little sense that they are "all right." Communication between the teacher and the children is likely to be cut off, and the teacher will be excluded from all the activities of the peer groups that have any real meaning to the children.

Thus the teacher, by the choices she makes in fulfilling her functions as a teacher, affects the peer-group relationships in her room, whether or not she is aware of it. It is within her power to establish a classroom climate in which children can freely associate with one another and can build up groups based on mutual acceptance and appreciation. There is every indication that the academic learning that the children are able to achieve increases as they work and play together in a friendly, accepting atmosphere.

Determining the Composition of Activity Groups

If the teacher plans the daily activities in such a manner that children are able to mingle freely with one another and to work together, she may find that in certain situations there is little or no value to a child in having to make choices frequently about whom he is going to sit next to, to walk down the hall with, to eat lunch with, to work with. She may find that having to face the worry each day about whether he will be chosen or whether the child he chooses will agree to be his partner is not conducive to easy relationships, that entering into competition daily for the privilege of being with certain other children can be a devastating process for many children. Such procedures are not likely to make for group stability and cohesiveness, as it is difficult for a feeling of mutual trust to grow up if each day a child fears his place may be taken by another.

Some sense of stability of arrangements must be communicated to the children, especially the younger children, if they are to be able to establish constructive group relationships. This may often be done best if the teacher determines the composition of groups with the aid of sociometric data.

The most effective groupings seem to be those that permit each child to be in a group with at least one of the persons he most wants to be with. (It should be noted that a child's playmates are not always the children he most wants to be with; they may be instead the available ones, the ones who are willing to play with him.) A teacher can best get the information about the real choices of the children by asking each child to write, in order of preference, the names of the three children he most wants to be with for whatever specific situation the teacher is going to arrange the grouping.

Obviously, every child cannot have his first choice, but each child is assured that he will be granted one of his choices. Usually, the unchosen children are the ones that are given their first choice (unless they should be rejected by the child they have chosen). The reason for this is as follows: according to the studies that have been made, a child's first choice is usually a child more mature than he himself is, usually one who can serve as a model or a guide, as a source of confidence in the very area that the child is having his greatest difficulty. (No clear pattern has yet emerged from the second and third choices.) It is the unchosen child who most needs the support of his first choice. On the other hand, the children who are chosen by a number of children are likely to be ones who are already quite successful in establishing relations with other children and who are likely to function well and with enjoyment in any group. Since the children's preferences are held in strictest confidence, no child knows what choices other children have made. An unchosen child knows only that he has been given one or more of his choices; he knows the others in the group have, too. So he feels that he has a right to be in the group. This in itself gives him a new feeling about himself, a new confidence. Under such circumstances it has been found that the unchosen children now make greater use of their capacities and act in a more mature manner.

Values of Teacher Determining Composition of Peer Groups

Thus one of the values that can come from the teacher using the children's choices as a basis for determining seating arrangements, or the composition of the groups in certain situations, is that those children who most need the help that comes from being part of a group are given an opportunity to be with one or more of the children they most want to be with. It should be pointed out that it does not necessarily follow that these children will build up a group feeling, will function as a group. The extent to which these aggregations of children will accept one another and will feel themselves to be a group will depend in part on the way the particular personalities of the children react to one another. By making sure that no child is put in a group with another child who rejects him, the probability of the children's being able to accept one another is increased. If the interest in the project is strong enough, the children may find enough in common as they carry through the project to establish genuine relationships among themselves.

Probably most important of all is the kind of climate, the atmosphere, in the classroom. As was mentioned earlier, if the teacher makes the children feel they are welcome, if they have opportunities for genuine achievement, then the feeling of confidence and security that a child has within himself makes it likely that in a situation of genuine interest such an aggregation of children will be able to feel themselves a group. If, on the other hand, there are few feelings of mutual trust and confidence permeating the classroom, devices such as sociometric tests are likely to be of little avail in helping those children who most need help. An unchosen child placed in a group may continue to be ignored.

When grouping of children is managed wisely by the teacher, the children themselves are not likely to form tight-closed cliques. They are more likely to form the kind of open and changing groups described by a committee of mothers and teachers in a certain school, as follows:

The groups are fluid. They are problem centered or interest centered, born of a common desire to get together for a purpose, dissolving when the goal is reached or when new, more pressing problems or interests develop. Individuals move freely from sub-group to sub-group and in the course of the day participate in a number of them.

Helping Individual Children into the Peer Group

There are certain ways in which the teacher may be able to help the individual child. In the preceding sections we have dealt with general procedures that concern the class as a whole. Now we come to the particular problems children may have in establishing relationships with their classmates and some suggestion of things a teacher may do to help the child who has such a problem.

1. In the second grade, a teacher may find children who still do not seem to know how to go about making friends, who do not seem sure enough of themselves to make overtures to other children, or who do not seem to realize that they would be acceptable playmates to some of the other children. If a teacher can find work situations in which the child feels at ease, and in which he has at least a fair degree of competence, then he may be able to relate to another child (or children) in terms of the work. He may accept help from them and establish a relationship that way. He may have good ideas to contribute and get acquainted with the others through an exchange of ideas. Sometimes he may establish a relationship by bringing something from home that is needed in the group work, or something that the others enjoy looking at or playing with. With each successful contact that he is able to make with another child his confidence in himself is likely to increase; his ease with other children will grow as he experiments with the different ways of approaching children.

2. Some children may try to make friends, may try to get into a group, but are ignored by the other children. This frequently happens if a child has ways of behaving that are annoying to the other

children. If the teacher can find some talent, some skill which such a child has, and can create a situation in which the child can contribute his talent or skill in a way *that would be valued or appreciated by the other children,* the other children may see this child in a new light and may be willing to accept him, even if in a limited area or limited way. As in the case above, with each success, with each new feeling of confidence, the child is likely to be able to establish better and better relations. We will use an incident reported by a teacher to illustrate.

A boy whose attitude and general conduct were rude and un- mannerly the first of the year expressed a desire to take part in the little Mexican play we were getting up. Thus far he had been ostracized by the group and left severely alone. When he demonstrated, however, that he could and would take a conspicuous part in the play and carry it out creditably, even before an invited audience, he was from then on accepted by the group in a far more favorable way; and when towards the end of the year another play was being planned, his name was one of the first selected by the committee to act out a leading part.

3. It may happen that inner conflicts may be so strong that the child is unable to establish any constructive relationships with the other children. He may be unable to exercise a sufficient degree of control over his actions to make himself at all acceptable to the other children. Probably each year a teacher has a child like this. Sometimes the child is so preoccupied by his own trouble that he does not even seem to be aware of his rejection by the other children. In any case, it is likely that there is no way the child will be accepted by the other children until he has been able to modify his behavior. In these cases the most important thing the teacher can do for the child is to help him understand that she can accept him as a person of worth, even with all his shortcomings. (This, of course, may not always be possible. Teachers have feelings, too, and sometimes a teacher just may not be able to feel sympathetically toward a child no matter what insights she has about his behaviors. In that case, it has been found that the best thing may be for the child to be transferred to another teacher who can take this particu- lar child in her stride. This, we realize, is not possible in every school system.)

If the teacher can at the same time find ways in which the child can gain a respect for his own abilities, either by doing jobs in the classroom like cleaning the sink or washing the blackboards, or by mastering some of the assignments, the child may gradually get a changed conception of himself and eventually he may be able to enter into some kind of relationships with the children even if he never becomes popular.

We quote another incident described by a teacher:

One boy had given a bit of trouble in disturbing the grade, talking, disregarding standards. It did not seem advisable to keep reasoning with him as the promises he made readily were broken the next day. He was a nervous, high-tempered child who was not happy nor did he want others to be. He was constantly hitting, pushing, quarreling, and I could see utterly unaccepted by the group. I visited his home and found he had always been like this. He has a good mind, however, and could be quite gentlemanly in manner towards adults. From time to time I showed him a little kindness, and when possible I commended his work. I let him see that in spite of his misconduct I was still his friend. Gradually I began to see a change coming. He began to smile more, enjoy a joke, and had less disturbing ways. Occasionally I would speak of his improvement before the class, and before long I could see some friendships springing up. He turned out to be a wonderful little football player and thus won the admiration of the group.

In helping children establish better relationships with a group it should be noted that all the teacher can do is to create a situation in which it might be possible for the group to see the child in a new role. It is not within the province of the teacher to dictate to the children whom they are to take into their groups, whom they are to like. This is the prerogative of the group. But if the teacher, within the limits of her situation, makes an effort to organize her classroom in such a manner that children have easy access to one another, if she creates an atmosphere in which she makes each child feel confident of his worth, then it is likely that the children will freely form groups and will be able both to offer and to accept help from one another in their problems of growing up.

CHAPTER 7

The Growth of the Mind [1]

THE PURPOSE of this chapter is to trace the course of mental growth from birth to adulthood, with special emphasis on the period of middle childhood, in order to help make clear the nature of the intellectual developmental tasks of this age period and their relation to the school curriculum.

By mental growth we mean the learning of word meanings and the learning of speech, which are the early stages, the growth of factual information, and the development of concepts and of the complex thought processes that are called reasoning, which are the later stages.

To a limited extent mental growth is analogous to the growth of bones and muscles, which seem to have a pattern of development within them, only needing for its fruition adequate nutrition and normal physical activity. Mental growth certainly depends upon the physical growth of the brain and nerves. But mental growth depends much more upon the social stimulation one gets than does physical growth. There are cases on record of children who were brought up in social isolation, but were fed adequately, and these children showed serious and, in nearly all cases, permanent retardation of mental growth, although their physical growth was adequate.

Mental growth takes place through learning. But why do we learn? We learn partly in response to social expectations or demands. The people who are in charge of us as children expect us to learn. However, it is probable that there are other and more direct rewards than social approval to the child for growing mentally. Remembering what he has seen, connecting things together in his

[1] The writer wishes to express his appreciation of the work of Ruth Nedelsky, whose memorandum on mental growth he used liberally in writing this chapter.

mind, learning words for things, building concepts, and reasoning from cause to effect give him the ability to predict and to some extent to control what will happen in his world. Thus there is a direct gain that encourages him and keeps him growing mentally. This kind of gain certainly persists up to the age of twelve or fourteen for all people in American society. Beyond that point a good many people may not experience much direct reward for further mental growth.

Goals of Mental Growth

Mental growth seems to occur in four broad movements, each directed at a specific goal. The goals are:

1. *To Separate Objective Reality from Fantasy*

Every person has some kind of a direct, immediate, and personal reaction as a result of each encounter with the world. For instance, one stands near two steel strips that stretch away into the distance. A light approaches, growing brighter all the time. One hears a hoarse, intermittent, but insistent sound. Then a rumble that grows to a roar as blinding light and booming sound and moving object bear down on the individual standing near their path. As the apparition thunders by, the experienced person remarks that a railroad train has passed, and proceeds to forget the experience. But what does this mean to the four-year-old child who encounters it for the first time? Is it some giant monster that may destroy him? Is it something like the thunderstorm that he has learned to watch from the window at home? The child assigns to each experience some kind of meaning that takes into account his own feelings as a result of the encounter. These meanings can be called the private meanings, the meanings unique to the individual. A very young child has no way of knowing that his way of feeling is unique to himself. As the child grows, and as the adults help him interpret the meanings of his experience, he comes to accept their interpretation as the objective meaning. Objective meanings are those held in common by the adults, they are the properties by which society identifies things, they are the meanings that for the most part can be tested empirically.

Learning to interpret the things round about in terms of their objective meanings is one of the aspects of growing up. It is a very necessary one. A child can communicate successfully with others only to the extent that he shares meanings in common with other people. A child can be successful in relating himself to the world in which he has to live only if he keeps expanding the objective meanings he holds about the behavior and functions of the things around him, because only then will his expectations be valid.

By the beginning of middle childhood the child is making strong efforts to arrive at an objective understanding of the objects and persons and events in his world. He apparently feels under a necessity that the child of three or four does not feel to separate sharply his own fantasies about an object from his objective understanding. For the younger child the line between reality and fantasy is a fluid one and the child moves with ease from the one world to the other. For example, he may have an imaginary playmate with whom he converses and plays when he wants to, moving in and out of this private world with ease and no appearance of distinguishing between the objective and private worlds. Perhaps the child holds the two worlds as equally real and equally true.

But by the age of five or six the child shows some recognition that adults do not place equal value on these two worlds. At about the same time the child begins to discover that other children do not share his private world and he must agree with them on an objective world if he is to play with them. By seven a child is normally able to make a sharp distinction between reality and his imagination and to recognize his imaginings as different and less real than reality.

Not all children are as mature as this. For instance, one first-grade boy told his teacher and the children about a pony of his that had run away, called a turkey buzzard that flew over the school his "pet pigeon," said his father was an airplane pilot and had given him an airplane ride, said that his grandfather was a locomotive engineer, said his father had a new Packard V-8 automobile, and claimed that it was his family's cow that had chased another boy. None of these things was true.

Most children from ages five to eight show a marked decrease in fantasy. Their make-believe in games is formalized and enacted

within a set of rules. Perhaps the predominance of rigidly structured games (such as ring-around-a-rosy) at this particular time
grows out of the need for children collectively to find some piece
of life in which their roles can be defined by the objective situation,
not by their inner feelings.

It is as though one of the developmental tasks for children at this
particular time is to *learn to live* in this objective world they have
been slowly coming to accept as the real world, the world of adults,
the world society recognizes, and the world they must learn to live
in if they are to play grown-up roles.

In early childhood, a child in his games and in his art is intent
primarily on expressing his feelings about an event, a thing, or at
times about life in general. But by seven, the child is shifting in his
art to a representational expression of the object or event. For
instance, a first-grade boy was busy making a Nazi flag. Another
little boy who had been looking on remarked, "If that's supposed
to be a Nazi flag, you have to paint it red." (The artist was making
it purple.) The teacher commented that she thought he was the only
child in the room who would have thought of a Nazi flag in terms of
its proper color. However, in another year it is likely that the
artist himself would have been concerned with painting the flag the
color that a Nazi flag really is. At six the child is still using color
primarily to express his feelings.

2. *To Explore Reality and Discover Its Orderliness*

The special mental activity of middle childhood is the exploration
and cataloguing of facts. The great wide world lies before the child,
who takes sheer delight in discovering one fact after another. His
mind is open, waiting to be crammed with knowledge. At first he is
satisfied with a hodge-podge of facts, but as the facts pile up in his
mind, he begins to sort them out and order them. He loves to
classify things, to make lists, and to dwell on the orderliness of his
knowledge.

3. *To Put Reality to Use*

Having absorbed enough facts about the world to feel at home in
it, the child becomes more selective in his interests. No longer is one

fact as good as another. By the beginning of adolescence he has some well-defined interests and tends to concentrate on them. A boy may be interested in sports and read widely about them, but may be uninterested in expanding his knowledge in other areas. A girl may become interested in dress-designing and read all the fashion magazines and books on costumes she can find. In general, the aim of the adolescent boy or girl is to learn things that fit his particular purposes and interests. He will not accept just any suggestion the teacher makes about what he should learn. The teacher must study him in order to find out what kinds of things will interest him.

Related to his selective attitude toward learning more about the world is his interest in learning the things that will be *useful* to him in such ways as preparing for a vocation, becoming more proficient at sports, or developing a musical or artistic talent. It seems that the adolescent grows mentally in ways that are related to the achievement of his several developmental tasks, while the boy or girl in middle childhood makes a developmental task out of growing mentally.

4. *To Find a More Basic Reality beneath the Surface of Things*

Together with the growing specialization of interests that comes with adolescence is a desire to get behind things, or to try to understand the fundamentals lying beneath the surface of things. This leads to the study of science and mathematics, and to the search for a grand, cosmic scheme of things. Though not so widespread as the search for useful knowledge, this still is a characteristic adolescent approach to reality, which lays a basis for the task of building a scientific world-picture.

Levels of Mental Growth

The four goals of mental growth just mentioned are related to the three levels of mental growth that dominate the ages of early childhood, middle childhood, and adolescence respectively.

1. *Immediate Physical and Face-to-Face Exploration of Reality*

During early childhood the child's main intellectual activity is that of building simple concepts of physical and social and moral reality out of his own direct experience. He does this by the most direct and immediate exploration that is possible: by seeing and feeling and hearing and smelling objects, by entering into a variety of emotional relations with members of his family and with other children, and by experiencing rewards and punishments for his behavior. The end product is a store of simple concepts dealing with things and with human relations.

2. *Mental Exploration of Concrete Facts*

Gradually the child's mind develops to the point where he can learn from a book, a movie, a television or radio program, a lecture. He no longer needs to have objects present to his senses in order to think about them accurately. His memory contains enough knowledge to be used as a basis for thinking about things not present to his senses. Having seen a camel at the zoo, for example, he can read about a llama and get a pretty fair notion of how it looks and acts.

Middle childhood sees this mode of mental activity added to the earlier one of direct exploration of reality. Gradually the child increases the proportion of his vicarious experience over his direct experience until by the fourth or fifth grade he is exploring reality as much with his mind and memory as with his senses. Still, though, he needs to deal in concrete imagery. He must read or hear about definite, concrete instances, persons, or processes. He can understand a specific geographical exploration, but not explorations in general. He can relate himself to a specific pioneer family, not to the westward migrations in general.

Intellectual Interests of Middle Childhood. There are indications that in middle childhood intellectual curiosity is channeled more in the area of impersonal relations, things, processes, and the exploration of the surrounding world than in the area of human relations. The latter are problems of immediate experience for the child, but not of intellectual quality. He is still *feeling his way* in human relations while he is already *thinking his way* into the world of nature.

Another characteristic of the interests of middle childhood is the preference for details rather than wholes. Children rarely attack the main thread or theme of a story or process; instead they are interested in sidelines, oddities, minor details. Toward the end of middle childhood and just before adolescence there is a pull away from the immediate present. This is an age when the far away and long ago has its greatest appeal. In an analysis of topics brought up in free discussions by sixth graders it was found that they rarely discussed anything that was an intimate part of their lives. This was a common pattern regardless of the socioeconomic background of the children or the type of instruction or school.

In order to throw further light on mental growth in middle childhood we shall turn to the questions children ask. A useful collection of such questions has been made by Emily Baker,[2] who asked 1,422 children in Grades 3 through 6 to write their questions. She secured 9,280 questions from children in sixteen cities ranging in population from 1,000 to 576,000 and spreading across the U.S.A. from the Middle Atlantic to the Northwest states.

One is immediately impressed by the wide range of interests of children and their avidness for detail. Some of their questions (with their original spelling and grammar preserved) are:

How do they make movies of Ghost, Giants and storms and all sorts of things like that?

Why does snapshot paper turn dark?

What makes static on the radio in rainy weather?

Does a motorboat burn the same kind of gasoline as a car?

What is the average speed of a Steam Ship?

Do the perople in Afrach have rowboat?

When you put on the brakes in a car how does a little light go on in back?

How long does it take to build an airliner, a steamer?

Are some airplanes made out of the material plastic?

What makes the landing gear of an airplane go down when on land?

Why do airplanes have wings?

How do they lay forms for a bridge in the river without water getting in?

What is ink made out of and what makes it different colors?

How is the lead we use in our pencils made?

[2] Emily V. Baker, *Children's Questions and Their Implications for Planning the Curriculum* (New York: Teachers College Bureau of Publications, Columbia University, 1945).

What do the orange men cut the oranges off the tree with?
How many men does it take to handle a big tree after it is cut?
How do men kill cows?
Why don't city people have cows?
Why is the river so terribly dirty?
I wonder how deep the water is at the Mississippi river is in the middle.
How does grass get green in the summer?
I would like to know how so many big rocks got into the woods.
What makes tungstung wire get so hot and not any hotter?
How does the light switch make the connection go on?
What makes the clock tick?
What makes hands move on a clock?
Why does the sun keep rising in the morning it can't keep up for ever.
When a person turns the waterfaucets on how is the water forced up through the pipes?
What makes bak soda and vinegar foam?
Why does soap take the dirt off of a person?
What makes a frog tern the culr [color] uve [of] the thing he is on?
How do birds and other living things get their color?
How do sea anamal make sea shells?
Why are cat's eyes usually green?
How can a train driver tell how to stay on the track?
How do people get plumbing round on the outside and hollow in the inside?
How do bombers release bombs?
How do men make bridges stay up?
How do you grease a car?
How do lightening bugs light?
How does a python dislocate his jaws to swallow something?
How do the straw roofs of houses in Africa stay on when there is a wind?

It is notable that many of these questions ask for information about *processes* that the child cannot comprehend from direct observation. Up to this time he has been able to understand his world and keep it predictable by exploring directly. Now he must use his mind, getting mental images and explanations, and so bringing the events around him into an understandable order.

There is also interest in the properties of things. "How deep is the Mississippi?" "How fast can a boat go?" "How high do airplanes fly?" "Why does snapshot paper turn dark?" "How do lightening bugs light?" The child of this age knows that physical exploration alone will not give him the answers. He could find out how deep a mudhole is by putting in his foot. But now he wants a knowledge that he knows will not come from tactile impressions.

Another kind of question that recurs frequently expresses an interest in the unique qualities of different animals and people:

Why do crabs or lobsters walk backwards?
Why does a snake or a worm crawl on its stimach?
Why do bees like flowers?
How come pigs are always so dirty?
Why are some animals tame and some wild?
Why is hair different colors? [may mean what causes a difference in hair coloring or it may mean why are there different colors of hair]
Why do some people have freckles? [again, two possible meanings]
Why do some peopl have red skins, some have brown skins and some yellow skins? [again, two possible meanings]
Why do birds make their nest in trees?
Why are some people fat and some skinny?
Why does the grasshopper have his ear on his abtomen when we have are ears on are head? [the question about the grasshopper verbalizes what the other questions only imply.]
Why do zebras have stripes?
Why do we have Elephants?
Why are ther so many animals in the world?
For what purpose were flies put on the earth?
Why do we have different kinds of birds?
Why is there children?

It may be that the child is trying to get behind the surface reality to some more general explanation of things. He may be trying to find a meaning for individual uniqueness within a larger framework. Possibly the question about the grasshopper's ears verbalizes what the other questions only imply. The child is trying to find out what there is about the grasshopper, or the zebra, or the lobster, that fits it into a scheme of life that includes all kinds of people, fat, skinny, freckled, red, brown, white, and yellow-skinned.

There are many questions concerned with "the first."

When was the first train build? How? Where?
Who was the first one to get the idea of sailing on water?
How was the first car made? When?
What did the first bug look like?
Who was first one earth, animal or man?
What made the first tree start growing?
How did the jungle start?
How was electricity first made?
How did peopel first discover music?
What was the first musical instrument invented?
How did they first make violins?
I like music very much so I would like to know who first made an organ.
Who was the first teacher to teach in the first school?
Where was the first school?
What was before God was alive?
How was the first man born?
Was man on the earth when it first started?
Was Adam and Eve the first peopler on earth or the cave men?
Who were the first people to make houses like we have today?
Who found the first watermelon?
How was fire first started and when?
How did men first discover paint?
Who was the first person to make a puppet?
Is there any of mans Frist clothing if so are ther any places where they can be seen?
Who discovered America?
Who really discovered America?
Who was the very first person that set foot on American soil?
When did the Indians first exest?
I know that Indians lived in America before white men but I would like to know what kind of people lived in America before the Indians.
Who was the first pony express rider and what kind of horse did he have?
What did the earth look like to the very first man?
How did men first learn to talk?
Where did man come from in the beginning?
What was the first kind of book that was written?
How was medicin first invented?

Who was the first doctor? dentist?

Who was the first king of Britain? the first ruler of germeny? the first king of egypat?

Was America all trees when the first people lived here?

Possibly these questions illustrate an attempt on the part of the child to push his knowledge to its beginning point, to establish the boundaries of his world.

Scattered among these thousands of questions are a number that are concerned with how we acquire our knowledge and how we know that our knowledge is true.

Why is the world flat to us but realy turning around?

How do they know that today is Oct 14 and that Oct 10 is on Saturday?

How do we know that cave man had fire?

How did the world find out about time?

How do book writers know what happened to George Washington and others?

How do people think of all the different designe for all the clothes we wear?

How did early explorers map the new lands they discovered?

In geography how do the people that make the population maps know the population of all the countries and where it is dense and where it is not?

I know states have boundaries but just hoe can a person tell where they are?

How did King James Virsion no how to write about God?

How did people find out how far the sun is in the sky?

What makes people think the world goes around, they never saw it.

If the earth keeps turning around why don't we get dizzy?

Why can't you feel the earth moving?

How do scientist know when a year is over?

How did the egyptian people discover so many things and make so much nicer things before any one else did?

These may represent another way of dealing with the problem of establishing boundaries. "I know states have boundaries but just how can a person tell where they are?" The child will feel more at home in his world if he knows how the explanations for things were arrived at. He wants not only to know that his world behaves in a predictable manner, but also to know that he can find out the patterns.

If this interpretation of the manner in which a child relates to his world in middle childhood is true, it suggests something for curriculum content and methods of instruction. The standard curriculum for school systems is based on giving the child certain methods and information and expecting him to take these as given. Teachers are seldom concerned about helping children understand how we, as adults, collected the information we have or how we arrived at the assumptions and the generalizations that we pass on to children.

From these considerations it seems that children are trying to do several things as part of their mental growth in middle childhood. Their efforts can be listed as follows:

1. Children are trying to find out the extent to which the larger world around them is predictable—how it behaves according to rules, how it follows a pattern that can be understood.

2. Children are trying to establish boundaries to their world; not necessarily a single all-inclusive boundary, but rather a series of boundaries for each of the various areas of interest or concern.

3. Children are working at finding or making some order in their world, at organizing its facts and incidents into a pattern that makes sense to them. Much of the intellectual activity of children at this period may have little intrinsic value from an adult standpoint, in that the particular facts, the particular information the children seek would be of little significance in solving the problems these children are likely to face as adults. But the children need the satisfactions, the sense of security they derive from organizing and arranging these data into wholes they can take hold of and understand.

4. Yet, at the same time that children take avid interest in all kinds of collections of data that have little in common with the intellectual preoccupations of intelligent adults, there are indications that children are trying to understand adults' processes of reasoning and of proof. Their scattered questions indicate a growing interest in how adults get their information, how they can be sure that information is really true, what are the processes by which the

validity of the information and the ideas it produces can be tested. Although, to a certain extent, one can say that children at this age live in a world of their own, it is not a world of secession from the adult world. Rather it is a transition world that constantly reaches up into the adult world but which permits children to grapple with some of the problems of the adult world in their own terms.

Levels of Complexity. During middle childhood there is gradual motion up the complex ladder of the thought process.

The making of categories starts as early as age seven or eight and reaches a peak of interest probably about twelve. A boy will make a scrapbook with pictures of ball players and newspaper clippings about their games. A girl will do the same for movie actresses. This is an age for collections, and many hours may be spent in sorting playing cards or postage stamps or sea shells into categories.

Understanding of causality develops during middle childhood. The word "because" can usually be divorced by a child of eight or nine from the notion that there must always be a human or divine will that "causes" every event. Purely physical and material chains of cause and effect will be described by the child if he has enough information. Many of his questions are aimed at getting enough information to describe events in causal terms.

In middle childhood an individual becomes able to make mental experiments. That is, he becomes able to visualize in his "mind's eye" a great variety of concrete situations. A child of seven or eight is able to face another person and tell in which open hand, right or left, the other person holds an object. Since the other person's right hand is on the child's left, this requires the child to put himself mentally in the position of the other. Often a child of this age will be seen to twist his shoulders slightly when asked to solve this kind of problem. He moves his body slightly as though he would put himself physically as well as mentally in the position of the other person.

From this beginning the child becomes able to visualize a complicated activity, such as a group of people arranged in complex patterns, and to follow imaginary changes in their position, or to visualize the positions of the checkers in a checker game several moves ahead.

Thus by the age of twelve or thirteen the child has usually achieved the developmental task of learning the basic concepts and mental skills which assure him that he lives in a predictable world, and which equip him with enough skill and knowledge to carry him through adult life, though perhaps on a slightly below-average level. By the sixth grade he can learn fairly readily the geography and history that require him to visualize the far distant in space and time.

He is able to acquire and use systematically information that is needed for the manual and the clerical occupations, as well as for homemaking, and for elementary citizenship.

3. *Abstract Thinking*

It is toward the close of middle childhood that the power of abstract thinking begins to show itself. When a child can move from the concreteness of numbers in his arithmetic to the abstractness of allowing x to stand for any of a set of numbers, he not only is ready for algebra, he is ready for abstract thinking. When a child can assume something to be true for the sake of the argument when he knows it is probably not true, he is ready for abstract thinking. He is also ready for the type of proof in demonstrative geometry which starts by assuming something to be true that looks patently false (such as that the sum of the angles of a triangle is *greater* than two right angles), and then deduces consequences which are so absurd that the original assumption is disproved logically, as well as empirically. The logical "therefore" enters into the child's idiom at this point.

The writer knew a sixth-grade boy who made a prodigious catalogue of minerals. This he did by reading a number of mineralogical books and copying down information about every mineral that was named. Eventually, he had a book two inches thick, which he spoke seriously of publishing. This boy carried the cataloguing of factual data to the extreme. Then, on coming back to seventh grade after summer vacation, he lost interest completely in his mineral catalogue and asked to be allowed to start the study of algebra. Being a bright boy, he was encouraged to do so by his mathematics teacher, and he covered the first year of algebra in a few months' time. Here we see a sharp transition from the level of mental exploration of concrete fact to that of abstract thinking. This seldom happens as early as the sixth grade, although the beginnings of abstract thinking can be found there if we will search for them.

On this mental level the child is ready to study science as an adult. He is ready to understand scientific and logical explanations. He is ready to go beneath the surface of reality in his search for rules and general principles.

CHAPTER 8

Developmental Tasks as Objectives of Elementary Education [1]

THE ELEMENTARY-SCHOOL PROGRAM contributes in one way or another to the child's achievement of every one of his developmental tasks. Whether consciously designed for the purpose or not, the school curriculum helps or hinders the accomplishment of every task, and every school is a laboratory for the working-out of these tasks.

Consequently, it seems useful to regard the developmental tasks as objectives or goals of elementary education, some more important in the school program than others, of course. Successful achievement of these tasks can be described in terms of observable behavior, and these descriptions may be used in evaluating the progress of a child.

This has been done in the following pages, for two age levels, nine and twelve. Achievement has been described at three levels of performance: high, medium, and low. High achievement represents outstanding success, medium achievement is what may be expected of the middle two-thirds of any group, and low achievement represents failure that is serious enough to deserve special attention and special help. The definitions could be subdivided further, as they are in Chapter 18, and used as the basis for a rating or grading scale.

[1] The main body of this chapter was first written by Robert J. Havighurst and Douglas M. More as a memorandum for use by the Educational Testing Service in its *Study of Outcomes of Elementary Education,* and has been published by the Educational Testing Service in the volume entitled *Elementary School Objectives* by Nolan C. Kearney (New York: Russell Sage Foundation, 1952).

Six of the developmental tasks of middle childhood will be defined in behavioral terms as outcomes of education in the following pages. These six tasks coincide with those listed in Chapter 4, but they do not include the tasks of *intellectual development,* which are so well described and so thoroughly understood as educational objectives that we could hardly add anything useful.

The six developmental tasks that will be discussed are:

1. Learning to care for and use the body in an effective fashion.
2. Getting along with age-mates in a constructive pattern of social interaction.
3. Learning an appropriate masculine or feminine social role.
4. Acquiring a set of values and an ethical system as guides for behavior.
5. Achieving personal independence from controls by others.
6. Learning appropriate social attitudes toward institutions and social groups.

Developmental Tasks at Age Nine

1. *Learning To Care For and Use the Body in an Effective Fashion* [2]

The foundations of most patterns of behavior in caring for the body are laid down by family training in earlier years. Still, many school systems have come to feel some responsibility for teaching simple rules of health in the early childhood years, such as brushing the teeth, washing the hands, personal neatness, and so on, often through the offices of a school nurse or doctor. The school realizes the necessity for providing adequate play and rest periods, and playground equipment and facilities for sports and games. In cases where a child appears to be functioning much below par the school may make various recommendations regarding food and sleep to the child's family.

Simple facts about biology, human and animal physiology, sex differences, and the reproductive process may well be woven into the general fabric of the curriculum, or handled through special counseling services. By the end of Grade 3 we might expect a sound foundation to have been provided in this area.

[2] See Developmental Task #2, pp. 29–30.

The task may be defined as the development of sound habits of caring for the body, of maintaining good health to the best of one's ability. The child seeks for and engages in appropriate exercise to insure good growth, the development of and use of muscles in physical skills, and the safe enjoyment of using the body. He gains an attitude toward his body as an organism for enjoyment and activity.

High. Is beginning to be self-directive in routine matters of physical care, such as washing, caring for teeth, going to bed at an hour to insure sufficient rest, diet, and the like. Takes bath, combs hair, adjusts light for reading. Boys spend considerable time in acquiring skill at throwing, running, kicking balls, wrestling and the like. Girls likewise practice physical sports, but need not achieve the level of high skill that the boy must show to be at the top level on this task. Uses simple tools—hammer, saw, screw driver. Rides bicycle. Seldom fatigued. High degree of physical coordination is noted. Has knowledge of and emotional acceptance of sex differences, and of the facts of reproduction.

Medium. Has to be reminded from time to time to follow out routine care of the body. Dresses self. Handles toilet needs independently, practices safe behavior in crossing streets. Not self-directive about maintaining adequate hours of sleep, or a proper diet. Average physical game skill is acquired by the boy. Coordination and balance are average. The girl may be rather resistant to vigorous exercise and still be average for her sex. Some accurate knowledge of sex differences may be expected, but there can be gaps in this knowledge that are of a fundamental nature.

Low. Does not engage in routine health care of the body unless forced to do so by adult supervision. May need help in dressing and bathing. Does not use tools. Is highly resistant to direction about maintaining sufficient hours of sleep. Fails to develop adequate skill in physical games if a boy. Appears to be awkward; actions may show poor physical coordination. Often appears to be a "feeding problem" in that meals are taken haphazardly and with little attention to getting either enough to eat or the right kinds of food over a long period of time. May seem unnecessarily fatigued much of the time, avoids sports. Has unusual or even bizarre notions about sex differences. Reproductive processes are seen as mysterious, or fearful attitudes of a magical nature are expressed about them.

2. *Getting Along with Age-Mates in a Constructive Pattern of Social Interaction* [3]

The peer group provides an important milieu for personal and social development. It seems to fulfill some needs and perform some functions that no other setting provides. In the peer group a child can work out a conception of himself and arrive at some estimation of how his contemporaries regard him. It is in such a setting that the idea of having coequals is possible, as it seldom if ever can be when trying to relate to the always more powerful and wiser adults. A sense of personal worth is partly developed through being able to make realistic comparisons of one's own abilities, talents, and accomplishments against those of persons at the same point of development. That is, the child must "try his muscles" [physically, emotionally, intellectually] against those of his peers, and not evaluate himself against those much farther advanced or retarded. Through being at the same level of development they can have similar feelings, share attitudes, experiment in equivalent skills. It seems that few, if any, children develop into happy, successful, well-adjusted people in later life unless they have been able to engage in continuing, positive, well-knit interaction with a peer group during these years of growth.

In the peer group a child really discovers and learns his social personality, his social stimulus value to other people. He learns the habits and attitudes of approach to people, avoidance of them, conflict with them, sympathy with them, which will be characteristic of him for the rest of his life. This task may be defined as the acquiring of ability to form and maintain constructive relationships with those of similar age. A measure of it is the person's degree of adjustment with a play group, club, clique, or gang.

High. Is a member of a group of his or her own age, who characteristically play together in an informally organized way. Has one or more acceptable and functional roles in such a group. Spends most of free play time with such a group. Follows directions given

[3] See Developmental Task #3, pp. 30–31.

by age-mates; gives directions clearly enough to be followed. One or more mutual friendship choices are found on a sociometric questionnaire. Gives and participates in parties with members of the group. Reported to have good social adjustment. Takes his turn in games and use of school facilities.

Medium. Has one mutual friend, but no more, on a sociometric inquiry. Average reputation for popularity with age-mates. Is a member of a clique, group, or gang, but not outstanding in it and plays no important roles in its functioning. Takes part in simple team games, such as cops and robbers.

Low. No mutual friends. Is forced to play alone most of the time. Made into a scapegoat by other age-mates. Expressions of dislike are directed toward the subject on sociometric questionnaires. Reported to have poor social adjustment. Never chosen as a "best friend" by peer group. Exhibits hostility to age-mates and rejects them as much as they reject him or her.

3. *Learning an Appropriate Masculine or Feminine Social Role* [4]

Behaving in a masculine fashion for the boy and a feminine fashion for the girl is an important developmental task at any age. What is "masculine" or "feminine" may vary from one social class to another. For example, playing some kinds of musical instruments and having an interest in "classical" music might be considered "sissy" in some lower-class groups, but it would be acceptable for a boy to do this in some middle-class groups. The child's background needs to be kept in mind while making such evaluations. The levels of achievement that are given below are described primarily from a middle-class standpoint. Beyond direct observation some instruments are useful in determining the level of achievement: 1) there are sociometric tests containing questions about neatness, cleanliness, daring, timidity, and so on, and 2) essays may be written on such topics as "The Person I Would Like To Be Like" and "Experiences I Have Had" or "Things I Like To Do Most." Physical maturity has relatively little bearing on evaluation of sex role at this age, but it may be involved somewhat in cases of extremely early or retarded maturation.

[4] See Developmental Task #4, p. 32

High. Boy:—active in games, boisterous, often somewhat unkempt. Reputation on sociometric instruments for being daring in
play. High interest in sports and popular sport figures. No noticeable interest in girls, but may tease them. Essays on "Person I
Would Like To Be Like" show masculine hero figures as ideals.
"Experience" essays indicate vigorous games and masculine activities. Girl:—relatively quiet. Sticks to "girls' " games and seldom
plays "boys' " games or with the boys if girls are available. Little
interest in opposite sex, may make a show of disregarding them.
Essays indicate females as ideal figures, and feminine experience as
being desired.

Medium. Boy:—moderately active in physical games with other
boys. Average sociometric reputation scores for daring, active, unkempt. Ego-ideal seen as a male, but not necessarily a strong masculine figure. Girl:—plays both girls' and boys' games and seems to
like active sports. No noticeable interest in boys. Ego-ideal is
female, but may be a masculine, strong, "career" woman. Average reputation scores for "ladylike" attributes. Lower-class girls
may show less difference from boys in some groups.

Low. Boy:—called a "sissy" and shows little or no interest in
active sports. Reputation for being quiet, fearful, timid. May be
seen playing girls' games or with girls. Ego-ideal shows little influence of strong masculine figures with possible exception of the
father. Acts as though he dislikes members of own sex. Girl:—(a)
tomboy, play boys' games with boys. Avoids playing with girls.
Is reported to be active, daring, unkempt. May wear boys' clothes
whenever possible. Essays show influence of male figures in ego-
ideal. Or (b) very timid, plays with dolls, etc., with much younger
girls. Avoids playing with girls her own age. Tends to be overlooked
in reputation questionnaires. No interest in boys. Ego-ideal in essays
is limited to the mother figure.

4. *Acquiring a Set of Values and an Ethical System as Guides to
Behavior* [5]

Basic patterns of belief about good and bad, right and wrong, are
laid down in earlier years in the context of the family. However,

[5] See Developmental Task #7, pp. 36–37.

these tend to be relatively crude formulations in the child's thinking. He moves into wider interaction in the school with others his own age, adults, members of different groups, and the like. Two kinds of development take place in middle childhood. One is the acquisition of a system or set of values that enables a child to act more and more consistently as an honest, responsible, and loyal person in a variety of situations. The other is the development of an ethical code based on experience in the give-and-take of games and other activities with the peer group. This code is more flexible, more open to modification by reason and experience, than the earlier code, which was taken in uncritically from the parents and without much grasp of its real meaning.

It is not expected the child of nine will show up as having a well-formulated and flexible value system; but this gradual development progresses to near completion in adolescence. He comes to take more and more responsibility for what he does. The accomplishment of this task requires the presence of discrete elements of a personal code of behavior and the integration of these elements into an attitude toward life that motivates the individual to act in a "moral" fashion. At the top a person has a reputation for being a "good" person, and at the bottom of being a "bad" one. Specific judgments need to be made on questions of honesty, loyalty, responsibility, consideration for others, and the like.

High. Takes the lead in adjusting rules of a game to the needs of the group with which he is playing. Keeps the rules himself. Seen on questionnaires of the sociometric variety as being highly responsible, not one who would steal, cheat, or lie. Makes it a point to take others into some consideration in deciding what is right to do. Accepts his obligations to others, especially when they are pointed out to him. Obeys important regulations, even when authority figures are not present.

Medium. Seen as average in reputation on moral items of questionnaires as judged by his peers. Argues about established rules of the game. Generally considerate of others' feelings, but occasionally may be rude or discourteous, hurting others' feelings. May express some unwillingness to accept obligations to others, even when under pressure to do so. Does lie or cheat about inconsequential matters from time to time. Respects property of others. Accepts parental rules concerning religion, morality, the school, without reasoning about them.

Low. Has a reputation with peers of lying, cheating, being dishonest. Is rejected by peers as a teammate because he refuses to abide by rules. Shows little or no respect for others' rights. Inconsiderate of others' feelings, privileges, and refuses obligations to others. Does not obey regulations except in the presence of a strong authority figure. Never one whom the peers choose for positions of responsibility in matters of mutual interest, such as games, projects and the like.

5. *Achieving Personal Independence from Parents and Other Adults* [6]

During preschool years and to a certain extent thereafter the child has been highly dependent upon adults for all sorts of decisions—when and where to go, what to wear, and so on. By the end of the third year in school a greater degree of self-assertion and an ability to make many kinds of minor choices should have developed. The child is beginning to combine some rebelliousness with a genuine struggle toward positive self-expression and increased individual integrity. He is trying to set some of his own goals in life and to establish his own standards of behavior. There may be questioning of the complete validity of "blanket" authority statements by older children and/or adults. The child is in the process of moving away from a life pattern in which nearly all the rules of behavior are "given" by stronger persons. Some tendencies toward autonomy in discerning, constructing, or accepting rules are beginning to appear. That is, he is changing from a morality of constraint toward one of consent.

High. Plans his own after-chool activities without asking for help from mother. Works for an hour or more at tasks that interest him. Moves around freely in the neighborhood, during daytime. Can deal with strangers who call at the home or on the telephone. Puts up with mild accidents without crying or asking for sympathy. Occasionally shows displeasure at the arbitrary way in which parents,

[6] See Developmental Task #8, pp. 38–40.

teachers, or other authority figures direct his behavior; expresses rebellion by such actions as disregarding commands, disobeying rules occasionally, arguing with adults. Seems to fail to "hear" orders when they do not suit his interest. Stays away from home two or more nights without expressing homesickness. Puts away materials after he has used them (but may have to be reminded). Works for the approval of teachers, but is not slavishly dependent on such approval as motivation for doing his best. Accepts decisions of teacher or parents when these people definitely assert authority.

Medium. Activities tend to be largely within adult-structured situations, where an adult is present and directs the activity. There is an increasing desire expressed of wanting to range beyond such limits. Goes to and from school with confidence. Can stay away from home one night in familiar surroundings not far from home but has no real desire to do so. Subject's ideal person is usually a parent or parent-surrogate, but may include a glamorous adult.

Low. Subject's ego-ideal is exclusively a parent or parent-surrogate. Constantly requires attention, reassurance, praise by parent, teacher, or other adult. Prefers to play near adults and is timid about venturing around the community without adults to accompany him. Accepts adult structuring and discipline in all activities with little or no show of resistance. Has temper tantrums when frustrated. Cries and complains when peer activities are not to his liking and will not play with peers unless he feels that an adult will come to his aid. May be afraid of animals.

6. *Learning an Appropriate Set of Social Attitudes toward Institutions and Social Groups* [7]

These, too, tend to originate in the family, but characteristics of one's peer group interaction may influence their direction, tone, and intensity to a marked degree. During the first three school years the usual child has had a number of experiences with public officials of all kinds—teachers, policemen, firemen, and others. The child may have had some experience with people of other religions, and perhaps gets to know people of other racial or cultural backgrounds

---

[7] See Developmental Task #9, pp. 40–41.

than his or her own. Some conceptions of government and politics and business arise. Whatever the influences of family, peers, and other elements in the community, it is a task of the school to provide a setting in which the attitudes we have come to see as surrounding a central notion of democracy can be developed.

The task itself is defined to develop attitudes that are basically democratic. These are feelings, attitudes, and characteristic behaviors toward the institutions that make up the structure of the community, such as school, church, elements of public government, and the like. They also include attitudes toward the members of other racial, religious, or socioeconomic groups than one's own.

High. Says he enjoys school and in an argument stands up for his own school. Takes active part in paper drives, cleaning playground, keeping halls orderly. May make occasional disparaging remarks about the police, but also realizes they have a positive and constructively protective function in the community. Admires firemen and some other public servants. Does not make disparaging statements about other racial or religious groups than his or her own, and will come to the defense of one so attacked, even when the source of the scapegoating is within his own clique, gang, or group. Is curious about, and takes a positive interest in, learning about how and why members of other groups behave in characteristic ways different from his own.

Medium. Says he likes school. Admires policemen, firemen, and the like only because of the "romantic" nature of their duties, and because of the force they display. Will make disparaging remarks about other racial and socioeconomic groups and persons of different religious affiliation from his own if he has heard such attitudes expressed at home or by teachers in school. Joins the gang when they are scapegoating a person in that fashion, not necessarily because of a basic attitude of that nature, but simply because he does not have the moral courage to oppose age-mates in such matters.

Low. Sees school as a "prison." Is highly disrespectful toward public servants of all kinds. May react to police either in an overtly delinquent fashion, or on the basis of extreme fear. Shows little appreciation of their positive function in the community and thinks of them in terms of caricatures or stereotypes. Refuses to play with

or have any dealings with or learn facts about persons of other
acial, socioeconomic, or religious groups. Calls minority groups
ɔy unpleasant names. Scapegoats such persons often, and uses
them to blame when he has done something wrong himself.

Developmental Tasks at Age Twelve

1. *Learning To Care For and Use the Body in an Effective Manner* [8]

At age twelve the relative physical maturity of the subject has
an effect on the level of this rating. The person who matures slightly
earlier (one to two years) has somewhat of an advantage. This is
not so for those who mature extremely early, however. Menarche in
girls and pubescence in boys ordinarily occurs between twelve and
fifteen, earlier for girls than for boys, somewhat after the peak rate
of growth in height. This "point" is what is meant when we use
the word puberty in these ratings. The pubertal growth cycle is
taken from the age at which a spurt of rapid growth in height begins
to when it later subsides to its childhood rate.

High. Thoroughly self-directive in routine physical care, such
as washing, caring for teeth, maintaining adequate diet and getting
sufficient sleep. Practices simple first aid for cuts, minor burns, and
the like. If a boy, may need some urging for cleanliness. Engages in
adequate exercise to develop muscular system and promotes physical skills. Knows safe behavior in traffic with bicycle. Handles tools
carefully. Can swim. Chooses adequately balanced diet when made
responsible. Possesses simple skills of housekeeping—bedmaking,
cleaning, lawn-mowing. Perceives the human body accurately and
through self-acceptance enjoys using it. Has sound knowledge of
and accepts sex differences. Knows facts of reproduction. The girl
is well into the pubertal growth cycle, and has warm acceptance of
her new "feminine" appearance. Boys are average or better in
physical maturity, but most have not reached puberty and still
exhibit preadolescent, rough-and-ready interests.

Medium. Average in self-directiveness about routine physical
care; has to be reminded to perform some of the functions men-

[8] See Developmental Task #2, pp. 29–30.

tioned above, either by a parent or other adult. Average in the physical growth cycle, or no more than slightly retarded. Is aware of sex differences, but not necessarily acceptant of them emotionally. Knowledge of reproduction is sound in the main. Exercise, play, and games are engaged in to a moderate degree, but the individual boy or girl is not thought of by peers (e.g., on sociometrics) as outstanding in game skills and techniques of using the body (ball games, dancing, etc.). Boys handle tools, but with carelessness and awkwardness.

Low. Still requires continuing pressure from adults or parents in order to assure routine physical care. May avoid games and exercise. May have known record of indulging in detrimental health habits (e.g., habitual smoking). Not aware of facts of sex differences or reproductive process and may express some relatively bizarre, definitely incorrect ideas about them. Tends to be noticeably retarded in the growth cycle, or unusually large and not acceptant of own physique. Awkward in behavior. Handles tools clumsily.

2. *Getting Along with Age-Mates in a Constructive Pattern of Social Interaction* [9]

High. Has two or more mutual friends on sociometric questionnaires. High scores for being popular. Is in a small gang or clique in which he has a secure and functional role. Can give and take directions from age-mates. Participates in group projects that take some weeks to complete. Can subordinate his own point of view and cooperate in a group decision. As chairman of a group, brings out the participation of others. Is able to state a contrary opinion in a group discussion. Plays a variety of games. Has the social skills necessary for the kinds of parties and games that are played by children in his community.

Medium. Definitely a member of a gang, or clique group, but may not have a mutual friendship choice on a sociometric questionnaire. Considered average in friendliness and sociability. More a follower than a leader in group activities. Average or slightly below in popularity. Plays games cooperatively. Occasionally over-

[9] See Developmental Task #3, pp. 30–31.

looked by age-mates when they are sending out invitations to a party. Seldom ends a play period with a fight.

Low. Socially rejected. Gets sociometric votes for being unfriendly, unsociable. May be made the butt of teasing, disparaging comments, or hostile aggressive attacks. "Poor" social adjustment is reported. Exhibits hostility to others and rejects advances from them even when they do occur, or may be a timid fringer in play situations.

3. *Learning an Appropriate Masculine or Feminine Social Role*[10]

By the age of twelve, most boys and girls have learned to accept, and to behave in accordance with, the socially approved masculine or feminine role. They pattern their actions in sex-typical fashion. Physical maturity is beginning to have some slight bearing on the evaluation of this task, so that earlier maturing persons are likely to enter the task and accomplish it ahead of some of their peers of the same age.

High. Boy:—continues to center activities mainly with boys. Is average in rate of maturation, or large for his age. Strong interest in masculine figures as ego-ideal shown in essays on such topics. Not much interest need be shown in the opposite sex, but gives them occasional attention, more in the way of teasing and aggressive behavior in an affectionate manner. Girl:—is beginning to show some slight interest in boys, walks home from parties with one of them, but interest is seldom centered on one boy in the sense of "dating." Grooms herself carefully to attract attention. Essays show the influence of feminine figures and may show an initial interest in marriage and motherhood in the more advanced girls. Some may have reached menarche, but this is not required for a high rating.

Medium. Boy:—continues to be boisterous and unkempt. Does not associate with girls even at the tentative level of the high group above. Average or retarded in the physical growth cycle, but not among smallest in group. Ego-ideal shows strong male figure, but this is without any connotation of adult sex roles. Girl:—is physically average in growth, or retarded with respect to other girls. Essays show influence of female figures on ego-ideal, but without

[10] See Developmental Task #4, p. 32.

connotations of the marital role. Has not reached menarche. May go to parties where boys are present, but shows no special interest in them individually or as a group.

Low. Boy:—physically small or very retarded in maturation. Only passive interest in the masculine sports and games. No interest in girls. Does not go to parties where girls are present. May be overly fastidious, reputed to be a sissy. Ego-ideal may be rather weak male figure. Girl:—small and physically retarded; or, if large, very self-conscious about her size and shuns boys. Menarche not attained. Immature play patterns with dolls; or is reputed to be exceedingly tomboyish. No acceptance of role of wife or mother can be discerned in essays, and no perception of adult sex role present.

4. *Acquiring a Set of Values and an Ethical System as Guides to Behavior* [11]

High. Essays and tests of moral judgment show presence of altruistic attitudes and desires to be of service to others. Has a high reputation among peers for honesty, loyalty, responsibility. Takes others' rights and needs into explicit account when group action is being planned. Sees and accepts his own obligations to others independent of pressure from authority figures. Adjusts rules of games to benefit of all who wish to play. Noticeably adheres to moral principles. Deals with lost property that he finds in accordance with prevailing principles. Understands the reciprocal responsibilities of partners, parent-child, employer-employee. Can explain the simple ethical concepts—honesty, responsibility, loyalty. Able to state reasons for own values regarding school, religion, or other groups and activities in which he takes part.

Medium. Evidence of altruism and "service motivated" feelings may be present, but tends to be immature, i.e., unrealistic, and inconsistent with time. Evidence on reputation for moral traits is neutral, but explicit incidents of flagrant dishonesty, irresponsibility, and the like, are not to be expected. Ordinarily follows rules of games, but cannot be counted on to do so. Conforms to what others do and expect, but without much knowledge of or respect for

[11] See Developmental Task #7, pp. 36–37.

values of an ethical sort. Needs help in controlling his impulses to follow his scale of values.

Low. Low reputation on sociometrics for moral traits. Essays emphasize egocentric needs without apparent feeling for others. Known instances of flagrant dishonesty, irresponsibility, and so on. Peers often refuse to take subject on a team because of his unwillingness to abide by rules or cooperate in the game itself. Either shows no knowledge of moral principles, or noticeably breaks them when it is to his own advantage and he feels he can get away with it.

5. *Achieving Personal Independence from Parents and Other Adults* [12]

Throughout this stage, the development of actively self-assertive trends continues. The twelve-year-old now sharpens his ability to inquire into the way the world operates with respect to himself, without having to defer these ideas to those of the home or the school. Primary focus of behavioral codes is predominantly in the peer group, especially as regards dress and language patterns.

High. Ego-ideal includes figure of glamorous adult. Regardless of pressure from adults, makes sustained effort to have decisions honored with respect to clothing, food to be eaten, hobbies, books to be read, people to associate with, movies to attend, way money earned is to be spent, areas of play activity. Plans use of money earned. Voluntarily reads newspapers, magazines, chooses books. Visits away from family for as much as a season without much noticeable homesickness. Travels alone by bus or streetcar. Has to ask adult advice only on major questions of behavior. Can disagree openly with teacher or other adult. Not timid about meeting people or going to business or professional offices when necessary. Works out constructive alternatives after failure on a project. Plans his time so as to get things done; but may need to be reminded of homework for school.

Medium. Ego-ideal is tied to a fairly unrealistic image of a glamorous adult. Plays with age-mates in spontaneous fashion much of the time, but willing for adults to structure many of his or her activities. Carries out his agreements with age-mates, such as pro-

[12] See Developmental Task #8, pp. 38–40.

viding food for a party. Only mild rebellion to parental and adult regulations is made evident. Can stay away from home occasionally if accompanied by a friend or an older sibling. Gives in fairly easily to parental dictates about clothes, movies, food. Noticeably timid about meeting strangers, going to business or professional offices.

Low. Ego-ideal is limited to parental figures. Does not go out of own immediate neighborhood to play with other age-mates, even though they are known at school. Either disinterested in the peer codes of behavior or is afraid to allow them to be his behavioral guides. Not capable of staying away from home for more than one night, even under rather favorable circumstances. Is noticeably dependent on parents and adults for decisions about what he or she is to do with regard to play, school, and home activities. Many show temper tantrums when frustrated.

6. *Learning an Appropriate Set of Social Attitudes toward Institutions and Social Groups.* [13]

Acceptance of social institutions at this age is less certain than for age nine because of the beginning of an "adolescent culture," which often is "trying its muscles" in opposition to any and all adult authority.

High. Says he likes school. Respects authority of police, firemen, etc. Stands up for members of racial, religious, or socioeconomic groups different from his own when they are attacked or disparaged, even by members of his own gang or clique. Although may definitely prefer interaction with own gang or clique, does exhibit genuine democratic friendliness when in larger gatherings that include members of other social groups. Begins to feel self as a responsible citizen. Has an active concern for children in other parts of the world. Has a protective attitude toward the underdog.

Medium. Accepts school and school authority, though perhaps without enthusiasm. May engage in minor misdemeanors against authority under pressure of the group. No direct evidence of disparaging other racial, religious, or socioeconomic groups, but is noted to avoid playing with them. Does not choose such persons to be on his team in large group games. Fails to stand up for some

[13] See Developmental Task #9, pp. 40–41.

out-group person when he is attacked or disparaged. Moral horizon limited to his own community.

Low. Sometimes a truant from school. Flaunts authority of school, police, firemen, etc. May be known as "ringleader" in destructive gang behavior. Scapegoats people of other groups, refuses to play with them. Is either overtly delinquent or reacts to forces of law with excessive fear and shows no appreciation of their constructive function in the community. Not interested in welfare of any except his family and their friends. Has a few vague stereotypes, but is essentially provincial and isolated.

PART THREE

Adolescence

CHAPTER 9

The Adolescent Peer Group

THE PEER GROUP becomes more and more important as the child moves into adolescence. Whereas it tended to supplement the home and the school in middle childhood, in adolescence the peer group often takes priority over these institutions in its demands for the allegiance of its members.

Actually a degree of hostility occasionally springs up between the adolescent peer group on the one hand and the parents, teachers, pastors, and other leaders who represent the authority of the adults. In a rapidly changing society this seems very nearly inevitable. If the situation is handled wisely by adults, the peer group experience can be valuable to the adolescent in helping him to achieve independence and to grow toward maturity.

Within the peer group the adolescent gets the experience necessary to master two of his developmental tasks.

1. ACHIEVING NEW AND MORE MATURE RELATIONS WITH AGE-MATES OF BOTH SEXES

Nature of the Task. The goal: to learn to look upon girls as women and boys as men; to become an adult among adults; to learn to work with others for a common purpose, disregarding personal feelings; to learn to lead without dominating.

Biological Basis. Human beings are divided into two sexes. Sexual maturity is achieved during adolescence. Sex attraction becomes a dominant force in the individual's life.

Social relations among adolescents are influenced by the degree of physical maturity they have attained. A slowly developing boy or girl may be dropped out of a social group whose pace of physical development is more rapid.

Psychological Basis. During the later years of middle childhood children grow more and more interested in being together. At first the groups are limited to one sex. This is the time of the "gang age" in boys, with a similar, though not so striking, phenomenon among girls.

From the age of thirteen or fourteen, most boys and girls are preoccupied with social activities and social experimentation. This is their most important business. They make the school their social laboratory. Within their own sex they learn to behave as adults among adults: to organize their athletics and social activities, to choose their leaders, and to create on a small scale the society of their elders.

With the other sex they learn the adult social skills: how to converse, to dance, and to play social games. As they become older they become skillful enough to drop out of the large, mixed play-group which is characteristic of ages fourteen to sixteen, and to form foursomes and twosomes for a more intimate kind of comradeship, leading to courtship and marriage.

The most potent single influence during the adolescent years is the power of group approval. The youth becomes a slave to the conventions of his age-group. He must wear only the clothes that are worn by others, follow the same hair style, and use the same slang. Yet this conformity seems limited to the externals of life. In their inner life adolescent boys and girls are still individuals, and sometimes individualistic to an extreme.

The task of adolescent social development carries through the high school and into the college. Only toward the later years of college do we find that students have learned the lessons of adolescent social life well enough to remove it from the focus of their attention.

Girls mature socially more rapidly than boys. At ages fourteen to eighteen they tend to be dissatisfied with the attentions of boys their own age, and are more interested in boys a few years older. This carries on through college, where most couples show an age-difference, with the boy being older.

Success in accomplishing this task means a reasonably good social adjustment throughout life, and a good chance, without unnecessary hindrance, at the other developmental tasks of adolescence. Downright failure means an unhappy adult life. Not only may marriage be made difficult, impossible, or unhappy, but the individual has also failed to learn to work with other people as equals, and in his later relationships with people he is limited to childish dependence or to arbitrary dominance.

Delay in accomplishing the task is frequently seen in the better students in high school and college. The studious young man in his twenties who is just learning his way about with girls has to learn things that everyone else around him knows, and without the protection the fifteen-year-old has in being one of a group who are all so busy correcting their own mistakes that they do not have time or inclination to laugh at their fellows. Delay is not apt to have serious permanent consequences, though it may mean a relatively unhappy adolescence.

Cultural Basis. Culture sets the patterns for adolescent social relationships. Patterns vary enormously from one society to another, and within a complex society.

American Middle Class. The middle-class American sets great store by his children's social success during their adolescence. He wants his children's friends to be of the same or better social status. He wants his boy or girl to have many friends of the opposite sex, the more the better because this precludes premature serious attachments. Wide social experience is the ideal, if limited to the same or higher social class. Marriage should be put off for five to ten years after biological maturity is attained.

In the middle class there is well-developed social life within one's own sex group up to the age of twenty or later. This life goes on in clubs, fraternities, sororities, and church organizations.

American Upper Class. The upper-class arrangements for this task are quite similar to middle-class arrangements, except that marriage is apt to terminate the adolescent social life earlier. Furthermore, there is more scrutiny of friends on the basis of family background.

American Lower Class. Social experimentation with the opposite sex nearly always involves sexual experience. Marriage tends to come earlier, terminating the adolescent social life earlier. In the cities there is a good deal of informal social organization into corner gangs and neighborhood social clubs which are analogous to middle-class clubs and fraternities. The lower-class social groups more often become involved in stealing and sexual immorality, and therefore tend to get a bad name.

The task of establishing new relations with age-mates is much simpler in lower-class society than in middle- and upper-class society, and probably does not require the relatively high development of social skills that is necessary for middle-class social life, with its emphasis upon clubs, organizations, programs, politics, and planning. This may be a part of the explanation for the almost complete lack of organizations and associational membership among lower-class adults.

Educational Implications. School and college people might as well get used to the idea that their institutions are laboratories for the learning of social skills. Becoming used to it, they might do some things to raise the level of accomplishment of this task, and to help some of the backward boys and girls. This does not mean that secondary school people should attempt to speed up the rate of social development of adolescents. Urban middle-class life has already pushed boys and girls into a kind of sophistication at the age of fifteen which their parents did not reach until two or three years later in life. This may be a bad thing. But the community sets the pace, and the school must follow.

The successful achievement of this task is especially important for lower-class boys and girls who want to rise in the social scale. Upward social mobility is as much dependent on social skills as on economic skills. For lower-class youth, middle-class manners, party behavior, and social attitudes can seldom be learned anywhere except at school. If the school aims to help some boys and girls to rise in the social scale, it must offer them opportunities to learn social skills.

The secondary school and college should work largely through informal non-academic activities, such as clubs, parties, student government, athletics, music, arts. The following procedures are suggested:

Provide for teaching social skills on as high an esthetic level as is practicable. This means instruction, as informal as possible, in dancing, party behavior, entertaining, planning parties.

Provide for satisfying social contacts. Boys and girls of similar tastes and interests should be thrown together for the social activities of the school. Since girls mature earlier than boys, it is a question whether boys and girls of the same age should be kept together in the same social unit. Any break in the school program with promotion from one building to another at the end of grades 8, 9, or 10 is particularly bad, for it leaves the girls of the highest grade without boys of the same level of maturity.

The socially backward boys and girls can be helped through being put together to learn by themselves, and also by individual coaching from a skillful older person.

Teach democratic political procedures. Adolescence is the age when young people can learn to work together as peers. For the sake of their future usefulness as citizens it is important that they should have experience in handling as much of their own business as possible. Even at something of a sacrifice of immediate efficiency, it is desirable for school and college officials to keep hands off to a considerable extent while students learn to work together on their own responsibility.

2. ACHIEVING A MASCULINE OR FEMININE SOCIAL ROLE

Nature of the Task. To accept and to learn a socially approved adult masculine or feminine social role.

Biological Basis. The pubertal growth cycle broadens the physical differences between the sexes. Women become definitely the weaker sex, in terms of physical strength. They also become physically attractive to men, and thus gain one kind of power while losing another.

Psychological Basis. Since the masculine and the feminine roles are different in our society, a boy has to accept the idea of becoming a man and a girl has to accept the idea of becoming a woman. For boys, this seems easy in our society, which offers its principal places to men. Most girls also find it easy to accept the role of wife and mother, with dependence on a man for support. But a number of girls find this to be difficult. They want a career. They

admire their fathers and their older brothers and want the freedom
and power and independence of the male. For them it is not an
easy task to accept the feminine role. Fortunately, our society's
definition of the feminine role is broadening to give more satisfaction to girls of this type.

Cultural Basis. The approved feminine sex role is changing.
Especially in the urban part of our society women are given much
more latitude than they were a generation or two ago. This means
that adolescent girls are under less pressure to adopt the traditional
feminine role. Some of them can choose to be independent, to go
into business or a profession, to be married without becoming
mothers, to do a number of things that would have been impossible
or at least unpopular in an earlier day.

Educational Implications. For most boys this task is so easy to
achieve that it hardly appears to be a task at all. Only a few boys,
who may have been brought up without much masculine attention or influence, or who have learned certain feminine or sexually neutral interests and habits, need help with this task. For
them, the school may provide help through guidance and counseling.

With girls, on the other hand, there is often much more hesitation among normally well-adjusted girls to assume the usual
feminine expectations of becoming a wife and mother. This is
especially true of girls in the upper middle class, where it is expected that the girls will go to college and prepare for a career
outside the home.

The school can *help girls to think through the problem of
accepting the feminine sex role.* In senior high school and college
there should be opportunity for girls, individually or in groups, to
discuss the problem of accepting a feminine role. Courses in psychology and in literature are probably best for this purpose. A
woman's college could deal with this problem through the study of
literature. Free class discussion with a skillful teacher would meet
the problem for most girls. Women who have been outstandingly
successful in the usual feminine role of wife and mother should be
available to lead such discussions, as well as women who have been
successful in other accepted feminine roles.

Behavior Description of These Tasks
as Outcomes of Secondary Education

The behavior descriptions given in this and the following chapters will define high, medium, and low performance for a sixteen-year-old.

Getting Along with Age-Mates in a Constructive Pattern of Social Interaction

High. Two or more mutual friendship choices on sociometric questionnaires. A solid member of a same-sex clique. Chosen by peers for some responsible position in a club or committee or team. Observers report good social adjustment. Spends most of free time in formal or informal interaction with peers. Gives and participates in parties of same sex as well as of mixed-sex groups. Knows all the social skills regarded as important by the peer group. Has one or more acceptable and functional roles recognized by clique group. Cooperates with people he may not like for common good of the group. Seeks to understand the point of view of others, in group discussion. Sometimes applauds efforts of opponents at play.

Medium. At least one mutual friend. Identifiable as a same-sex clique or gang member, but not conspicuous in it. Average social adjustment reported. No conspicuous choice by peers for a responsible position. Only occasional attendance at mixed-sex parties; unsure of self in heterosexual area. Noticed as engaging in periodic solitary activity, when might easily be with other age-mates. Indefinite or neutral roles in peer group activities. Takes part in club or committee activity as a follower and supporter.

Low. No mutual friendship choices. An outcast, or reputation for being a "lone wolf." Not invited to same-sex or mixed-sex parties. Is scapegoated by peers, who may express overt attitudes of dislike or distaste toward subject. Retaliates by hostile and rejecting behavior toward peers even when being tentatively accepted by them. Observers report overt social maladjustment. No contacts with opposite sex, or, *if a girl*, some reputation for extreme "looseness." Alternatively, is seen as very shy, and is practically invisible to age-mates.

Achieving a Masculine or Feminine Social Role

At this age sexual impulses tend to be present in considerable degree for members of both sexes. Successful accomplishment of this task at this level means that the nature of such affectional heterosexual feelings is perceived and that the individual has acquired an adequate pattern of socially acceptable ways of expressing them. Failure implies a) non-recognition, or b) grossly inappropriate ways of expressing sexual feelings, or c) fixation of affectional feelings on members of same sex, or d) use of sexual relationships in a hostile or exploitative manner. The role at this age also includes development of concern to acquire appropriate masculine or feminine "occupational" status.

High. Boy:—mature sexually. Through with pubertal growth cycle or nearly so. Enjoys parties and other group affairs with mixed sexes. Interested in opposite sex. May occasionally "date" a girl, but not necessarily one individual over a period of time. Is careful to be well-groomed. Essays show strong influence on ego-ideal of masculine *qualities*, with the ideal figure being an attractive young man or a composite imaginary character. Active in sports. Exhibits interest in becoming prepared to work in an area characterized as a "man's job." Looks for work experience. Girl:—physically mature, with feminine body build. Interested in matched interaction with boys, "dates" with opposite sex are average or frequent, if these are permitted by the social group. Feminine tastes in dress predominate. Essays show acceptance of goals of marriage and motherhood. Ego-ideal contains concept of loving female figures. Interested in baby-sitting and babies.

Medium. Boy:—may be mature, but not necessarily through pubertal period. Little or no effort to "date" girls, but will attend mixed parties. Essays show influence of masculine qualities in ego-ideal, but there may also be doubts, fears, or rejection of an adult heterosexual role. Only mild interest in sports. Grooming may be seen as indifferent. Girl:—physically mature, but may lack feminine body build. Often wears boys' clothes, or uses unfeminine taste in dress. Engages sometimes in masculine sports. Feminine influence on ego-ideal is seen in essays, but hesitates to accept goals of marriage and motherhood and may insist on wanting a career. Definite emotional fear of the sexual implications of marriage may be expressed to an interviewer. Attends mixed parties, but rarely if ever has a date.

Low. Boy:—physically immature. No interest in girls. Avoids mixed-sex groups. At best passive in sports. Reputation of a "sissy." Lacks masculine body build. Weak masculine figures or unrealistically glamorous ones are seen in essays on ego-ideal. Unkempt; or overly clean in little-boy fashion. Grooming may be characteristic of boy three or four years younger than self. Girl:—late maturing. May not have reached menarche. Appearance of "little girl" in body build and dress. No interest in opposite sex. Plays with much younger girls. *Or alternatively:*—a tomboy, with masculine interests and "masculine" females as friends. Influence of male figures seen in ego-ideal. Shuns boys as heterosexual partners, but may play with them "as one of the boys" herself.

CHAPTER 10

The Development of Personal Independence

ADOLESCENCE is a period when growth toward autonomy and personal independence proceeds normally to the point where a person becomes independent emotionally, financially, and intellectually. This process occupies most of the adolescent's time and energy. Whereas we called it a developmental task during middle childhood, it is so inclusive during adolescence that we use the phrase "developing personal independence" to include six developmental tasks of adolescence.

3. ACCEPTING ONE'S PHYSIQUE AND USING THE BODY EFFECTIVELY

Nature of the Task. The goal: to become proud, or at least tolerant, of one's body; to use and protect one's body effectively and with personal satisfaction.

Biological Basis. The pubertal growth cycle, coming at the beginning of adolescence, involves a series of endocrine changes with development of adult sexual characteristics and adult physique. Adolescence is the time when a person learns what his adult physique will be—whether he will be tall or short, wide or narrow.

During puberty, girls develop faster than boys. A thirteen-year-old girl is closer to being a woman than a thirteen-year-old boy is to being a man. As early as nine or ten the average girl slows down her growth, preparatory to a spurt of two or three years' duration which ends shortly after the menarche. Boys go through a parallel growth cycle, but lag behind girls a year or two. Thus girls are more mature than boys between the ages of about ten and sixteen. They are actually larger than boys, on the average, at the age of thirteen. Their advanced maturity shows clearly in their skeletal development. The long bones develop faster at their ends, where growth takes places, and the last of the long bones cease growing in girls by about sixteen. Nearly all girls have reached their adult height at fifteen or sixteen. Boys continue growing in height until eighteen, and even beyond in many cases. At the time they enter college they are often still growing, while girls of their age have reached mature size and proportions.

There is great variability of the ages of beginning and end of the pubertal growth cycle. For example, in a group of a hundred eleven-year-old girls several will have already reached the menarche, while several in a group of sixteen-year-old girls will not yet have reached that point. Boys are equally variable in their time of achieving an adult appearance of the genitals. The age of greatest variability of physical size and physiological development is about thirteen. There is also great variability in the duration of the pubertal growth cycle, which may be extended over seven or eight years for some, and may be compressed into four years for others.

Psychological Basis. The internal physiological changes of adolescence are paralleled not only by external changes in body size and shape, but also by changes in attitudes and interests. For example, a group of thirteen-year-old girls was divided into two groups of the same average chronological age, one group having begun regular menstrual cycles while the other group had not yet achieved this sign of physiological maturity. The post-menarcheal girls were more interested in the opposite sex, and more interested in clothing and personal adornment, while the pre-menarcheal girls were more interested in active games and other occupations of younger girls. Similar differences have been observed in boys of the same chronological age but different stages of physiological maturity.

Everyone in our society goes through adolescence with a lively interest in his developing body. He constantly compares himself with his age-mates. Slowness of development is almost sure to be a cause for concern. The girl asks herself why her breasts are not developing. The boy is worried because his genitals have not grown as much as those of the other boys he knows. Shortness in a boy, and tallness and large feet in a girl, are often causes of concern. Both sexes are worried about crooked teeth, acne, obesity, and many other physical characteristics which they may define as inferior. It is a rare youngster who is never worried during this period with the question: Am I normal?

Cultural Basis. Our society sets great store on physical appearance, and on "growing up." We teach boys and girls to be concerned about these things because we praise them for being "good-looking" and for growing faster than their age-mates. For women there are fashions in body form. Girls with slender, mannish forms are made to feel proud of themselves for a decade, then "curves" come into style and another type of girl is favored.

Educational Implications. Since we teach boys and girls to evaluate themselves so largely on the basis of their physical development, we must expect this to be a source of interest, pride, assurance, doubt, worry, or inferiority feeling, depending upon the accident of the individual's particular physique and pattern of growth. Many problems of behavior and low achievement in school can be solved by reassuring boys and girls that they are "normal" even if their pattern of development is not that of the average person. Even in college there are always a few freshmen who are slow in physical development and for this reason need special help in understanding and accepting themselves.

The secondary school should take the following steps to help boys and girls with this task:

Use criteria of skill and physical development in grouping students for physical education. This is being done increasingly. The less skillful ones, and those whose growth is slow, are given a chance to compete among themselves in games, without suffering the recurrent disgrace of being chosen last and scoffed at for ineptness whenever a game is played.

In biology or hygiene, teach about the physical changes of adolescence, stressing the normality of variability. This has not yet been done to any appreciable extent. Yet this kind of knowledge would set at rest the worries about their normality of all boys and girls except the few who have serious emotional disturbances.

Apply criteria of physical development in grouping students at the junior-high-school level. Since chronological age is such an inadequate index of physical status in the age-period from eleven to fifteen, efforts should be made to put pupils together who are of approximately the same stage of physical development. This has been done successfully in physical education classes. The principle should be extended to other parts of the school program, such as industrial arts, home economics, and social activities. However, criteria of mental development will also need to be used in grouping pupils for "academic" subjects.

Use dancing and painting to build up appreciation of the beauty of the human body. A few schools with exceptional facilities have used esthetic dancing, and drawing the human form, to give adolescent boys and girls more freedom and enjoyment in the use of their own bodies, and a more wholesome attitude toward the human body.

Make it easy for a student to ask for information and assurance with respect to his own physical development. Every school and college should have someone who is easily approached and who is prepared by personality and by training to discuss with students their concerns about their physical development. This person will usually be a doctor, a nurse, a teacher of biology or physical education.

4. ACHIEVING EMOTIONAL INDEPENDENCE OF PARENTS AND OTHER ADULTS

Nature of the Task. The goal: to become free from childish dependence on parents; to develop affection for parents without dependence upon them; to develop respect for other adults without dependence upon them.

Biological Basis. Probably there is a biological basis for this task in the sexual maturing of the individual. Since the adolescent boy and girl cannot find sexual satisfaction within the family, they must go outside the family and establish emotional ties to people of their own age. This can hardly happen without some change in the emotional ties that bind them to their parents.

Psychological Basis. In our society, adolescents and their parents are worried and confused over this task. In psychological terms, we say that they are ambivalent. Boys and girls want to grow up and be independent, yet the adult world is strange and complicated, causing them to wish for the continued security of parental protection. Parents want their children to grow up, yet they are afraid of what the world may do to innocent and inexperienced youth. In this confused situation adolescent boys and girls often rebel when parents assert their authority, and then become dependent children just when parents want them to be responsible adults.

Rebellion against parents is sometimes transformed into rebellion against teachers. School and college teachers are often the targets for hostility really meant for parents. Especially when parents are very strict and authoritative, allowing no freedom to their children, boys and girls are apt to use the school as a place to assert an independence which they are not strong enough to establish at home.

Teachers often play an important part in the process of "psychological weaning." An attractive woman teacher gives boys a point of attachment after they break free from their mothers and before they become attached to a girl of their own generation. A young man teacher does the same thing for girls.

Adults who have failed in this task are dependent people, often still tied to their parents, unable to make up their minds on important matters, unable to move about freely in our adult society because they are still children, emotionally. Failure in this task tends to be associated with failure in the task of establishing adult relations with age-mates. Marriage is often a difficult matter for such people, and successful in a limited way only when a person finds a father-figure or a mother-figure for a mate. The great majority of boys and girls accomplish this task successfully, though seldom without a good deal of friction with their parents. They are able to establish new families of their own, and to take their rightful places in the adult society.

Cultural Basis. Study of other cultures shows that conflict between the generations is not a universally necessary part of growing up. Margaret Mead has demonstrated this in her study of adolescence in Samoa. The causes of the conflict that surrounds this task in our society are two. First, there is the fact of rapid social change, which introduces a gulf between generations. Recreational habits and mores change so rapidly that the elder generation lacks experience in the ways of the younger generation. Second, there is the close tie-up of marriage and independence from parents. Boys and girls usually cannot get married until they are economically independent. This postpones marriage, and lengthens the period of residence within the family. It keeps young people in a position of dependence for several years beyond the time when they want to be independent.

American Middle Class. The task seems to be more difficult in middle-class life than in the upper or lower classes. Middle-class parents are highly protective of their adolescent children and worried about what life can do, especially to their daughters. The long period of education, with economic dependence on parents, and delayed marriage, cause the difficulties referred to above.

American Upper Class. Upper-class parents appear to be somewhat more "relaxed" in their attitude toward their adolescent children. While the period of economic dependence is very long, this does not cause the difficulty that it brings about in middle-class families, because money is seldom something to be worried about in upper-class families. Since economic support requires little or no sacrifice on the parents' part, young people can accept it without feeling dependent. The fact that upper-class children are more frequently sent away from home to boarding school in their early teens probably aids them in accomplishing this task.

American Lower Class. The task is a fairly easy one in most lower-class families. Economic independence is achieved by the age of sixteen or eighteen. Parents are more relaxed about the moral behavior of their children. The causes of friction which operate between middle-class parents and children are largely absent. However, in lower-class immigrant families there is often a great deal of conflict between parents with their old-world ways and children who have picked up the new American ways.

Educational Implications. Education cannot assume primary responsibility for helping boys and girls accomplish this task. It is primarily the responsibility of the home. But school and college can do some things to raise the level of accomplishment. The college, in particular, has a chance to help young people who are away from their parents for the first time. College students, as a group, have more difficulty with this task than any other large group of young people.

The following procedures would be useful:

Study the conflict of the generations in literature. This is such a common theme in literature that the teacher who advises young people on their reading is embarrassed by a burden of riches. There are novels of two or more generations of family life, such as *The Forsyte Saga* and *Buddenbrooks.* There are novels dealing with intense personal conflicts, such as Arnold Bennett's *Clayhanger* and D. H. Lawrence's *Sons and Lovers.* The problem appears in Shakespeare's *King Lear,* Turgenev's *Fathers and Sons,* Dickens' *Dombey and Son,* Gosse's *Father and Son,* and Sidney Howard's *The Silver Cord.* The teacher should not recommend these books indiscriminately, but should advise his students in the light of his knowledge of them as individuals.

Study social change as it affects morals. The teacher of social studies or history could help boys and girls understand how social change causes children to have different experiences from those of their parents, and thus lays a basis for misunderstanding between the generations.

For teachers: Learn to play a useful role in the process of psychological weaning. Teachers should learn enough about adolescent emotional development to understand the reasons for the attachments which some students will form to them and to help their students on to the next stage of development.

Help parents to understand the problem and to attack it constructively. Through individual conferences with parents and through study groups and parent-teacher association meetings, schoolteachers can do something to help parents with their side of this task. Some parents will get help from reading about adolescent development—such a book as Katherine Whiteside Taylor's *Do Adolescents Need Parents?* is often useful. Middle-class parents need some constructive outlet for the energy which they so often use to obstruct a desirable freedom for their children. For example, instead of complaining about the evil influences of night clubs and forbidding their children to go to such places, parents might get together to establish social clubs under responsible supervision which would be attractive to boys and girls.

5. ACHIEVING ASSURANCE OF ECONOMIC INDEPENDENCE

Nature of the Task. The goal: to feel able to make a living, if necessary. This is primarily a task for boys, in our society, but it is of increasing importance to girls.

Biological Basis. There is no necessary biological basis for this task, although full adult physical strength and skill are useful.

Psychological Basis. The desire to "grow up" is deeply rooted in American children. The most convincing symbol of "growing up" is ability to earn a man's wage. Studies of young people made during the depression of the 1930's showed that fear of unemployment and worry about getting established economically were major concerns. During the period of adolescence in our culture there is an enforced delay between the desire for adult status and its fulfillment, and the paralyzing forces of anxiety set in unless somehow the adolescent becomes sure of his ability to become an adult.

Cultural Basis. In most simple societies this is not a great task, for boys become economically useful before they reach their 'teens, and girls commence doing women's work at six or seven. But in our complex modern society there is a gulf between the adult economic system and the life of the child.

American Middle Class. Probably every middle-class man remembers clearly the time he first did a full day's work. From that day he felt himself to be a man. The middle-class boy of today is under strong social pressure to show that he is a man by finding and holding down a job. When jobs are plentiful this is an easy task for an American boy. A part-time or a summer job gives him all the assurance that he needs. It is not necessary for him actually to earn his living, as long as he is sure that he can do so. During the recent depression many boys had to go through adolescence without the assurance that comes of earning money. Not a few fathers actually arranged secretly with employers to give their sons work to do, and paid their boys' wages out of their own pockets.

American Upper Class. There is probably less pressure here to become economically self-sufficient than in middle-class life. Since his family and associates do not value the act of earning so highly, the upper-class boy does not take this task so seriously.

American Lower Class. Except in times of severe unemployment, this task is easily accomplished by lower-class youth. They quit school and start an earning career as early as they are allowed by law to do so.

Educational Implications. When work is plentiful the school is little concerned with this task. But during a period of unemployment the school is called upon to help boys get work experience. Some school systems operate job placement bureaus for their students. Others provide jobs in and about the schools for as many young people as possible.

Another approach to this problem lies in trying to reduce the importance of earning money as an end in itself, and to give recognition to economically useful activities that do not result in immediate earning. Boys may be taught to look at their education as society's investment in them and thus to gain a sense of assurance from working at their studies. Their success in schoolwork demonstrates their economic adequacy.

The voluntary work camps conducted by the Friends' Service Committee and several other organizations also help youth to achieve this task. Although there is no earning of money, a boy does a man's work and develops confidence in his ability as a workman.

6. SELECTING AND PREPARING FOR AN OCCUPATION

Nature of the Task. The goal: to choose an occupation for which one has the necessary ability; to prepare for this occupation.

Biological Basis. Since adult size and strength are reached by about the age of eighteen, occupations requiring strength or dexterity can be learned at this age.

Psychological Basis. Studies of the interests of adolescents show that occupational planning and preparation are the principal interests of boys and of many girls in the age-period fifteen to twenty.

Studies made with the Strong Vocational Interest Inventory show that interests which have an occupational significance stabilize by about sixteen, so that guidance into a general family of occupations may safely be given at that age on the basis of an interest inventory.

Testing for vocational aptitudes shows much promise, especially for aptitudes related to clerical and mechanical work. Aptitude tests for the various kinds of professional work are not so satisfactory.

The amount of specific occupational preparation that can usefully be given to the majority of boys and girls is limited. From three-fifths to four-fifths of the actual jobs in business, agriculture, and industry require no specific previous preparation. It is understood that the worker will learn on the job. Employers want workers who can read and write, and when the labor supply is plentiful, employers like to insist on a high-school diploma as a prerequisite. This is a convenient way of selecting people who can learn a new job fairly rapidly.

A general occupational training in high school, as distinguished from preparation for a very specific job, seems to have advantages over a general program without a vocational bias. The Regents' Inquiry in New York found that high-school students who had taken vocational courses and had then gone to work adjusted better and made better records than students who had taken general nonvocational courses and had then gone to work. This suggests that occupational training which gives one familiarity with the basic materials of a group of occupations is useful. For example, a general familiarity with tools and materials and with working arrangements in a shop is good preparation for a boy who will become a manual worker. A familiarity with business procedure and with clerical activities is good preparation for clerical work.

Cultural Basis. In American society lifework is the most important single thing about a man. He has been taught to evaluate his worth to society, and sometimes even his worth in the sight of God, by the level of his occupation and the quality of his performance in it. Consequently, the choice of an occupation and the preparation for it are matters of great concern to most boys. They are increasingly matters of concern to girls, as women go more and more into the vocational world.

Occupational choice is unusually free and open in our society. The number of occupations to which entrance is restricted are very few—perhaps only the practice of medicine and of certain manual arts, where professional associations and trade unions control the avenues of entrance.

The particular skills required for a given occupation, as well as the number of workers needed in a given occupation, change rapidly. Consequently, the ancient pattern of apprenticeship is inadequate in all but a very few skilled trades. Industry or the educational system must train the vast majority of workers.

Change of occupation is frequent. For the ordinary young man the process of finding the right occupation is one of trial and error. He starts toward something on the accidental advice of someone, or because he happens to be attracted to a certain older man. When the times comes to go to work he must choose from available jobs. He knocks about from one job to another until he finds something that suits him.

Over a hundred years ago, Pestalozzi spoke of education as "the staircase in the house of injustice." In modern society this is even more true Upward social mobility, so greatly desired by so many in our society, is achieved mainly through occupational mobility. Either one starts at the bottom of a business and works up the job ladder, or one prepares in college and professional school for a job which will place him above his father.

All this mobility and fluidity of occupation is in contrast to what we find in simple societies where the economic activities are not so finely subdivided nor so highly specialized.

American Middle Class. For middle-class youth this task is especially important. Yet, as noted above, there is a great deal of fumbling about, without guidance, which results in a substantial number of vocational misfits. Those who go to college are often encouraged to put off vocational choice until after they have completed two years of "general education." Yet college is definitely a vocational school for this group. The two largest vocational out-lets for college graduates are business and teaching. Those who are going into teaching prepare explicitly for this occupation in college. Many of those who are going into business major in busi-ness administration or in economics in college.

For girls, college is not so largely a vocational school. Still, there are very few college girls who do not plan their college courses with half an eye to a job after college. The proportion who definitely plan on a business or professional career is in-creasing.

The long period of preparation required for many middle-class occupations makes this task take precedence over others for young men and women in their twenties. Thus this task actually inter-feres with the successful performance of other developmental tasks, such as those of becoming a responsibile citizen and the head of a family.

American Upper Class. This is an important task for upper-class youth but not so important as for middle-class youth, since the future position and prestige of upper-class youth do not de-pend so largely on vocational success. The occupations toward which upper-class youth aim are the same as those for which the upper middle class prepare.

American Lower Class. This task is not taken so seriously by lower-class youth. Lifework for them is a means of making a living, nothing more. They shift from one unskilled job to another, and learn on the job. School does very little to help them with this task, beyond making them literate.

Educational Implications. For the middle- and lower-class groups, it seems that the educational system has a major respon-sibility in connection with choice and preparation for an occupa-tion. The efforts of school and college should be directed toward:

(a) helping students to choose an occupation in line with their abilities and interests;
(b) helping students to choose an occupation in the light of its value to society;
(c) helping students to get general educational values out of occupational preparation.

School and college should adopt the general principle that the last formal schooling should be mainly vocational. This means that the last years of college should stress occupational preparation for those who will end their formal education with college, and the same principle should apply to junior college and high school. There are, however, two partial exceptions to this general rule. Boys who quit school at fourteen or sixteen can hardly profit from training for a specific vocation, unless it be farming. Boys of this type should get some general acquaintance with tools and with work in a shop, through what is usually called a "general shop" course in junior high school. Many girls should not have specific vocational training, but should have in its place an educational program directed toward homemaking and child rearing.

The school and college should take responsibility for scientific vocational guidance of their students. This can be done with relatively little extra expense. Some school systems now operate Vocational Guidance Services, and others offer courses in occupations which give a student a chance to study his vocational possibilities before making his choice.

Schools and colleges should experiment with liberal or general education in a vocational setting. We commonly suppose that it is impossible to pursue the values of goodness, truth, and beauty while pursuing vocational studies. But this assumption should be examined. The student preparing for business administration certainly can study questions of right and wrong as related to business. The student preparing to be an architect obviously must study questions of beauty as related to architecture. The student preparing to be a chemist can study questions of philosophical truth as related to science. The high-school student preparing to be a factory mechanic can study questions of right or wrong as related to labor unions.

The skills aimed for in general education certainly can be taught in a vocational setting. English composition can be taught in relation to business practice in high school. Certain engineering colleges have related freshman English to the vocational interests of their students with most encouraging results, both in the literary performance and the literary appreciation of their students. Foreign language can be related to the vocational interests of a young scientist or one preparing for work in foreign trade. Graph-reading, which is a skill all good citizens should possess, can be taught in relation to business, engineering, or scientific interests.

Standards should be raised in certain high-school courses that lead to professional occupations. A considerable part of the college preparatory curriculum in the high school is really preparation for an occupation. This is true of advanced algebra, trigonometry, geometry, foreign language, physics, chemistry, zoology, and botany. While these subjects, if rightly taught, undoubtedly have educational value apart from their vocational value, yet they are usually taught as preparatory to more work in the same field in college. In courses of this sort it seems desirable to maintain standards that would be too high for the average student, since the average student has very little chance of succeeding in the occupations for which these courses prepare. If students of less ability or students without a vocational use for the subject want courses in these fields, they should be given courses designed for their general educational value rather than their vocational value.

7. PREPARING FOR MARRIAGE AND FAMILY LIFE

Nature of the Task. The goal: to develop a positive attitude toward family life and having children; and (mainly for girls) to get the knowledge necessary for home management and child rearing.

Biological Basis. Normal sexual maturation results in a strong attraction between the sexes, which is one of the bases of marriage.

Psychological Basis. Adolescents show great variability in attitudes toward marriage. Some are antagonistic toward or fearful of marriage. Others look forward with pleasure to marriage as the most important thing in life. The great majority accept the idea as a matter of course. These attitudes are probably very much affected by experiences in the home. Most high-school and college girls show a strong interest in young children. Some older high-school boys also display this kind of interest.

Studies of success and happiness in marriage (such as the study

by Burgess and Cottrell) indicate pretty strongly that similar
tastes and similar social backgrounds make for satisfactory marriage.

Cultural Basis. It is impossible here to do more than call to
mind the fact that marriage and the family have many forms. Marriage is the central institution of social life, and will vary as society
varies. Children adopt the ideas and ideals about marriage that are
prevalent in their society.

American Middle Class. Marriages are relatively stable, and
have a strong legal and religious basis. Small family units are the
rule. Birth rate and death rate are low. Contraception is practiced
increasingly. The typical family unit consists of only two generations, without grandparents and without extended kindred such
as aunts and uncles or cousins.

A young man getting married is expected to be economically independent. This causes relatively late marriage in this middle class.
Sexual satisfaction is expected to be found only within marriage.
Many of the satisfactions of marriage and family life in the middle
class tend to be limited by the desire to rise in the social and economic scales. Most middle-class families sacrifice some of the
comforts of life in order to give their children a good education.

American Upper Class. Married life falls into two patterns. For
the established upper-class youth, marriage comes rather early.
It is not postponed until the young husband can earn his living.
Size of family need not be limited by a desire to get ahead in the
world. The grandparents and other relatives are more closely knit
to the family unit. For another section of the upper class marriage
is very unstable and intimate family life seems to be practically
non-existent.

American Lower Class. Marriage is unstable. There are occasional illegitimate children. Marriage is not dependent upon economic independence, since a young couple may live with their
parents, and the children may be brought up by the grandparents.
Birth rate is relatively high. Death rate is also high, except in cities
where free clinics and child welfare services are available. Sexual
satisfaction is not tied closely to marriage.

Educational Implications. Accomplishment of this task is largely dependent on family factors which the school and college cannot influence directly. The best preparation for marriage and family life is the successful accomplishment of two of the developmental tasks previously described: achieving satisfactory relations with age-mates of the other sex, and achieving emotional independence of parents. Still, the popularity of college courses on marriage and family shows that students want something which they think they can get from books and teachers. The following procedures are suggested:

Institute high-school and college courses in home management. This hardly needs more than passing mention, since it is so well established, especially at the high-school level. The courses are usually given for girls only, but some interesting experiments have been made with home management courses for boys, and for mixed groups, in the high schools.

Provide experience with young children. For girls of sixteen to eighteen this seems to be especially valuable. Some high schools operate a nursery school in which the older high-school girls get experience with young children. Sometimes a young baby is kept during the daytime, and cared for by the girls under the supervision of a nurse.

Provide expert advice on sex and courtship problems. College and high school should give young people a chance to get individual guidance on problems of boy-girl relationships, and preparation for marriage.

Offer college courses in marriage and the family. The popularity of these courses argues that they meet a need. In the writer's judgment these courses can be made extremely valuable to middle-class youth. They should do at least two things: first, help young people to define in appropriate and workable terms the roles of husband and wife in modern urban society; second, encourage young people to expect a great deal of satisfaction from family life and to be ready to make the necessary investment of time and money to obtain such satisfaction.

8. DEVELOPING INTELLECTUAL SKILLS AND CONCEPTS NECESSARY
   FOR CIVIC COMPETENCE

Nature of the Task. The goal: to develop concepts of law, government, economics, politics, geography, human nature, and social
institutions which fit the modern world; to develop language skills
and reasoning ability necessary for dealing effectively with the
problems of a modern democracy.

Biological Basis. The brain and nervous system reach adult size
at about the age of fourteen. There probably is a further maturation
after this age, with chemical changes and growth on a microscopic
scale. However, it seems safe to say that the biological basis for
adult mentality is present by the age of fourteen.

Psychological Basis. As a result of a combination of innate biological differences and differences in experience, adolescents exhibit a great range of mental ability. A few adults never get beyond
the level of mental ability of the average ten-year-old. They have
to plod through the simplest news story and they cannot do long
division. At the other end of the scale are a few people who commonly think so rapidly and handle abstract concepts so easily that
they get out of touch with the ordinary man, and find great difficulty
in communicating with him.

Individual differences in mental development show themselves
principally as differences in:

(a) acquiring language and meanings,
(b) acquiring concepts,
(c) interests and motivation.

By the age of fourteen, an average high-school student knows about
thirty-eight thousand words, but some know twice as many words
and others only half as many. More significant than difference in
size of vocabulary is difference in semantic competence. The degree of skill in using and understanding abstract words and in discovering meaning from context varies from almost zero in some
people to the level of genius in others.

Concepts are formed out of experience, both the direct experience of the senses and the vicarious experience of reading books

and making mental experiments. People of low conceptual ability must remain very close to direct, concrete experiences in their concepts. A subject with a medium degree of abstractness, such as algebra, is beyond the conceptual ability of perhaps a half of the adolescent population. Many of the complex concepts of modern economics and politics are forever beyond their reach. On the other hand, everybody can and does form his own concepts of abstractions such as democracy, justice, and freedom. The experience of living through childhood and adolescence affords a basis for these concepts.

There is no doubt that high interest and high motivation raise the level of the individual's learning ability. A person pays closer attention, and remembers better, the things in which he is interested. Since interests and motivation are extremely varied, we have here another source of individual differences in mental development.

Cultural Basis. Modern society poses many problems for the individual which require a high level of concept formation and reasoning ability. This is mainly due to the fact that the consequences of a given act extend so far in space and time in our interdependent world. Social processes are complex. Effects are not clearly related to causes. A person with the best of character may make serious mistakes if he is uninformed or unintelligent.

Our democratic society requires its citizens to decide complex matters of social policy. It takes advantage of the fact that the common man may be a better judge of men than of abstract problems, and allows us to elect representatives to think through some of our problems. Yet we have to vote directly on many issues. Democracy places a premium upon intelligence and education.

American Middle Class. Intelligent citizenship is expected. Members of the middle class are expected to inform themselves. It is generally said that they are not as well informed as they should be, and that they do not use their mental abilities on civic problems as well as they do on their own occupational and economic problems. Yet any movement for civic education is well received in middle-class circles.

American Upper Class. The best of upper-class people feel

an obligation to be well informed and a responsibility for civic leadership. This is a motivation that causes many upper-class youth to achieve this task reasonably well. How they compare in numbers with the other upper-class people who are selfish and self-centered and complacently ignorant we have no means of knowing.

American Lower Class. Lower-class people do not participate much in civic affairs. If they vote, they do so on the basis of purely personal interest. Their young people feel little obligation for civic competence. Lower-class youth are handicapped by an environment that fails to motivate them to apply their minds to civic problems.

Educational Implications. The secondary school, and the college to a lesser extent, make education for citizenship a principal objective. As ways of realizing this objective we can point to a few things that are being done quite successfully in many places.[1] The procedures most generally approved are:

To provide experiences on the basis of which students can form important concepts. For example, experiences in student government, community and regional surveys, field trips, participation in local civic projects.

To study contemporary social problems. Though some social scientists criticize this type of course, the weight of opinion among teachers is that a course of this type is useful at the late high-school or early college level. The principal criticism of this type of course, that it is superficial and does not give the student a chance to get to the bottom of problems, has been at least partially met by a group of university social scientists and high-school teachers who have published a series of "source units" for teachers under the joint auspices of the National Council for the Social Studies and the National Association of Secondary School Principals.

To differentiate the courses in history and social studies so as to enable the more intelligent students to go more deeply into these

---

[1] Good practices in education for citizenship at the secondary school level have been reported by the Educational Policies Commission in an excellent book entitled, *Learning the Ways of Democracy* (Washington, D. C.: National Education Association, 1940).

subjects (?) This procedure is not generally accepted, though it is followed in a great many secondary schools. In view of the great range of mental abilities among students in the ordinary high school, the advantages of grouping the abler students together are obvious. However, this procedure has been criticized on the ground that people of a wide range of abilities should learn to work together and to respect each other's views on problems of general social concern.

Behavior Description of Two of These Tasks As Outcomes of Secondary Education

Some of the developmental tasks described in this chapter are more obvious and more central objectives of secondary education than others. Two of the most important tasks are described as if they might be considered to be outcomes of education for a sixteen-year-old boy or girl.

Accepting One's Physique and Using the Body Effectively

High. Thoroughly self-directive in all routine health care. May engage in long-range health or training programs on own initiative to attain some particular goals. Boys engage in systematic hard exercise (team play); girls need be no more than moderately vigorous. Possesses skill in some individual sport—tennis, swimming, etc. Perceives human body and sex differences accurately and through self-acceptance enjoys the use of his or her own body. Factual knowledge of reproduction. Can be trusted to choose own diet. Warmly accepts her "feminine" appearance, if a girl; his masculine appearance, if a boy. Learns to use and gain peer acceptance through physical skills, choosing those for which best suited and not vainly attempting sports for which abilities are lacking. Boy is handy with a variety of tools—chisel, plane, brace and bit. Girl has some skill in sewing and cooking. Careful of grooming. Has good posture.

Medium. Fairly self-directive in routine health matters. Not able to maintain long-range training program without continuing adult supervision. Average exercising for both sexes, but may tend to be sporadic about this. Moderately accurate perception of human body and sex differences. Some attitudes of non-acceptance of own body, or of sex differences, may be present. Accurate knowledge of reproduction, with some irrational fears of it (in girls). Physically mature, or just passing out of puberty. Occasionally attempts to engage in noticeably inappropriate games or skills for his or her particular abilities. Knows ordinary safety rules with bicycle. Has simple homemaking or home-repairing skills.

Low. Poor health habits and resists attempts at correction by adults. May "dissipate" in matters of sleep, food, tobacco, liquor. (Chronic overeating to point of obesity places person here.) Tends otherwise to be physically immature. Distorted perceptions of human body and sex differences. Expresses distaste for own body configuration. May worry about delayed maturation, or about deviant physical appearance. Inaccurate or bizarre ideas about sexuality and reproduction, or pathological fears are expressed in this area. Makes ludicrous attempts to perform in grossly inappropriate physical skills. May express desire to be of the opposite sex. Boy is unhandy with tools.

Achieving Emotional Independence of Parents and Other Adults

In adolescence, the young person begins to define his life goals realistically. He has a growing perception of the total community and perhaps attempts to become integrated in it independently of his own family. He develops the ability to arrive at, carry out, or defend his own point of view. At this period, too, he tries out adult responsibilities.

High. Beginning to build relationships with some young adults in community. Plans with adults for community, church, etc., projects. Accepts the consequences of his own mistakes without complaining. Has a job of some kind. Can travel alone by train or airplane. Knows safety rules for automobile. Buys small items of clothing for self. Does a number of things because he likes to do them, regardless of approval of teacher or parent. Resists parental authority on many matters, but gives in on crucial family issues. Seeks parental or adult advice only on troublesome issues. Has some independent intellectual interest—a hobby, or a field in which he has specially developed knowledge. Does outside school assignments without adult supervision. Meets failure with rational efforts to do better, without prolonged depression or regression to dependence on parents. May try to circumvent age limitations on such things as tobacco, driving license, and so forth.

Medium. Ego-ideal influenced by young adults, or glamorous unreal figures. Resistance to adult authority seen only in minor issues. May fluctuate between insistence on "adultness" and a polar attitude, of still "being a child." Requires emotional support of adult when entering new or difficult tasks, or when meeting failure. Puts up strong resistance to parental dictates in regard to clothes, leisure activities, companions, books, use of money. No homesickness when away from family. Can take care of self in journeys around the community or on familiar routes. Plans his time successfully for most activities, but may have to be reminded about things he does not like to do, such as school assignments.

Low. Ego-ideal definitely parent or glamorous unreal person. Spends much leisure time with parents. Accepts authority of parents or other adults in structuring his activities and directing interests without protest, and even seeks such direction. May make occasional but unsuccessful attempts to do something "on his own." Needs familiar company if away from home. Some timidity is seen by observers. Seeks parental or adult support in difficult situations.

CHAPTER 11

Developing a Philosophy of Life

THE CROWNING ACCOMPLISHMENT of adolescence is the achieving of a mature set of values and a set of ethical controls that characterize a good man and a good citizen. This is the process that started in early childhood with the forming of ethical concepts, the dawn of moral conscience, and the beginning of moral responsibility in one's relations with others. The individual's relations to social groups and institutions and his concepts of the place of man in nature are involved in the two developmental tasks described below.

9. DESIRING AND ACHIEVING SOCIALLY RESPONSIBLE BEHAVIOR

Nature of the Task. The goal: to participate as a responsible adult in the life of the community, region, and nation; to take account of the values of society in one's personal behavior.

Biological Basis. None. This task seems to be entirely due to the influence of society on the individual; unless we wish to postulate a "social instinct" in man. Also, some have supposed that the observed altruism of many adolescents is a result of sublimation of the sex drive.

Psychological Basis. The process of binding an individual to his social group goes on from birth. He early learns to define his own welfare in terms of the welfare of his family, and to sacrifice certain individual pleasures for the good of the group. This process is extended steadily during childhood and adolescence. The child learns to be a participating member of his own age-group, with the give-and-take that are involved. The adolescent is ready to become affiliated with the community and the nation. For this process to take place, there must be both sacrifice and reward. The adolescent must sacrifice some things for the greater good, and be rewarded by social approval and the privileges of an adult.

During the 1930's, there was serious interference with this normal process of affiliation of young people with the adult society. When young people were not wanted in the labor market, when society seemed to have no use for them and they seemed to be a redundant segment of the body politic, they could not make the usual sacrifices of time and energy nor secure the usual rewards of money and adult privileges. School became a custodial institution to keep them out of mischief. The welfare of society was seriously threatened. World War II solved the problem in a dramatic way, by making young people the most important age-group in society, and giving them a chance to make sacrifices.

Certain ceremonies or dramatic rituals serve very effectively to make the individual loyal to his social group. The Fourth of July and Memorial Day celebrations of a small community are good examples. The Catholic Church makes effective use of the Mass in very large gatherings, sometimes using a stadium with fifty or one hundred thousand people participating. The ceremonies appeal to the emotions, and thus bind people together who have the most diverse intellectual abilities. Whatever we may think of the social wisdom of using this means of bringing about social cohesion, we must recognize its effectiveness.

It has been observed that many young people during late adolescence are highly altruistic. They desire to assume social obligations. They are ready to think in terms of the good of the community and larger social groups.

Cultural Basis. Our modern society lacks a counterpart for the initiation ceremonies by which an adolescent in many primitive societies is made a possessor of tribal mysteries and is assigned responsibility for continuing the tribal life. We do not have a ritual for making a young person responsible for the welfare of society, such as the Athenians had when the young men were given their shields and made responsible for the safety of the state, or such as culminated in knighthood for young men of the Middle Ages. Only in some rural parts of our society are young people still subject to strong influences that make them feel responsible for the good of the community.

Search of our society for experiences that might give young

people a sense of responsibility to a community or to a section of
the community yields the following: playing on community athletic
teams, belonging to a cooperative society, belonging to a fraternal
order, owning property and paying taxes, rearing children, playing
in a community orchestra, singing in a community chorus. Consideration of this list, with any supplements the reader may think of,
shows that such experience is not easily available to young people
in late adolescence, and that very little of it ties a person into the
life of the community as a whole.

There is no period of life when a person is on his own so much
as the period just before adulthood in our society. Previous to this
time, the person, as an adolescent, has been one of an age-group—
"the sixteen-year-olds," "the fourteen-year-olds"—which has a
common social life of its own. By the age of eighteen or twenty,
unless he goes to college, he begins to lose touch with members of
his age-group. He enters a period of courtship and marriage which
is highly individualistic. The choice of a marriage partner is an
individual responsibility.

The first year or two of marriage find a young couple preoccupied with becoming adjusted to each other. At the same time, a
young man is getting started in an occupation, trying one job after
another, often moving about in search of better opportunity. There
is a period of five or even ten years of this highly individualistic
life before a young man or woman is really established in the adult
society, with a status as a worker, parent, church member, stable
citizen, lodge member, and so on. It is no wonder that in urban
society young people tend to grow up into individuated, rootless,
secular, essentially lonely people, with no feeling for the values
of community life. If they could speak their true thoughts, many of
them would repeat the words of the poet, "I'm a stranger and
afraid in a world I never made."

American Middle Class. Middle-class youth lead a highly individualistic life during late adolescence. They go away to college,
many of them without any thought of returning to the community
where they were reared. Probably less than half of all middle-class
youth outside of large cities stay in the community in which they
were educated. What social loyalties they have must be attached to

larger social units than the community, such as the nation, or a church, or a labor union. Without the basic experience of social solidarity within a local community it is difficult for them to develop the more abstract loyalties to distant social groups.

American Upper Class. Upper-class youth often develop a very strong sense of social obligation and responsibility, as is evidenced by the quality of the leadership we get from members of this class who go into politics. On the other hand, many upper-class youth grow up to be irresponsible and selfishly individualistic. What is there in the social experience of an upper-class youth to teach him loyalty to society? The writer would suggest that a family tradition of public service together with a relatively easy start into adult life without intensely individual efforts are factors in creating a sense of social responsibility in these young people.

American Lower Class. There is very little feeling of responsibility to the community or the nation on the part of lower-class youth. The family and sometimes the extended family and a few neighbors comprise the social unit to which lower-class people are really loyal.

Educational Implications. If this task is taken to be an essential one for youth in America, we must recognize that it is very poorly accomplished, and that the educational system is the agency that offers most promise of improving the situation. The following procedures seem to be indicated:

Study and improve the local community. At the high-school level students can study the history, physical and economic geography, business, industry, government, and religious and cultural life of their community, through reading and first-hand experience. Such a study will always open up possibilities for service to the community which should be made a part of the school program. In England a nation-wide land utilization survey was carried out through the cooperation of school children in every locality.

Study the literature and history of the region and the nation. In a country as large as the United States some encouragement of regional loyalty is probably desirable. Literature is an especially good vehicle for this purpose. Dealing with the Middle West, for example, are the following: Cornelia Cannon's *Red Rust,* Donald

Culross Peattie's *Prairie Grove,* Hamlin Garland's *Trail-Makers of the Middle Border,* Bojer's *The Emigrants,* Willa Cather's *My Ántonía* and *O Pioneers!,* Eggleston's *The Hoosier Schoolmaster,* Sandburg's *Abraham Lincoln,* Edna Ferber's *Cimarron,* Rolvaag's *Giants in the Earth* and *Peder Victorious,* Herbert Quick's *Vandemark's Folly,* Margaret Wilson's *The Able McLaughlins,* Sherwood Anderson's *Tar.* Every region in the Middle West, from Ohio to Nebraska and from Minnesota to Oklahoma, has been celebrated in fiction and biography. The lore of the rivers has been collected in books about the Mississippi, the Ohio, the Wabash, the Illinois, the Missouri, and the Wisconsin. Many towns have their stories told in fiction by minor novelists.

Beyond helping boys and girls develop a feeling for their own region, we should help them develop a similar feeling for the nation. For this they might read such books as Bradford's *History of Plymouth Plantation,* Franklin's *Autobiography,* Parkman's *Oregon Trail,* Booker T. Washington's *Up from Slavery,* the *Letters of William James, The Education of Henry Adams,* Turner's *The Frontier in American History,* Jane Addams' *Forty Years at Hull House,* Lewis Mumford's *Sticks and Stones,* and some of the state papers of our greater presidents.

Use ceremonies to inculcate loyalty to community, nation, and the greater society. While it is idle to speak of recapturing the spiritual unity of a simple folk society through ceremonies and rituals imitating those of such societies, there certainly is a place for ceremonies in the education of youth in modern society. We now use Christmas and Easter in many schools as means of developing feelings of loyalty and solidarity within Christendom. We use Thanksgiving and Washington's Birthday to develop loyalty to the nation. There should be more ceremonial occasions which bring young people both in and out of school into the life of the community. The hundredth or two- or three-hundredth anniversary of the founding of a town, the annual harvest festival, a yearly First Voters' Day, are examples of occasions which the schools can use for this purpose.

Require a period of service to the community or the nation? This proposal is introduced with a question mark because it has some questionable elements. In the form of universal military service it probably is not desirable in America. But a year, or a half-year, of national service would have much to recommend it, particularly in times of unemployment when it is necessary to keep youth out of the labor market as much as possible.

Another possibility is to organize a plan on a community or county-wide basis, tied into the school program. At the age of fourteen or fifteen all boys and girls might give two or three hours a day to community work, supervised by members of the school staff. The work projects should be chosen to raise the standard of living of the whole community, so that the individual would have the experience of sharing the results of his work with all members of the community.

There might be projects such as: clearing land for a park, cleaning up alleys and vacant lots, caring for a community forest and camp site. In our large cities this project might be used to attack the bad American habit of littering parks and streets with refuse. By systematically picking up waste material, the school children might reform the habits of the adults of the community and develop such habits of their own that this unpleasant feature of American life would be eradicated in a generation.

10. ACQUIRING A SET OF VALUES AND AN ETHICAL SYSTEM AS A GUIDE TO BEHAVIOR

Nature of the Task. The goal: to form a set of values that are possible of realization; to develop a conscious purpose of realizing these values; to define man's place in the physical world and in relation to other human beings; to keep one's world picture and one's values in harmony with each other. Definition: a value is an object or state of affairs which is desired.

Biological Basis. None.

Psychological Basis. It is an observed fact that many young people have great interest in philosophical and religious problems. Although this is not true of a substantial proportion of college students, and certainly not true of more than a small proportion of the whole population of young people, still, the group who do have this interest are superior people and are worth special attention from educators.

A person's values and ideals fall into a hierarchy, and a scale of values emerges as the child becomes an adolescent and the adolescent becomes a man. Analysis of values becomes possible, though it is not undertaken explicitly by very many people.

The primary source of all values is the fundamental physiological drive of the organism. This drive expresses itself first in desire for food and warmth, later in desire for physical activity and for stimulation of certain zones of the body. These are the only values for an infant. All later values are built upon them.

The primary values are patterned and channeled into a host of derivative values by experience in the family and in the culture. This process of building up derivative values takes place through the agency of persons who stand in special relations to the individual. The first agent is the mother, or the person who acts as a mother. Her face and her smile, being associated with food and warmth, become values in themselves. The child learns to desire the love and attention of the mother. Later other things which win him the love and attention of his mother become values—such things as cleanliness, respect for property, learning to talk, learning table manners, etc.

Formation of values through association of certain behavior with love or approval by the mother is the first example of a process that goes on through life. The individual desires the love and approval not only of the mother, but also of the father, teacher, other adults, and of age-mates and those slightly older than he. He learns to value the things that win him love and approval from these people. The values thus formed exist side by side with the early physiological values, and may become as deeply rooted. For example, a person may endure hunger or pain for the sake of his belief in the rightness of some principle, or for the sake of helping someone who is in trouble. The physiological values have no prior place in the mature individual's hierarchy of values.

There appear to be six ways by which a person comes to desire an object or state of affairs. They are:

1. *Through satisfaction of physiological drives.* Food satisfies the hunger drive, and hence the child comes to value food. Climbing on things satisfies a drive for physical activity, and so the child comes to value climbing. Caressing someone of the opposite sex satisfies the sex drive, and hence the adolescent comes to value such caresses.

2. *Through satisfactory emotional experience.* This is very close to the preceding method of forming values, but is worth separate treatment. Certain sound arrangements, color arrangements, form and line arrangements, rhythms, scents, etc., are pleasant to some people, while others are unpleasant. These are values or aversions in themselves. They may also be associated in a person's experience with other things, and thus those other things may become values. For example, obedience to certain religious rules, sacrifice for patriotic reasons, or attendance at a certain school or college may become values because they are associated with satisfactory emotional experience.

3. *Through concrete reward and punishment.* This also is related to the first method of forming values. If a person is consistently rewarded for doing certain things, he comes to value those things. For example, if a child is given money or a treat of some kind every time he does some chores at home, he will gradually come to value doing chores. However, this method is apt to be ineffective in turning an initially unpleasant act into a pleasant one.

4. *Through association of something with the love or approval of persons whose love and approval is desired.* The difference between this and the preceding method is that this method relies on the intangible rewards of love and approval. If keeping clean wins the approval of the mother, the child values cleanliness. Learning to play games well wins the approval of age-mates, and therefore comes to be valued. Keeping one's hair combed and one's clothes in order wins the approval of the opposite sex, hence the boy of fifteen comes to value these things.

5. *Through inculcation by someone in authority.* There may be some learning of values through fear or respect of someone in authority, even though there is no reward of love and approval. Thus the Ten Commandments are handed down from super-

natural or fearsome authority, or the catechism may be impressed upon the child by the stern pastor who is a surrogate for God.

6. *Through reasoning or reflective thinking.* Some people learn to reason out some values. They analyze behavior, reflect on its possible consequences, and then decide on a desirable course of action. Or, instead of analyzing behavior, they may study a work of art to find its value. In this case they look for evidence that certain esthetic principles have been applied, or they analyze the effect of the work of art upon their own senses, and arrive at a judgment concerning its value.

Two of these modes of value formation are especially relevant to education at school and college levels. They are the fourth and sixth. They will be discussed more thoroughly.

Identification with and Imitation of Persons. The term "identification" is here used rather loosely to indicate any close attachment of one person to another who has prestige in his sight. The individual identifies himself with many people during his lifetime, and with various degrees of closeness. The first identification of importance is that which is made with the mother. The next is that with the father. There is abundant evidence to show that the child assimilates himself to or identifies himself with his parents. He imagines himself to be the parent, and behaves as if he were the parent.

It is this identification with the parent that lays the groundwork for the conscience. The "inner voice" which tells us what is right and what is wrong is fundamentally the praising, reproving, and warning voice of the parent incorporated by the child as part of the process of identification. The conscience is later modified through identification with other adults and with age-mates, as well as through reflective thinking.

One aspect of identification is imitation. The individual imitates those with whom he identifies. For the most part the imitation, like the identification of which it is a part, is unconscious. The five-year-old boy imitates the walk and the mannerisms of his father. The fifteen-year-old girl imitates the posture and the hair style of a popular young woman of her acquaintance or a glamorous movie actress.

Imitation goes beyond external manners. The individual imitates the likes and dislikes, the values and aversions, of the people with whom he identifies. Thus he absorbs values, for the most part without reflecting on them. Most of his values are "caught" from other people.

There appears to be a rough sequence of identifications followed by the average person in the process of growing up. This sequence is as follows:

(a) parents;
(b) teachers and parent-surrogates, such as club leaders and adult neighbors;
(c) successful age-mates and persons just older than the individual;
(d) glamorous adults, such as movie stars, soldiers, airplane pilots, athletes, outlaws;
(e) heroes read about, such as Abraham Lincoln, Florence Nightingale, Louis Pasteur;
(f) attractive and successful young adults within the adolescent's range of observation.

Several of these types of identification may exist at the same time. Identification with successful age-mates occurs at all ages from about six years up to old age. Identification with parents persists as a controlling factor throughout life. Identification with "glamorous" adults is probably the most ephemeral. Identification with attractive and successful young adults comes last in the series, and is, the writer believes, essential for the achievement by the adolescent of personal maturity.

Reasoning and Analysis of Values. Civilized life is full of unforeseen conflicts of value, in which the individual must make the choice on his own responsibility, because no moral rules have been made to cover such specific cases. Furthermore, many of the value choices must be applied to extremely complex situations in which one should take account of the most distant moral consequences of his acts—distant both in time and place.

Members of our society are constantly faced with problems of this nature from the age of early adolescence. Those who go to high school and college show their concern about such problems by their readiness to engage in discussions of general moral questions, by their interest in the rational aspects of religion and ethics, and by their readiness to appeal to moral principles in deciding what practical courses to follow in the solution of social problems.

Those with limited intellectual ability and those who become early preoccupied with the economic problem of making a living and getting a family established tend to avoid reflective thinking on such matters by appealing to an authority, or by imitation of someone who seems to be meeting similar problems. In this they are closer to the members of a primitive culture.

Cultural Basis. Every society develops a view of the nature of the physical world and of man which is consistent with its dominant values. There is a constant interaction between values and world-view. Henry Adams illustrates this in the chapter of his *Education* entitled, "The Dynamo and the Virgin." He takes the dominant value of medieval society to be Love, symbolized by the Virgin Mary. The medieval world-view, supported by medieval science, is presented in Dante's *Divine Comedy.* This world-view makes the Love of God the central force of the universe. Medieval man's conception of himself, his relations to other people in society, and his place in the universe, is in harmony with his system of values. Henry Adams then uses the dynamo as the symbol of modern society, whose chief value is power. He feels that there is no satisfactory harmonizing of the modern scientific world-picture and the power which it magnifies with the Christian values, and so he turns his back on the twentieth century.

Modern man and modern education are faced with the task of developing or discovering a set of values which are in harmony with modern knowledge of the nature of the world and of man. At present a large part of modern society lives in a state of moral anarchy, half-heartedly obeying traditional moral principles which people are afraid to analyze because they feel certain the old principles cannot stand the scrutiny of modern eyes. And so modern man recognizes no divine moral law, but bows to elaborate necessity, economic and political.

Modern society divorces its world-view from its value-system.

This is not deliberate, and no one is happy about it. The result is bewildering to a young person. He seems to be alone with the task of formulating his own goals and aspirations in the light of his scientific knowledge of the nature of man and the universe. Too often, his teachers and his parents do not or cannot help.

American Middle and Upper Class. What has been said about modern society applies especially to the middle- and upper-class American. He tends to accept the scientific view of the physical world without much difficulty, but he has trouble with the scientific view of the nature of man. This is obviously in conflict with the orthodox religious view of man's nature. The middle- or upper-class youth who goes to college is apt to be bothered by problems of this sort.

American Lower Class. Lower-class people have relatively little difficulty with the task of building a set of values in relation to a scientific world-view. They ignore it. One group accept the solution given them by authoritative or fundamentalist religions. Another group live on the basis of an elemental set of values hardly developed beyond the animal level.

Educational Implications. There are three related educational problems:

(a) to inculcate a truly democratic set of values;
(b) to teach students a process of applying these values;
(c) to help students bring these values into accord with a modern scientific view of the nature of the world and man.

There is no general agreement on how the first two of these problems should be attacked, and the third problem has hardly been touched by educators. Some notion of the variety of answers we get to the question of how moral education should be conducted is gained by reading the results of a questionnaire sent to many distinguished people by Michael Sadler some years ago, in the course of an investigation of moral training in the English schools.[1] We quote the answers given by two distinguished Americans.

[1] M. E. Sadler, ed, *Moral Instruction and Training in Schools* (New York: Longmans, Green, 1908), p. 94.

"(In response to the question, 'If you had a free hand, what reforms would you introduce in courses of study, or in educational organization or otherwise, in order to increase the ethical efficiency of school training?')

1. Dr. William James, Professor of Philosophy, Harvard University, U.S.A.

   I should increase enormously the amount of manual or "motor" training relatively to the book-work, and not let the latter preponderate till the age of 15 or 16.

2. Dr. G. Stanley Hall, President of Clark University, Worcester, Mass., U.S.A.

   (a) I would have a manual for each grade made by a committee somewhat like the French books for *Instruction morale et civique.*
   (b) I would introduce selections from the Bible and have religious instruction in the school.
   (c) I would have text-books in practical and personal morals, beginning with rules of health, training for volition and without disowning the spiritual basis of ethics.
   (d) I would rely much on *honour* to supplement *conscience.*"

The following propositions are offered as having some psychological basis and some relevance to the present situation in schools and colleges.

1. *People are important, as objects of identification and imitation.* Teachers should be selected who have the qualities (a) that make them admired and attractive to students, and (b) that students should imitate.

At all levels of education there should be a systematic use of biography.

Recognizing that the leaders among a group of children or adolescents have tremendous moral influence on their age-mates and those slightly younger, schools and colleges should pay special attention to these leaders.

2. *Experience with age-mates is an important source of value formation.* Children get the experience of moral autonomy in their games, where they must make and enforce their own rules. Here they learn fair play, tolerance, respect for law. But they can also

learn to bully, to be intolerant to people who are "different," and to break the laws of adult society. Consequently, adults must supervise and occasionally direct the play activities of children and adolescents.

3. *Study and analysis of values is important.* The student should be made to feel that his moral convictions are important to the teacher.

The principal school subjects providing opportunity for study and analysis of values are history, literature, art, and philosophy. History can be used to arrive at understanding the development of social and ethical values. Certainly an important use of American history is to help students understand and be loyal to the democratic values of our nation. Literature is especially good for helping young people to organize their goals and aspirations.

Such books as the following are profitable: Maugham's *Of Human Bondage,* Samuel Butler's *The Way of All Flesh,* Fielding's *Tom Jones,* Santayana's *The Last Puritan,* Joyce's *Portrait of the Artist as a Young Man,* Dickens' *Great Expectations,* Romain Rolland's *Jean-Christophe,* Conrad's *Lord Jim* and *The Shadow Line,* Melville's *Moby Dick,* H. G. Wells' *Ann Veronica,* Arnold Bennett's *Hilda Lessways,* Edith Wharton's *Ethan Frome,* Thomas Wolfe's *Of Time and the River,* Aldous Huxley's *Eyeless in Gaza,* and Dostoievski's *The Brothers Karamazov.* Autobiographies are also useful in this connection; for example, the *Autobiography of Lincoln Steffens, The Education of Henry Adams,* and Thoreau's *Walden.*

The study of art and literature can, of course, serve as a means of analysis and development of esthetic values. It is often contended that esthetic and ethical values are so related that ability to analyze and judge esthetically can be made to transfer to ability to analyze and judge ethically. The philosophical study of values should certainly be a part of the general education of all college students and possibly of senior-high-school students. A number of college teachers of philosophy appear to have done a good job with such courses.

4. *Ceremonies are important.* Ceremonies that give emotional satisfaction are powerfully effective in the inculcation of values.

Furthermore, they have a wider appeal than the studies that require intellectual skill. Wherever it is desired to bring all kinds of boys and girls together in a common value-building experience, dramatic ceremony is probably the most effective instrument. Celebrations of Thanksgiving, Christmas, Washington's Birthday, Easter, Memorial Day, and Fourth of July are examples.

5. *There should be study of the meaning and significance of modern science.* At the high-school level all students should get a picture of the origin and development of the physical world and of life in this world. This calls for imaginative and artistic presentation. It also calls for a sympathetic understanding by the teacher of conflicts that may arise in the minds of students who have been given an outmoded world-picture through religious teaching.

Very often the teacher will himself be puzzled and uncertain about the relation of his scientific world-view to his ethical values. In this case there is real question about his fitness to teach boys and girls the scientific world-picture. He may teach them science, but he had better confine himself to "straight science" and avoid the problems of philosophy and value. Only if the teacher has made strong value affirmations which he believes are consistent with his knowledge of the nature of the world and of man should he undertake to teach students in this area.

Behavior Description of These Tasks As Outcomes of Secondary Education

The educational implications of these two tasks indicate that secondary education can be expected to help adolescents greatly in achieving them. The behavioral descriptions that follow indicate what may be expected of sixteen-year-olds in this area of life.

Desiring and Achieving Socially Responsible Behavior

High. Thinks and speaks of self as a "member" of student body, church group, or junior community-based organization. Works on projects related to community welfare. Thinks about and can discuss realistic reasons for obeying laws and regulations of community institutions. Exhibits unquestioned democratic attitudes in interaction with other socioeconomic, religious, and racial groups. Stands up for groups who are attacked on the basis of such "differences." Will go against even close friends who attempt to gain preferential treatment on basis of these differences, and will struggle to see that rules are applied justly and equally to all under them. Interested in world affairs and problems of war, population, etc. Reads about them. Understands roles of organized groups in labor and business. Favorable toward conservation of natural resources. Expects growth and change in a democratic society. Participates actively in student government.

Medium. Definitely appears to prefer social interactions of all kinds with own socioeconomic, racial, or religious groups; but also shows no noticeable tendency to disparage other groups. Exhibits democratic attitudes in situations where this is the popular prevailing atmosphere. Ordinarily seems indifferent to discriminating treatment of other groups, so long as he feels his own group is benefiting. Shows dim appreciation of the constructive roles of school, church, or community government. Sees self at best as a titular member under such designations. Beginning to be interested in politics, elections, etc. Generally favorable to democratic practices, but uncritical of situations where undemocratic practices are popular.

Low. Delinquent behavior toward authority of school and government forces is in evidence. Disparages and may attack physically members of groups other than his own when he thinks it at all "safe" to scapegoat them. May try to organize some of peer group to oppose democratic treatment of some special religious, racial, or socioeconomic segment in the community. Openly professes belief in sole rightness of ideology of his own group membership. Or— completely provincial and isolated.

Acquiring a Set of Values and an Ethical System as a Guide to Behavior

Growth of an integrated set of ethical values. Concerned with civic and social problems. Is finding a personal "philosophy" of life. Applying ethical principles reflectively to new situations.

High. Excellent reputation on moral "traits" of honesty, loyalty, responsibility, etc. Clear evidence of some altruistic attitudes, tak-

ing others' feelings and rights into account in deciding course of
own behavior. High order of self-control. Accepts obligations not
only to peers and family but also to broader community, cooperates
in community projects (e.g., Cleanup Week). Some evidence of
being able to modify strong moral "beliefs" as a result of experience
plus rational revision. Can think through moral problems. No need
for a "referee" in games. Interested in problem of ethics and religion
and discusses such problems seriously. Makes distinctions of *degree*
of goodness and badness. Can analyze the behavior of others
rationally.

Medium. Average reputation on moral "traits." Essay may show
altruism or service motives, but of an immature, unrealistic nature.
Can explain the simpler moral concepts—honesty, responsibility,
loyalty. No flagrant examples of dishonesty, irresponsibility, etc.—
but also not one who is depended on without some reservations.
Referee must be present to insure following rules of games. More
apt to consider personal needs than rights of others in deciding
and carrying out action. Is reluctant to cooperate in community
projects, but will under group or adult pressure.

Low. Definite evidence of dishonesty, cheating, or other non-
moral behavior. Persistently inconsiderate of others' feelings—rude,
discourteous. Rejected by others in team play because of flagrant
disregard of rules. Forceful authority must be present if regulations
are to be followed. Marked evidence of opportunistic motives. Refuses to cooperate in group or community projects and disparages
those who do support such constructive goals. No evidence of guilt
about behavior or impulsive acts.

CHAPTER 12

Developmental Tasks and the School Curriculum

SCHOOLS were created for the sole purpose of helping children to grow up properly. Since different societies have different ways of bringing up their children, their schools differ accordingly. Our own American society makes a different use of the school than it did a hundred or even fifty years ago.

The Marks of a Modern School

The modern American school has the following important characteristics:

1. The staff consists of people who specialize in assisting the development of children. Besides the classroom teacher in the elementary school who is an expert in her own right, there are specialists in health who assist in the healthy physical development of the child, experts in the teaching of reading to children who are poor readers, specialists in the teaching of music and art, and experts in the various vocations and subject matters that make up the curriculum of the high school.

2. Teachers become "significant persons" to children. A "significant person" is one who is more than a part of the human furniture in the child's neighborhood. Such a person is linked by strong emotional ties to the child—he is one whose love and respect is desired by the child. Father and mother are significant persons to the child, as are older brothers and sisters, and not very many others before the child reaches school age.

Relatively few teachers become significant persons in the life of any particular child. Most teachers remain outside the shell of his emotional attachments. Most teachers are seen by the child as faintly hostile persons, to be called by almost derisive names such as "Old Man Lemon Peel" for Mr. Peale who teaches science, or "Old Lady Crack-a-smile" for Miss Craigmile, the fifth-grade teacher.

But a few teachers find a place within the inner circle of significant persons and exercise a deep influence on the child's development.

3. The child learns by identification with and imitation of the teachers who are "significant persons" in his life, as well as by the direct instruction he receives from these and other teachers. Imitation is a habit that is learned unconsciously very early in life by the child. He learns to imitate the people who are emotionally close to him and have prestige in his sight—namely, the significant persons in his life. He learns to imitate their manners, language, attitudes, and values. Every child learns more from example than from precept. And, while every teacher is a teacher of many children in the formal and mechanical sense of giving instruction to them, every teacher is also a model for imitation by a smaller number of children who are drawn emotionally to the teacher and find him or her to be a significant person.

4. In the school there is formed a peer group that has profound teaching effects upon children, some good and some harmful, depending upon the way the peer group develops under the observation, guidance, or sometimes the neglect of the teachers.

5. Finally, society is putting more and more responsibility upon the school for assisting children with their social and emotional developmental tasks, as well as the intellectual ones.

The Curriculum

The curriculum consists of the *planned learning experience of the child*. In the old-time school, the curriculum consisted of the 3 R's—the mental skills of reading, writing and calculating. But the modern school goes beyond these bounds and helps children with a variety of their developmental tasks, through learning experience in the following areas:

Knowledge of the Social World. The history and the present facts of government, trade, industry, agriculture, population, the family, religion, nations, world interdependence, intergroup relations, vocations, occupational trends, etc.

Knowledge of the Physical World. The origin and development of the physical universe, the structure of matter, geography, weather, the nature of animal and plant life, the evolution of life, technology, etc.

Knowledge of Self. The body and its machinery, how the human being grows, diet, disease prevention, emotions and their relations to behavior, sex, and reproduction.

Esthetic Appreciation. Music, art, architecture, literature, drama.

Ethical Values. The nature and values of democracy, the ethical systems of the world's great religions, the ethical aspects of everyday behavior in school and community.

Physical Skills. The skills necessary for competence in ordinary games. The skills of homemaking. Vocational skills.

Teaching Materials and Methods

The curriculum uses materials and methods of various kinds.

Reading

Reading is a tool for the achievement of developmental tasks because it gives knowledge, esthetic enjoyment, and a supply of vicarious experience that is nearly inexhaustible. Over and beyond the evaluation of reading material as examples of good writing and as aids to vocabulary building, the teacher may choose literature as a means of aiding the emotional adjustment and the formation of values in her pupils.

Children and young people, especially in the intermediate grades and the high school, read more for personal satisfaction than for knowledge. Through reading they prepare themselves for the victories they will win later in real life; also they get relief and escape from the more intense conflicts they face at the present moment. Their reading provides them with heroes and models with whom they can identify and thus set their level of aspiration and frame a clear picture of their goals.

Because reading has these kinds of values for young people, a number of teachers and librarians in recent years have drawn up lists of books which are related to one or another of the developmental tasks of youth.[1] From these lists the following examples are taken, of books for boys and girls in junior and senior high school. The books on these lists are not classics that will live forever; they are current books that were chosen from recent booklists by interested teachers. Such lists can be kept up to date by committees of teachers.

ACHIEVING NEW AND MORE MATURE RELATIONS WITH AGE-MATES OF BOTH SEXES

BRYANT, BERNICE. *Miss Behavior*. Indianapolis: Bobbs-Merrill, 1948.

DUVALL, EVELYN MILLIS. *Facts of Life and Love*. Association Press, 1950.

EMERY, ANNE. *Senior Year*. Philadelphia: Westminster Press, 1949.

The heroine has permitted herself to become too dependent on her girl friend and the boy who lives down the street. When circumstances separate her from them she learns to make her way by herself.

JONATHAN, N. H. *Guidebook for the Young-Man-about-Town*. Philadelphia: Winston, 1948.

Could very well be subtitled, "How to get along with girls," but after giving a very irritating chapter in which the author attempts to type women, there is much common sense on various aspects of a boy's social life.

[1] The illustrations given below have been taken from the following sources: Alice R. Brooks, "Integrating Books and Reading with Adolescent Tasks," *School Review*, 58 (1950), 211–19.

Eloise Rue, Chicago Teachers College, materials from classes in Library Science taught at the University of Michigan and the Arizona State College at Tempe in 1951 and 1949.

Intergroup Education in Cooperating Schools, *Reading Ladders for Human Relations*, (Washington, D. C.: The American Council on Education, 1949).

ACCEPTING ONE'S PHYSIQUE AND USING THE BODY EFFECTIVELY

FEDDER, RUTH. *A Girl Grows Up.* New York: McGraw-Hill, 1948.

The problems of acquiring self-confidence, becoming emotionally adjusted, and living harmoniously with others.

FELSEN, HENRY GREGOR. *Bertie Comes Through.* New York: Dutton, 1947.

Bertie, a fat boy, tried out for all the teams and was proficient in nothing. He persevered and succeeded in becoming a happy and popular boy.

MCKOWN, H. C., and LEBRON, MARION. *A Boy Grows Up.* New York: McGraw-Hill, 1949.

Concerned with the problems of health, growth, family relations, vocations, and hobbies.

STRAIN, FRANCES BRUCE. *Teen Days: a Book for Boys and Girls.* New York: Appleton-Century, 1946.

Discusses such teen-age problems as allowances, entertainment, jobs, dating, sex, and growth. Brief sections on "Help for the Shorties," "Help for the Skyscraper," and "Gain in Weight."

SUMMERS, JAMES L. *Open Season.* New York: Doubleday, 1951.

A series of short articles and stories showing how adolescents meet handicaps, both mental and physical.

ACHIEVING EMOTIONAL INDEPENDENCE OF PARENTS AND OTHER ADULTS

FRANKLIN, BENJAMIN. *Autobiography.* Boston: Houghton-Mifflin, 1928.

An outstanding example of one who achieved emotional and economic independence at an early age.

FULTON, REED. *Stevedore.* New York: Doubleday, 1949.

Ben Saunders, young stevedore, faces the task of making himself an adult among adults. He masters this task on the Seattle waterfront where death, mystery, and intrigue shadow the activities of the working man.

HOWARD, SYDNEY. *The Silver Cord*. In Thomas H. Dickinson, ed., *Chief Contemporary Dramatists*. Boston: Houghton Mifflin, 1930.

Self-centered and domineering mother whose possessive love for her two sons renders them spineless. This all-consuming mother love causes marital unhappiness until one son's wife enters the struggle.

STERN, ELIZABETH G. *My Mother and I*. New York: Macmillan, 1918.

A poignant story of an immigrant mother in an American ghetto, who helped her daughter become a part of America, even though she herself could not understand America.

TURNBULL, AGNES. *Bishop's Mantle*. New York: Macmillan, 1947.

For the young minister in this book, the task of aiding youth to become independent formed a major part of his work. He brought love and understanding to the people of his community and wise counsel to youth.

SELECTING AND PREPARING FOR AN OCCUPATION

COREY, PAUL. *Corn Gold Farm*. New York: Morrow, 1948.

By his practical knowledge of scientific farming, young Carl Blake is able to rehabilitate an old, worn-out agricultural area.

DELEEUW, ADELE. *With a High Heart*. New York: Macmillan, 1944.

The wisdom of a college teacher sends the young girl of the story to a small-town library, when she had dreamed of being recommended for the large, well-supplied library of a near-by city. The added duties of the bookmobile bring her to the realization that people here need her and she needs them.

HAMRIN, S. A. *4 Square Planning for Your Career*. Chicago: Science Research Associates, 1946.

Helps reader to evaluate his own abilities, interests, and personality in order to make thoughtful, independent decisions about educational and job plans.

MACDONALD, ZILLAH K. *Marcia, Private Secretary*. New York: Messner, 1949.

Essential qualities—friendliness, patience, and the will to succeed—help. Marcia faces all the tasks of making a living. Her preparation took place in high school.

RUSSELL, SHEILA MACKAY. *A Lamp Is Heavy.* Philadelphia: Lippincott, 1950.

An amusing and yet serious story of Sue's life in nurses' training.

DEVELOPING INTELLECTUAL SKILLS AND CONCEPTS NECESSARY FOR CIVIC COMPETENCE

BAILARD, VIRGINIA, and MCKOWN, HARRY C. *So You Were Elected.* New York: McGraw-Hill, 1946.

The high-school club is a laboratory for developing effective techniques of democratic leadership and membership. The authors offer practical suggestions for getting the most out of clubs, ranging from parliamentary procedure to social events.

FLESCH, RUDOLF. *The Art of Plain Talk.* New York: Harper, 1946.

HERZBERG, MAX. J., editor. *This Is America.* New York: Pocket Books, Inc. 1951.

This inexpensive anthology contains not only excerpts from the basic writings of American democracy, but many patriotic poems, stories, and essays as well.

SCHERF, C. H. *Do Your Own Thinking.* New York: Whittlesey House, 1948.

Careful and critical thinking as a co-requisite of civic and social competence in a democracy.

DESIRING AND ACHIEVING SOCIALLY RESPONSIBLE BEHAVIOR

WHITE, WALTER. *A Man Called White.* New York: Viking, 1948.

The life work of a man who chose social responsibility.

WHITNEY, PHYLLIS. *Willow Hill.* Philadelphia: McKay, 1947.

Faced with an unfavorable community reaction to a government housing project bringing in a Negro population, a group of high-school students do something constructive about racial prejudice in their school and community.

WILLIAMS, BERYL. *Lillian Wald, The Angel of Henry Street.* New York: Messner, 1948.

The transition of a young society girl into a fine nurse and ultimately into the founder of the Henry Street Settlement House.

YATES, ELIZABETH. *Nearby.* People's Book Club, 1947.

A young teacher takes over a country school, giving herself equally to all her children, rich or poor, and teaches democracy in the face of bitter class prejudice.

PREPARING FOR MARRIAGE AND FAMILY LIFE

DUVALL, EVELYN. *Family Living.* New York: Macmillan, 1950.

A textbook for high-school courses in Home and Family Living.

GILBRETH, FRANK B., JR., and CAREY, ERNESTINE GILBRETH. *Cheaper by the Dozen.* New York: Crowell, 1948.

Hilarious biography of a large family. Through the humor there is much good sense to be absorbed.

WUNSCH, ROBERT, and ALBERS, EDNA, editors. *Thicker Than Water: Stories of Family Life.* Philadelphia: Lippincott, 1939.

Short stories that enable the reader to understand family relations better, and how to handle some of the problems of intimate living together.

ACQUIRING A SET OF VALUES AND AN ETHICAL SYSTEM AS A GUIDE TO BEHAVIOR

FITCH, F. M. *One God—and the Ways We Worship Him.* Boston: Lothrop, 1944.

Highlights of Jewish, Catholic, and Protestant forms of religion make us feel a reverent sympathy for all religions.

GOLLOMB, JOSEPH. *Albert Schweitzer: Genius in the Jungle.* New York: Vanguard, 1949.

An example of social responsibility on an international scale, with one of the modern prophets as the hero.

HILTON, JAMES. *Goodbye, Mr. Chips.* Boston: Little, Brown, 1934. The story of a beautiful character—a young man of great sincerity and simplicity who earnestly pursues the profession of educating boys.

Solitary Work with Materials

A second method used in the school is solitary work with materials, or laboratory work. Though narrower in scope than reading, this kind of work has special value for building concepts, for developing certain vocational skills, and for laying a basis for reflective thinking.

Group Activities

A third method is one that involves group activities. A group of children may plan and work together to do a play, to build a store, to make a garden, to assign responsibilities for reports on a history unit, to organize a student government. The group may sing or dance together, or take turns reading to the group, or play games, or meet as a club, or carry on a panel discussion.

Group activities may contribute especially to achievement of the developmental tasks of:

Learning physical skills and using the body effectively.

Getting along with age-mates.

Learning an appropriate masculine or feminine social role.

Developing conscience, morality, and a scale of values.

Learning an appropriate set of attitudes toward social groups and institutions.

Preparing for marriage and family life.

Desiring and achieving socially responsible behavior.

Criteria for Value in Group Activities. Group activities are not necessarily good in and of themselves. We should judge the value of a group activity in school by asking whether in fact it helps children achieve their developmental tasks in a democratic society. We might ask such questions as the following about a particular activity.

Does it give children emotional support—a feeling of solidarity and mutual help?

Does it teach children to work in a group for a common purpose?

Does it offer satisfaction and rewards to all children who make a constructive effort to help in the project?

Does it teach children social skills of getting along with age-mates?

Does it help children learn to use their bodies skilfully, or their voices, or their hands?

Does it give children a chance to practice masculine or feminine social roles?

Does it give children practice in thinking together in a reasonable, dispassionate, and critical way?

Drill

Drill, either alone or in a group, is another method that is useful for tasks requiring knowledge or skill.

Observation

Finally, the method of observation, or watching and listening, rounds out the methods of the curriculum. Pupils may take a field trip, watch a motion picture, or television, listen to a broadcast or a recording, observe a demonstration by the teacher or some other expert, listen to reports by members of the class. There is also the educative effect of observing the personalities and the manners and morals of teachers and administrators, visitors, and older students, and popular age-mates.

The Importance of Reflective Thinking

The methods and materials that have been described can be used in the schools of a variety of societies. For instance, an authoritarian society could choose materials and organize methods so as to train children for membership in such a society. In contrast, a democratic society makes use of similar methods but organizes them and chooses materials so as to teach democratic values and habits.

For education in a democratic society, which is also a *changing society,* the highest quality of performance of developmental tasks requires *reflective thinking,* or *thinking through* the situation before acting. The boy whose father and grandfather made buggy whips may without thinking much about it go into the buggy-whip business in an unchanging or a slowly changing society. But in a rapidly changing society the boy must think ahead, and determine, if he can, whether buggy whips will continue to be needed when he grows up.

Suppose a high-school class is studying the question of the proposed St. Lawrence Seaway, which is expected to bring ocean-going ships into the ports of the Great Lakes, give the steel mills of Ohio, Indiana, and Illinois cheap access to iron ore from Labrador, and develop new quantities of electric power. The arguments pro and con are known to the class. Some pupils are for the proposal, and some are against it. Can the class make headway with this problem by thinking ahead ten or twenty years, imagining what the economic situations of the U.S.A. and Canada will be at that time, foreseeing what needs there will be for iron ore and power, foreseeing what effects the proposed Seaway would have on American railways which tie the Great Lakes region to the Atlantic seaboard? In the end can the members of the class arrive at answers to the questions of economic and political policy involved? This procedure is far better than asking what the tradition of economic cooperation has been between Canada and the U.S.A., or finding out how the local newspaper editor stands on the question. Though their answers may still be less than complete, the class will have gone a long way toward getting the best answers there are, and all because they have used reflective thinking on the problem.

Reflective thinking at its best involves thinking ahead and foreseeing both the moral and the material consequences of projected actions, and then choosing the plan of action that promises to have the best consequences as measured by the values of our democratic society.

At what age can reflective thinking be started in the school? Are children in the elementary school too young for it? The answer is that a skillful primary-grade teacher can help her children to learn reflective thinking on their level, just as a good teacher of social studies can stimulate the process with teen-age boys and girls at their level, as in the illustration just given. For a group of third graders the process may take the form of discussing what will happen if the plants growing in the classroom are not watered over the Christmas vacation, or whether it is wise to have parking meters installed on the downtown streets.

The Individualization of the Curriculum

We have said much about the values of group activities in the curriculum, but this does not mean that children should all do the same things together. Actually, children should be doing a variety of different things, even when they are working together. Because they differ from one another in their level of achievement of the various developmental tasks, they should work at various levels on these tasks, and give varying amounts of attention to the different tasks.

Really, what is needed is a kind of diagnosis of each child, with reference to his standing in the various developmental tasks, and then an educational prescription that will help him to get ahead with his own particular tasks.

For instance, Joe may be doing very well on the development of mental skills and concepts, on the development of conscience and values, and on developing desirable social attitudes; but he may be lagging on the development of physical skills, the learning of a masculine social role, and getting along with his age-mates. In this case the teacher should seek ways of helping him with the tasks where he is lagging. But she should not seek to discourage him from working on the tasks he does better, for success in these tasks may give him self-confidence and fortitude to work on the ones that are more difficult for him. Nor should the teacher encourage him to escape from the tasks in which he does poorly by concentrating on the tasks he does best. She can help him to establish a balance between the things he does most successfully and the things he must work hard on even to achieve mediocre performance.

Fortunately, there are many different satisfying and socially healthy ways of achieving some of the tasks, such as getting along with age-mates. A few people may become leaders and idea-givers, while many may become maintainers of social action and just average citizens who are necessary and valuable in any social enterprise. Choice of a vocation may be achieved in many satisfactory ways. The masculine and feminine social roles are loose and varied in our society, and permit a great deal of individual difference.

Thus the modern school is doing its best when it is giving pupils opportunity to achieve their developmental tasks in a wide variety of ways. By enriching the school program so that the most talented boys and girls can find plenty of interesting things to sharpen their wits on, by individualizing the curriculum so that each child is helped to work at his own best speed on his own special developmental problems, the school can meet its obligations to all kinds of children.

Curriculum Variations To Meet Group Needs

Many schools serve children of particular religious or socioeconomic or nationality groups. These children will have special needs in connection with certain developmental tasks.

Children of underprivileged families, living in urban or rural slums, find in the school the source of opportunity to rise on the social and economic scales. To do this they have special need of help to learn the social skills, language, and manners of the middle class group to which they aspire. Also they need help in selecting an occupation and in planning a course of study to prepare for it.

For the substantial group of high-school boys and girls who will go into jobs or into homemaking immediately upon leaving high school, the developmental tasks of preparing for an occupation and preparing for marriage and family life are especially vivid. To help them with these tasks the vocational courses in the high school are generally available. For the task of preparing for marriage and family life there is a growing number of courses in the field of human relations, or home and family life.

Boys and girls going to college have a longer perspective on occupational choice and preparation. For them, the "college preparatory" curriculum has vocational values as well as the values of general education. For them, the emphasis in high school may well be on experience that leads to social and civic competence, as well as that which leads to individual independence and to a high order of personal skill in communications, in the art of study, and in reflective thinking.

Evaluating the Individual Child

In evaluating the growth of a particular child through his developmental tasks, two general procedures can be used. First, the individual's growth can be measured and evaluated in relation to the growth of his age-mates. Second, the individual can be measured and evaluated in relation to where he stood in the past.

Both kinds of evaluation are useful. Both should be used by the school as part of its guidance program.

Ways of Evaluating the Child's Development

The ideal teacher knows how each of her pupils is succeeding with each of his developmental tasks. Few of us are perfect, but many teachers can tell with surprising completeness and accuracy where most of their children stand on most of their developmental tasks.

The tests and other procedures that may be used to evaluate a pupil's progress can be discussed in relation to various types of behavior, as follows:

Mental Skills. Standardized achievement tests are good for this purpose, since they place the child in relation to his age-group and also give a record of his progress in relation to his earlier performance. In addition to the typical tests of achievement, an intelligence test is useful in giving a notion of the extent to which the child is living up to his capacity.

Physical Skills. There are several tests of physical performance and physical fitness which can be administered in groups by teachers of physical education. In addition, ratings on skill and spirit in playing games are useful. Performance in games is the thing we are after, and is sometimes better measured by an over-all rating than by measures of specific physical skills.

Concepts of Social and Physical Reality. A number of standardized tests are available, especially at the high-school level.

Social Attitudes. Measurement of social attitudes is more difficult and less reliable than measurement of mental skills and concepts

Nevertheless, attitude inventories are available and can be useful if employed with caution. They are more valid in the elementary school than in the secondary school, because younger children are more likely to report their true attitudes than older children who have learned to cover up the expression of attitudes which they think might be unpopular with the teacher or tester. Better than testing, probably, is a set of ratings by teachers and also by other pupils, if these can be obtained.

Values. Measurement of values suffers from the same difficulties as measurement of attitudes. Several procedures are possible, such as value inventories, and essays on topics such as "The Person I Would Like To Be Like When I Grow Up," "What I Would Do If I Were 22," "My Heroes." Ratings by teachers and age-mates are probably the most valid procedures.

Social Relationships. Evaluation of the quality of social relations with age-mates and other people is best done by ratings made by teachers and by age-mates.

Personal Independence. This quality is best assessed by sensitive and observant adults who know a good deal about the child. It might also be rated on the basis of psychological analysis of a child's responses to "projective" tests such as a sentence completion test or the Thematic Apperception Test.

Recording Performance of an Individual on Developmental Tasks

Using objective test data and ratings based on observation to evaluate a child's performance, we can record his performance (1) in relation to other children in his class or age-group and (2) in relation to his own performance in the past. To illustrate this pro-￢edure we will evaluate the performance of the boy, Jed, who is the subject of Chapter 13. Jed was rated by a research group who had studied all the information that was available about him.

In the first figure we see how Jed stood in relation to his age-group when he was 13 years old. He is rated on a scale of ten equal intervals. If his rating is 5.5, he is just at the middle of his age group. If his rating is 2, he is second from the bottom in a group of ten, or twentieth from the bottom in a group of 100.

HOW JED RATED IN COMPARISON WITH HIS AGE GROUP
AT AGE 13

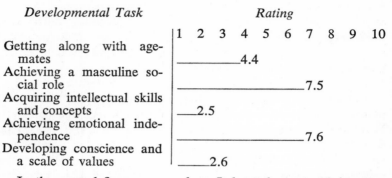

Developmental Task	Rating
	1 2 3 4 5 6 7 8 9 10
Getting along with age-mates	_____4.4
Achieving a masculine social role	_____7.5
Acquiring intellectual skills and concepts	___2.5
Achieving emotional independence	_____7.6
Developing conscience and a scale of values	____2.6

In the second figure we see how Jed rated at age 13 in comparison with himself at age 10. In this case he has made no striking changes in the past three years, in comparison with his age-mates.

HOW JED RATED AT AGE 13 IN COMPARISON WITH AGE 10

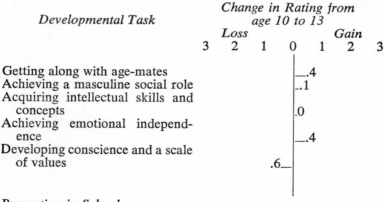

Developmental Task	Change in Rating from age 10 to 13
	Loss .... Gain
	3 2 1 0 1 2 3
Getting along with age-mates	___.4
Achieving a masculine social role	__.1
Acquiring intellectual skills and concepts	_0
Achieving emotional independence	___.4
Developing conscience and a scale of values	.6___

Promotion in School

The developmental-task concept suggests that promotion in school should be related to the child's over-all developmental task rating. In general, the child should be placed with other children who are at about the same level with him on most of the developmental tasks.

This would justify placing a child with older children if his achievement on the social and physical developmental tasks is superior as well as his achievement of the intellectual tasks.

On the other hand, a child with poor achievement in the physical and social tasks as well as poor achievement on the intellectual tasks should probably be "kept back" and put with children of younger chronological age.

The child with mixed performance—good on some tasks and poor on others—presents a special problem in grade placement. Here the judgment should be made in the light of all the information that can be obtained. Probably the child's social and emotional level is the safest one to use in placing him, but it must be considered that poor intellectual skills may cause emotional and social difficulties for a child who is placed in a group far advanced over him in intellectual development.

Most parents of unusually bright children are now properly wary of allowing their children to be advanced into a class dominated by much older children. Unless a child is unusually large and socially mature for his age, he may have a good deal of difficulty in making a good social adjustment if placed with older children, even though he is mentally their equal. But bright children can be safely accelerated a full year if they are above average in size and social maturity.

Conversely, children who are below average in their mental development and also below average in their size and social development can wisely be retarded a full year and occasionally even two years.

Evaluating the School Program

A good school program is one that makes a maximum contribution to the performance by children of their developmental tasks. In a good school program the staff will know which developmental tasks they wish to emphasize. There will be general agreement that the family and other institutions do a good job helping children with certain tasks, and that the school should specialize with certain other tasks.

The questions we might ask, in evaluating the program of a particular school are:

1. Does the school know where each child stands in his achievement of his developmental tasks? And does the school assist each child where his need is greatest?

2. Does the school have a clear policy and program for assisting children especially with certain developmental tasks, based on discussions with parents, churches, and youth-serving organizations, while these institutions take more responsibility for assisting with other tasks?

3. Does the school understand the strengths and weaknesses of other community institutions in assisting children with their developmental tasks, and does it aim to help where help is most needed?

4. Do the teachers and other school personnel exert an effective informal influence by their examples as people and through their relations with children so as to help children with their developmental tasks?

5. Does the school definitely and systematically teach reflective thinking in the performance of developmental tasks?

CHAPTER 13

A Boy Who Failed and What the School Might Have Done: The Case of Jed

The Boy and His Family

JED'S FATHER was born in 1895, of Swedish descent, came to Prairie City in 1929, and never worked steadily. He was on WPA during the depression, worked off and on at one or another factory in Prairie City between 1939 and 1943. In the latter year he went to Louisiana to work in a shipyard, but returned after a few months and got a job on the county roads in Prairie County. Then he worked for a time as a guard at a munitions plant near Prairie City in 1945; was reported "out of town" early in 1946; and returned in that summer to work as a machine operator in a local factory. At this time he told an interviewer that he had to go south for his health every few months. "You know, you stay up here and get the rheumatism and neuritis mighty bad. But once you cross the mountains in Tennessee, they don't trouble you any more."

When he is away from home his wife and the children must fend for themselves; he does not send money home to them. But they are always glad to see him return, and Jed says he would like to work and to travel with his father. Mr. J. only went to the second grade in school. He is a small, wiry, weather-beaten man, with a cheerful grin and large blue eyes. He likes to see his sons independent. When he was asked about the job that one of Jed's older brothers had just got in Chicago, Mr. J. said that he did not know what kind of a job it was. "He's pretty much on his own. That's the way I like my kids to be. I want to see them able to stand on their own feet. We haven't raised no 'candy kids'!"

Jed's mother is two years younger than Mr. J., and they were married when she was eighteen, after she had worked as a waitress for about four years. She finished the eighth grade in school. By the time Jed was ten years old there were ten children, but three older sisters had married and moved away and one older brother was in the army. Mrs. J. kept the home together, working part of the time when she was not having a baby, and getting help from the County Welfare Department when she could not work. A social worker on the staff of the Welfare Department said:

"No matter how hard up they were, they always seemed to be happy and make the best of things. During the depression I would go there sometimes and they would have nothing but bread and potatoes and oleomargarine and yet they would act as if they were having a good dinner. Of course, I think it's the mother who makes the difference in that family. Despite having as many children as she has, nine or ten, she's a darn good-looking woman, even now. And the kids are nice-looking. They all seem good-natured and they are attractive kids.

"The J. family has never paid rent on the house in which they live; it is owned by someone who lives out of the state and no effort has ever been made to collect rent from the family. At one time both the father and mother were working in defense factories and there was a good deal of money coming into the house. You'd think they would have bought a few things, but they didn't—not one improvement. You can go into that house today and they haven't done one thing to it. Maybe there'll be a new kerosene stove, but that's all. They're really a very interesting family. To know the kids you would never guess they came from a background like that. Still now, they're not so bad. Just yesterday I came by there and happened to notice there was a big washing on the line and it was a darn good-looking washing. Clean, and none of the clothes were ragged or anything. They were all in good condition.

An interviewer called on Mrs. J. when Jed was thirteen and describes the house as follows:

"The house in which the family lives is very dilapidated and badly kept up. In addition, it is littered with trash and clothing, odds and ends of all sorts. The front porch was extremely dirty and the roof leaks so that no matter how neatly it was arranged, it would probably be damp and messy. The milk was cooling on top of the icebox; probably there is no refrigerator in the home and apparently they do not get ice when the weather is cool as it was on the day when I visited them. The living room and what I could see of the other room, which is probably used as a dining room, were jammed full of furniture, children's toys and odds and ends of clothing, cushions, books, papers, everything imaginable. I doubt whether any effort had been made to pick up the house for days; whether it is ever any better, I don't know. Each of the three times I have been there I've gotten the same impression. Their baby's clothes were hanging on the line at the rear of the house and there were also diapers strung across the dining room-kitchen, adjoining the room in which we sat. The living room is heated by a coal-burning stove. When I came in, Mrs. J. was sitting at a table listening to a play on the radio. I do not know how many members of the family live at home. On the afternoon I called, Mrs. J. was there, two of her daughters, Alice who probably is in her early twenties, and the younger girl, perhaps nine or ten, whose name is Tessie.

"Alice, an older sister, has two children but is not married. She and her children, Patsy and Bub, live with the family and Alice helps her mother with the housework."

The interviewer reports:

"All the time we were talking, Patsy and Bub were running about the house, eating cookies, climbing onto the studio couch, into their mother's lap, and playing about with Tessie. Tessie was constantly grabbing at Bub and playing with him, pulling him into her lap, hammering him with her fists, and giggling and tickling him. Apparently they are trying to make the child as tough as possible. She would hit him hard, but in a joking way, and ask him if he wanted more, and he always asked for more. Patsy was pretty much ignored by the family, except when Bub went over to her and put his arms around her; at which his mother said, 'Are you going to love your sister?' Bub took one look at his mother and proceeded to slam Patsy across the face, at which the whole family laughed. Then he began chasing her around the room and into the dining room and back. Whenever he could catch up with her, he would first hit her, and then put his arms around her and kiss her. The whole family seemed highly amused at his antics.

"At one point, Tessie seized Bub and said several times in a loud voice, 'Do you like me, Bub? Do you like me, do you like me, do you like me?', very insistently; and when Bub finally said, 'No,' she grinned delightedly and spanked him again.

"It is hard to describe this scene to give the actual impression of the situation. The children were not let alone for one single instant while I was there; no effort was made to give them something to play with and let them stay by themselves. They were constantly being grabbed at, played with, shouted at, and encouraged to fight between themselves."

A middle-aged woman, active in church work, told about some of the children who had gone to Sunday school:

"Alice had her first illegitimate child when she was about seventeen, and was still going to the Young People's services on Sunday evenings. The father of the child was reported to have been a teacher in the Sunday school, John Waverly. He had to quit because of this; that is, they made him quit teaching Sunday school, but let him continue coming to church. One of the smaller J. boys is in my Sunday school class now. He is always half asleep and sometimes he stretches out on the table and goes to sleep with his head in his arms. Last Sunday when I was talking to the class about Negro settlements in northern cities, I asked them if they knew what a tenement was. Well, one of the girls immediately spoke up. 'Yes, a tenement is one of those houses like Cal J. lives in.' Well, the little J. boy looked up sorta blankly but I think he was so much asleep that he didn't know what was said. He just looked up, because he thought he heard his name."

Jed is the seventh of ten children. Older than he were four sisters, only one of whom, Alice, was at home when he was ten years old. Of two older brothers, one was in the army in 1942, and the second one lied about his age so as to be accepted in the army in 1943. None of the children has graduated from high school, although Earl, the oldest of the boys, went to high school for three years and then dropped out to take a job driving a truck, before he joined the army in 1941. George was in the tenth grade and sixteen years old when he got into the army in 1943. Younger than Jed are Cal, Tessie, and Chuck.

Earl and Jed were closer than any of the other children and Jed used to follow Earl around to the high-school football and basketball games, when Earl played on the team. Jed was nine years old when Earl joined the army, and eleven when George left home in 1943 for the army.

Speaking about the way in which she reared her children when they were infants, Mrs. J. said that she nursed Tessie all the way through but did not have enough milk for the others and had to put them on a bottle. They all drank out of a cup when they were seven or eight months old. She got them toilet trained at one and a half years old, except for Cal, who was three and a half. When asked whether they wet the bed beyond that age, she said, "Oh, Jed has always wet the bed up to three months ago. (He was fourteen at that time). Cal just quit this summer. I guess it was just laziness with them."

Jed, she said, "always eats like a horse. He was a big baby." He never had any serious illnesses and never missed school until the time he broke his arm when he was in the third grade. This happened when he was fighting with some other boys. His mother said:

"He was fighting downtown and the kids just took his arm and twisted it till it broke. He didn't know what was wrong till he got home. It healed up, but still it bothers him a little bit in basketball."

About his disposition, his mother said:

"He just is so excitable and nervous, he can't stand anybody to tease him or make fun of him. Why, even here at home if the kids make faces at him, he gets so mad and screams and is terribly excited. I tell him, 'What difference does it make, those children making faces at you?' but he just can't stand it. He hates to be teased or to have anybody look at him or make fun of him in any way."

As for school, she said:

"Well, he gets along all right. Of course, he has trouble with some of the teachers. But some of them are not good teachers and they pick on certain kids. Now, there's Miss Kable—my children always had trouble with her. Earl and George didn't like her, but they knew how to handle her and Jed did the same thing. If she'd come up to him, he just went like this." She demonstrated, lowering her head and butting it forward, and then she laughed.

"And then Miss Meeks. We had lots of trouble with her. She's just an awful person. I think a teacher's disposition has a lot to do with it, don't you? It really has a lot to do with how she handles the children. Even if she is sort of severe, if she's fair and nice, the children like her anyway. Some of them are just terrible.

"But he likes school, and he gets good enough grades, and he really likes being there. Sometimes, when I'm going to be away from home and ask him to stay home with the kids, he refuses to do it, and I have to ask Alice to stay home. He always wants to go to school."

JED AS A TEN-YEAR-OLD

Jed was a slender blond-haired boy, thought by his teachers to be rather nice-looking, though his age-mates rated him as one who never bothered to comb his hair, to dress up, or to wear clean clothes. On the school playground he was all over the place, never playing long at one particular thing. On one particular afternoon he played first with a rubber ball, throwing it against the building, then passed a football with two other boys, then played tag. He could always find someone to play with. Going to and from school he never went down a street if he could help it. He always cut down alleys and driveways. The following are some accounts he wrote of how he spent his time:

Yesterday, October 27

I came to school and worked for a while then had airplane club then went home for dinner then came to school played come in and then had recess then went home.

I was going to have a fight but he went down to the Catholic School and waited for his Uncle so I went home.

Yesterday, November 3

I got up, ate breakfast came to school went over to John Bradys' aunts and ate with him then wint down after two girls (not menenigs names) and brought them to school and took the bikes over too Johns aunts, came to school and then had a fight then played football then came home.

Yesterday, November 12

I got up and went over to Thompsons and got a resapy for my Girl Scout sister whom is trying to learn how to cook and bake, and she made a cake that I went after and then got the things to make it with then lite the oven, then went over to Thompsons to help Russ to clean the chicken house out, then come home, went down to Jim Barrys grandmothers with him and got his paper sacks and then went down after the papers. I got my bundle and brought it home and folded them.

While he was in the fifth grade he began to have trouble with teachers, especially Miss Meeks. She was a big strong woman who ruled her class with an iron hand. Most of the children disliked her and nearly all of them were afraid of her, but Jed stood up against her. One day when he said something that annoyed her, she seized his ear and pulled him out of his seat. Jed wriggled loose, grabbed her arm and twisted it behind her back until she screamed with pain. She called the principal who took Jed out and gave him a whipping, but he was a hero to his schoolmates.

Miss Crane shared the fifth and sixth grades with Miss Meeks, and she had difficulty with Jed, too, but she was more tolerant of him. She said:

"Jed's a sweet kid. All of the J. kids are—I don't mean that he can't be a vixen. At times he is just as obnoxious as he can be. Miss Meeks was just unreasonable to him though and he got to disliking her more as time went by. It got so that she wouldn't let him in the room half the time. His mother got so sick and tired of her sending Jed out and making him write his lessons outside the room that she told him he could go home any time it happened. Well, I never punished him unjustly myself and I felt sorry for him—but I never let on to him that I felt he was being persecuted. I caught him going home one time. I stopped him in the corridor and told him what the school law was. I said:

" 'Listen here, Jed, you're just being a white feather. You've just got to learn to face things. That's no way to do. The next time you go home see some teacher first. Any teacher in the building can excuse you. If I catch you going out of here again I'm going to call a policeman over here. That's a promise and you know that I keep my promises.'

"He told me that his mother had told him he could leave any time he was put out into the corridor. I said:

" 'Now, Jed, your mother is a good woman, and she wouldn't like you to run up against the law.' (I knew Mrs. J. didn't care what the rules were—that she didn't want to have her kids stepped on at any cost—but that's what I told him. She supports them 100 per cent. She doesn't give a hoot about authority.) 'She just doesn't know what the school law requires—and you just better see that you pay attention to it yourself or you're going to be thrown out on your ear.'

"Well, usually Jed and I got along all right but he could make himself annoying whenever he didn't feel like doing something. One time, we were finishing up the Palmer handwriting exams and Jed just refused to write his sample. He was supposed to stay during the noon hour to finish it but when I looked for him he had gone home. I asked some of the last kids to go—they told me he had gone home—that he said he wasn't going to write that old test. Here he was advertising this to the other kids.

"Well, I just had to go to see Mr. Swanson (the principal) as much as I disliked doing it. I said:

" 'Mr. Swanson, I promised Jed I'd get the police after him the next time he left school without permission.' Mr. Swanson didn't like to do it but he agreed that we'd have to go through with it.

"Well, the Chief of Police, Mr. Sykes, brought a very tearful and persecuted Jed back. I said, 'Mr. Sykes, I don't enjoy bothering you or humiliating Jed.'

"John Brady and Roy Jordano were still hanging around. They asked if they could stay and hear what I'd have to say. They wanted to stand by Jed.

" 'Jed,' I said, 'You've always had the idea that you have no friends and here these friends of yours have given up their whole lunch hour just to stay here with you.'

"Well, Jed and I went to bat more than once over Miss Meeks. I told him, 'Now, you've got to promise me to work with Miss Meeks.'

"He said, 'Miss Crane, I've tried but I've got three strikes against me already. I can't grin out of the right side of my mouth without her jumping on me or sending me out of the room.'

"When Jed came up against Meeks he wanted to let her know it was 'mule meet mule.' All the kids in the room would think up mean things for him to do. One day I told him, 'You're just the boob that does the dirty work for the gang. Now, Jed, you're too smart for that kind of a program. You've done just everything they could think up to annoy that woman.' "

Jed's school grades in the fourth grade were four C's and two D's, the latter being in grammar and history. For the fifth and sixth grades he got about the same number of C's and D's, and ranked forty-fifth in his grade of seventy-two pupils. Yet he had better than average learning ability (I.Q. about 110), and should have been in the upper third of his class. When given standard tests toward the end of the fifth grade he rated at about the average of fifth graders generally.

Jed Writes about Himself

The following essays were written by Jed when was in the fifth and sixth grades. He and the other pupils were asked to write on these subjects.

THE PERSON I WOULD LIKE TO BE LIKE

When I grow up, I would like to be like John Brady. When I'm about 20 years old. He is a friendly person and don't hurt people unless they need it. He dresses in good clothes and I don't know what he is going to be when he grows up, but I am going to be a forest worker. I don't think John would like to be though.

When not at work he would probably be in a canoe fishing for bass or some other fish or be home in a garden.

IF I WERE SIXTEEN

A trip to Oregon with my little brother and Uncle Jim.

We would spend about two or three months maby stay there out there. In a little cabin on the side of a moutian side. We might stay in a house in the moantians.

We could go fishen hunt bears, dear, or go to the show or coast down the mountians in a wagon or on a bike.

Good Things To Do	Who Would Praise You?
Help America	The President
Save on tires	Gov't.
Save on gas	Gov't.
Don't start fires	No one
Don't put tacks in tires	Governor

Bad Things To Do	*Who Would Blame You?*
Don't help America	Gov't.
Start fires	No one
Put tacks in tires	Gov't.

I was happy when:

I thought I was going to Florida.
I saw "Prairie Gamblers" on the stage at the show.
Seeing Arkie on the stage.

I was sad when:

I found out that my dad left without me to go to Florida.

I was afraid when:

I just about drowned.

I was angry when:

I couldn't go to Florida.

The *Best Thing* that could happen to me is to:

Go to Florida without paying or nothing to get there in a few hours.

The *Worst Thing* that could happen to me is:

To get KILLED.

Answering a questionnaire on family relations when he was eleven years old, Jed answered "very often" to the following questions:

Do your parents approve of your friends?
Are you allowed to invite your friends into your home?
Are you allowed enough time to play?
Are you allowed to spend your money as you please?
Do your parents have confidence in you?
Do you get a square deal at home?

He answered "almost never" to the following questions:

Do your parents object to your going to meetings such as Boy Scouts, 4-H Club, etc.?

Do your folks ever visit with the parents of your friends?
Do you go to bed at a regular time every night?
Do you go to movies or games with your parents?
Do your parents demand immediate obedience of you?
Do you talk to your parents about your problems and worries?
Does either of your parents ever seem to like one of your brothers or sisters better than you?

As His Peers Saw Him

Jed's reputation with his age-mates for certain traits of character when he was eleven years old was as follows:

Loyalty	Very low
Honesty	Very low
Moral Courage	Low
Responsibility	Very low
Friendliness	Low

At this time he had the reputation of being a show-off, and of being quarrelsome. He was named by his age-mates more often than anyone else for these traits. He was also named as active, and always ready to ask questions.

As His Teachers Saw Him

Jed's teachers reported on him as follows when he was eleven years old:

Loyalty	Very low
Honesty	Low
Moral Courage	Low
Responsibility	Very low
Friendliness	Average

JED AT THIRTEEN YEARS OLD

At thirteen Jed was stretching up, better than five feet three inches tall and weighing about 106 pounds. In the seventh and eighth grades he played basketball on the junior-high-school team, but was finally dropped because of low grades. He liked his basketball coach, who was also one of his teachers in the seventh grade. The coach said about him:

"Well, he was a mediocre player, but I carried him along. I never keep a boy from playing if he really likes it. Then his grades got so low that he was not eligible. He was bright enough, but he couldn't get along with some of the teachers. He had a scrap with Miss Conklin when he was in the seventh grade, and he shoved her all over the room. He's got the idea that the world's against him. When they have that you've got a hard time getting it out of them. It takes a lot of time. That's why teaching itself is just a sideline to me—I get so interested in these kids in a personal way. People do so darned much talking about juvenile delinquency but nobody does anything to prevent it. Why, I've got three kids paroled to me now.

"Now, about Jed, he hasn't a chance in this world. The only thing in his favor is that his mother is a wonder woman. She does what she can. I've been in and out of there at different times of day enough to know how things run. She's all right. Last year we were to have the basketball banquet. She was so proud of Jed, she wanted to go. She told me: 'Mr. Johnson, I ain't got the clothes to go in but I'll pay my part of it'—and by golly she did pay her share.

"But I think she pets her kids too much. She's overindulgent. You can tell that Jed is spoiled. If a thing suits him, he'll do it! Otherwise he won't. She's the kind who would rather shovel her own coal and get the kindling than to bother about asking them.

"I've got the impression that the J. kids like their Dad, but he's not home very much. Jed always talks about his Dad's opinions—'Well, my Dad says . . . , My Dad does that. . . .'"

As Adults Saw Him

When he was thirteen, his teachers rated Jed as follows:

> Physical Courage—Very high.
> Self-Confidence, Self-Centeredness, Energy Output, Overt Hostility—All above average.
> Health, Covert Hostility—Average.
> Ambitiousness, Optimism, Creativity, Emotional Stability—Below average.
> Strength of Conscience, Self-Sufficiency—Very low.
> Sociability—Above average.

    Loyalty—Low.
    Honesty—Low.
    Moral Courage—Average.
    Responsibility—Low.
    Kindliness—Very low.
    Self-Control—Very low.

School grades were barely passing, and he almost failed to graduate from the eighth grade. At this time he took standard achievement tests that showed him to be about a year behind the average for his grade in school. However, he was in the top quarter on a test of mechanical ability.

As His Peers Saw Him

At the age of thirteen Jed and his age-mates took a sociometric test that shows how he was regarded by his peers. He had the most extreme score of the group for being bossy, and was tied with another boy for the highest scores on being restless and unkempt. He received average scores as being active in games, daring, and enthusiastic, and being fun to be with.

    Sociability—Above average.
    Loyalty—Below average.
    Honesty—Low.
    Moral Courage—Very high.
    Responsibility—Low.
    Kindliness—Below average.
    Self-control—Low.

He was definitely more popular than he had been at age ten. His ability to stand up against teachers won him some admiration and gave him a reputation for moral courage. But his claim to popularity was pulled down by his bossiness, irresponsibility, and temper; and his unkemptness, though an asset at age thirteen, would be a disadvantage as he moved into high school.

Jed started having dates while in the seventh grade, and he especially liked Jean, the daughter of a grocer. He took her to school parties, and during eighth grade he took her to the movies twice. She was the only girl he seemed to like.

Jed Writes about Himself

Since he was ten, Jed had earned his spending money, first doing odd jobs for people, and then carrying the afternoon newspaper. He was a fairly steady worker.

On an Interest Inventory, Jed scored high on interest in Aggressive Activities, average in activities that expressed Acceptance of Impulses, and very low in things that involved Submission to Authority.

On a test of moral judgment he received an average score, and showed a better than average ability to evaluate moral behavior objectively.

THE PERSON I'D LIKE TO BE LIKE

I wish I were Don Ameche with his black mustache. He is about 35 years old, a movie star, good looking and works as a movie star and he's a golf player and pretty.

IF I WERE SIXTEEN

My friends would be (list of ten). In the morning I would go swimming, eat dinner, go hunting for about to hours come home eat and go to the show at night,

I was happy when:

    I passed all of the time I've been in school.
    Being on the basketball team
    Learned how to dive from high positions

I was sad when:

    The death of my nephew
    The death of my brother-in-law
    The death of my closest friend

I was afraid when:

    In my dreams
    When I just about drowned
    When I was hit by a car on my bike

I was angry when:

> When some boy took my girl friend
> When Miss Conklin sent me to the office
> When we lost our one and only game in the tournament

I was ashamed when:

> I hit Miss Conklin.

The *Best Thing* that could happen to me is:

> When I get out of school

The *Worst Thing* that could happen to me is:

> When I fail in school

JED AT SIXTEEN-SEVENTEEN

By the time he was sixteen Jed had dropped out of school twice. The first time he quit was in his freshman year in high school, when he had trouble with the principal. He had been cutting some classes and the principal asked Mr. J. to bring Jed to school. Jed said he didn't see that he was learning anything in school, and the principal offered to give him a permit to leave school if his father would sign it. Mr. J. would not sign the request. Mrs. J. told an interviewer:

"Well, as long as he has his mind set against it he might as well quit. That's what I told his father. His father had to go out of town. He told me to go and sign the permit, but I was afraid that the school would think we didn't agree. I try to talk Jed into school. I say, 'You almost have to have a high-school education to get anywheres nowadays.' Jed likes to sleep late and he hates to get up for school. You know he's been working nights at the bowling-alley—and he makes more than his father can make. The last couple of weeks, he's been bringing in $36."

Another reason for Jed's dropping out of school was that his grades were too low to permit him to play basketball. He did drop out, and he worked at one job or another until the next autumn when he started school again. This time he stayed until March, and played on the junior varsity team. He was still tall for his age, and played center.

About this time Jed talked with an interviewer about himself and his family. He remarked that he was a good deal like his older brother Earl, who was in the Marines.

"I look just like his pictures when he was my age. And he used to be king and now I'm king."

Interviewer: "Oh, I see, you are the oldest boy at home and your father is away."

Jed: "I'm the biggest one in the family now. I'm not the heaviest but I'm the tallest. I buy my own clothes with my own money now."

When basketball season was over Jed dropped out of school again, but he returned the following September. Again he started to play basketball, but this time his school attendance was so irregular that he was told not to come back to school unless he was ready to stay. The interviewer described him at this time (age about seventeen) as follows:

"Jed would be a nice-looking boy if he were better dressed. His jacket, shirt, and sweater were all very noticeably dirty and his clothing was wrinkled. He has heavy blond hair and rather startling blue eyes which look at you very directly."

The interviewer asked Jed to write on some questions for her. The first was: Describe briefly any important or unimportant difficulties you have had at home, at school, at work.

Jed: "At school, I can't get along with some women teachers. I skip school without caring much about it but I want to go."

Describe briefly some conditions or situations in which you had a lot of unpleasantness or disappointments.

Jed: "In my ex-girl friend, she does some things I don't like."

This was Jean, the girl he had dated in seventh grade. She had given him the cold shoulder after he began dropping out of school.

Describe briefly some conditions or situations in which you had a lot of fun and enjoyed yourself.

Jed: "When I go roller skating and meet people; when I play basketball and football."

What special abilities do you have? What abilities that you do not have would you like to possess?

Jed: "I can learn mechanics pretty fast. I can meet girls and have fun kinda fast. I can play football and basketball fairly good. I wish I could play baseball good enough to play with the Cubs."

How does what other people think of you differ from what you think of yourself?

Jed: "The Coach don't think I am good enough to play in Varsity basketball. I don't care what other people think of me."

This interviewer saw Jed several times during the spring, and he became quite attached to her. One evening he came to her apartment about seven and stayed until ten o'clock. She reports:

"Jed was dressed better on this occasion than any time I've seen him. He wore a pair of light tan slacks that were cleaned and pressed. He had a light sweater and new shoes. We talked over some of the aptitude tests he had taken, and then he said, 'I've had a brilliant idea for next year. I might go over to Diamond Hill and stay with my sister and brother-in-law and go to school over there. You know I've been going with a girl from there. She's valedictorian of the graduating class.'

"Later, Jed said suddenly, 'Has Jean been up here lately?'

"I said I hadn't seen Jean except for a couple of times on the street. Jed said, 'I guess she's too busy writing to her boy friend. He's up in Chicago now.'

"At one point in the conversation Jed said, 'I feel like going out on another window-breaking spree.'

" 'Another one?' I said, 'When was the last one?'

" 'Didn't you read about it in the paper?' Jed said. 'The police thought it was some drunk. They didn't catch us. We were roller skating, and then we got this idea. First we went out to the judge's house, and we threw a big stone through his front window. He called up the police and by the time they came we'd gone out and done the same thing for the newspaper editor. Before we quit we'd busted windows in five houses, all of people we didn't like.'

"Jed went on to say that a year ago they had done something similar and had been caught. 'We just had to pay a little fine, though; it was worth it.' "

The Person I Would Like To Be Like

I'd like to grow up to be like Bill Nicholson. Bill stands at six feet one inch and played Baseball for the Cubs and now the Phillies. He can hit a home run just as easy as a single and I like to watch him play and hit homer's. He is 34 years old and still hitting homers. My brother says he is slow but I've seen him hit infield hits and make it to first, hit a blooper into right field and get to second and run in and snare bloopers from deep right field. I've watched him play in about 30 games and he hit a homer in about 15 of them, 2 in the same game, once with the bases full and once with two men on. Of course his occupation is playing baseball and he goes fishing for recreation. He runs around in sports clothes and is always smoking a cigar. While he plays baseball he chews tobacco. He is very much alive, ask any National League pitchers, they'll tell you. I've seen him get walked 3 times out of four times at bat. The other time he hit a home run with two men on.

When I'm Twenty-Two

I'll probably be running a bowling alley for my boss. I'll be getting pin boys and taking money from bowlers. Fixing pins, selling pop, and maybe I'll be tending bar once in awhile.

As His Peers See Him

On sociometric tests Jed continued to maintain a low reputation for loyalty, responsibility, and self-control. He was dropping out of the social group of the high school, and had his own gang of several aggressive, delinquent boys. Jean, the girl he had gone with during seventh and eighth grades, had dropped him.

As Adults See Him

Jed's reputation was better as a sixteen-year-old than it had been earlier, as far as adults were concerned. He was noted by them as average on loyalty, honesty, responsibility, kindliness, and self-control, and high on moral courage. Teachers varied among themselves in their opinions about him. The high-school principal, a man, rated him above average.

Vocational Choice

By the time he was seventeen, Jed had worked at a variety of unskilled jobs—farm hand, railroad section gang, newspaper delivery, laborer on a construction project, pin-setter in a bowling alley, gasoline station attendant. None of these jobs had a future for him. On a questionnaire he was asked:

Q. When you leave school, what will you probably do for a living?
A. Labor of some kind.
Q. If you could have your choice of anything, what would you like to do for a living when you leave school?
A. A big slugger in the major leagues.

Although he did well in several tests of mechanical ability, Jed did not seriously follow this lead. On the Kuder Vocational Preference Test he came out with a high score on preference for science. When he learned this he asked to take the test again, because he thought he didn't like science. On the retake his science score was down. Jed grinned and said, "I purposely marked down everything in science so it wouldn't be high because I don't like it."

His high-school algebra teacher said that Jed had a very good head for mathematics. However, Jed said that he would not take any more than the one year that was required. "I have to do so much writing on these problems. I can figure out the answer and put that down but she doesn't want it that way. She wants me to put every step down."

Jed showed a close attachment to a young man who owned a filling station, and for whom he worked at one time. This man, Frank Wamsly, took Jed with him to baseball games in Chicago, and placed a good deal of responsibility on him for operating the filling station when he (the owner) was away on a fishing trip. Wamsly was long on ideas for making money but short on capital to put the ideas into effect. He formed the idea of building a motel and restaurant and service station on the outskirts of town, and promised Jed a job as assistant manager. Since he had no more than a couple of thousand dollars capital, he asked the local bank for a loan of $50,000 on the project. This was declined and he then tried a Chicago hotel corporation. Jed went with him to Chicago, and visited some friends while Frank saw the corporation vice-president.

Wamsly was not well received, and he proved to be a bitter companion on the drive back to Prairie City. "There just isn't any opportunity in this God-damned country any more," said Frank. "That guy sitting there behind a big desk insulted me. He practically said that I had no business taking his time. He said I'd have to put up at least half of the capital for this job."

Jed's Self-Concept

Like every other adolescent boy, Jed has a vague and shifting picture of himself, which he cannot or will not put completely into words. Some of it comes out in his interviews with people whom he trusts. More of it can be discerned in the stories he tells in response to certain picture-tests that are designed to bring out a person's feelings about himself in ways that do not hurt or embarrass him. The self-concept which emerges from these sources, but of which Jed himself is only dimly aware, is the following, as phrased by a psychologist who studied the tests on Jed:

1. I want to be active, friendly, and kind, and have the constancy of human relations marked by affection.
2. I need to figure myself out and to gain self-direction (I need psychological space in which to do this).
3. I am really a lone wolf and must be left to myself to find my own directions.
4. But people keep interfering with me and demanding things of me.
5. I wish I knew how really to act friendly and not be bothered and upset by people's demands upon me.
6. The only way I know to fend off people's demands is to kick back at them and to refuse to accept their ways of behaving (especially certain adults).
7. And to refuse to become emotionally tied to them.
8. Someday I will get what I want and will find the direction and peace I need, but I'm afraid I'll also be very lonely when I do.

JED'S ACHIEVEMENT OF DEVELOPMENTAL TASKS

A research staff of eight people studied all the material they could get concerning Jed and then rated him on his achievement of four developmental tasks. They rated him at ages 10–11, 13–14, and 16–17. They placed him on a scale from 1 to 10, in relation to other American youth of these ages.

Getting Along with Age-Mates

Age	Average Rating
10	4.0
13	4.4
16	3.8

In this area Jed was below average throughout, but not far below. His activity, desire to be with people, willingness to be in on everything that was going on, all count in his favor; but his bossiness, chip-on-the-shoulder attitude, irresponsibility, and poor self-control count against him.

Achieving a Masculine Social Role

Age	Average Rating
10	7.4
13	7.5
16	6.8

Jed has always put up a tough, masculine front, in spite of his wanting to be loved and cared for. In his environment, aggressiveness and toughness are rewarded, and he has learned his lesson. But there are signs of a wistful longing for a less tough value system. The masculinity he shows is broken into by an unstable relation to women—either he hates them or he is overdependent on them. This reduces his rating.

Achieving Emotional Independence of Parents and Other Adults

Age	Average Rating
10	7.2
13	7.6
16	7.2

This boy has become independent of his parents perforce, because his parents have given him so little chance to be dependent. In his relations with other adults he is generally independent and

somewhat defiant. Actually, though, he falls short of the most
desirable level of emotional independence because of his lack of
inner direction. He looks for older people (Frank Wamsly) who
will gratify his impulses without requiring too much maturity of
behavior for him, and on such people or in such situations he
becomes quite dependent.

Developing Conscience and a Scale of Values

Age	Average Rating
10	3.2
13	2.6
16	2.5

Jed's ratings must be low in this area. He has a weak moral
conscience, and a narrow moral horizon. His impulses of the
moment are apt to overpower him. He gives lip service to such
values as education and moral respectability, but he cannot with-
stand the temptations of immediate pleasure and cannot stand out
against the crowd he is with, even though he knows it to be a bad
crowd.

Selecting and Preparing for an Occupation

Although no ratings are made for this developmental task, there
is sufficient evidence to show that he must be rated low. A boy with
definite mechanical ability which he himself recognized early, with
above average mathematical ability, with strongly developed scientific interests, would make a success in a technician's job in a
factory or laboratory, and might have done well in an engineering
school. But Jed stays away from these areas that would require self-
discipline and hard work in return for a reward some years in the
future. He takes whatever unskilled job comes to hand, and yearns
vaguely to be a major-league ballplayer.

What the School Might Have Done

It seems clear from this case history that a boy who might have
become a happy man and a useful citizen is going to become an
unhappy man and a poor father, worker, and citizen. What are
the causes of Jed's difficulties? From the writer's study of the case,
there are three basic lacks in the life of Jed:

1. Lack of moral training in the family tied in with treatment giving emotional security.

There appears to have been little or no discipline in the home and not enough deeply focused affection. While there has been a good deal of affection between members of the family, it has a kind of superficial quality, and it has not been tied in systematically with self-control and self-discipline. Consequently, Jed is not sure of the rewards for self-control.

2. Lack of a stable and responsible father-figure.

3. Lack of a stable feminine person who will tolerate Jed and give him affection in return for self-control and self-discipline. Three women in this history seem to have offered him some of this kind of support, but for various reasons none of the three stayed by him. Miss Crane, who taught him part of the time in fifth and sixth grades, was not available to him after that time. The field worker to whom he formed the beginning of an attachment when he was 16–17, was in the community only a short time. Jean, the girl he dated at 13–14, was a strong, rather driving girl, who probably could not stand Jed's lack of self-control and self-discipline, and dropped him when he showed his weakness by dropping out of school.

On the other hand, Jed had several important assets:

1. His family was a close-knit, loyal family, who supported each other with a fair degree of affection. However, we believe this affection was not deep enough nor systematically given in connection with moral training.

2. Jed was a sociable, rather likable person. He made friends easily, though superficially. As he said of himself, "I can meet girls and have fun kinda fast." He could meet anybody and strike up a friendly relationship quickly.

3. Jed responded positively to stable and tolerant men and women. He seemed to enjoy being with them, and made himself open to their influence.

Signals for the School

By the time he was nine or ten years old Jed was showing symptoms of maladjustment. Even if he had not had a series of older brothers and sisters to alert the teachers to the probability of trouble, his own behavior was enough to call attention to his need for help. He was thought to be quarrelsome and a show-off by his classmates, who rated him very low on loyalty, honesty, responsibility, and friendliness. His teachers also rated him low on these characteristics. Of a list of traits that are predictive of delinquency, he showed a marked degree of quarrelsomeness, fighting, disobedience, defiance, temper, and he was a disturbing influence in school. The school should have studied every child who showed so many signs of maladjustment.

If school personnel had studied the boy, they probably would have come out with some such procedures as the following:

(a) They would have found teachers who could tolerate Jed. In the record we see two of them—Miss Crane and Mr. Johnson. Although not indulgent of the boy, these teachers treated him with affection and respect, and he responded by real attempts to work with them. The principal or guidance counselor should have spoken to the other teachers about Jed, attempted to help them see his needs, and then if they still could not tolerate him, he should have been taken out of their classes. There are usually some children who cannot get along with some teachers, or vice versa, and the school should establish the expectation that incompatible children and teachers should be separated, without discrediting either the teacher or the child.

(b) They would have helped Jed to find a stable father-figure. This man might be a teacher or later an employer, or a Scout leader. Jed himself found an older man to be with in the person of Frank Wamsly, but the latter was too unstable and immature to do Jed much good. What Jed needed was a man who could set him an example of realistic planning for a vocation, and of sacrifice of present pleasures for future gain, so as to help him make the effort to study in school or to work his way up in some job with a future.

(c) The school could have helped Jed to get into the kind of schoolwork where he could do his best. He had above average learning ability, and superior mechanical ability. He scored high in science interests. He had a good head for mathematics. Thus there was a good deal to build on. Possibly a male shop or science teacher could have been found to become a teacher, father-figure, and counselor, all in one person.

(d) The school could have provided personal counseling for Jed. He was a confused, uncertain boy, with inner conflicts that he could not clear up unaided. A skilled counselor could have helped him to understand himself, to see himself more objectively. By gaining insight into himself, Jed might have been able to take himself in hand.

Results of Such Treatment

Looking at the record of Jed's performance on his developmental tasks, we see that he was short in getting along with age-mates, developing conscience and scale of values, and selecting and preparing for an occupation. How would the proposed treatment by the school have helped him in these developmental tasks?

Through the help of firm, friendly, and stable teachers and employers, Jed might have developed more self-control and more self-discipline, and a better scale of values. These people would have set an example for him in these areas, and they would have rewarded him by their approval of his achievement in this direction. The counselor's efforts, also, would probably have counted in the same direction.

Any gain in self-control and improvement in scale of values would have been reflected in a better relation with age-mates, for what cut him down in their esteem was just his lacking self-control and his failure to live up to the peer values of responsibility and loyalty.

Similarly, Jed's vocational performance would have improved whenever he gained more self-control and a scale of values that gave a higher rank to vocational success, planning for the future, and saving money.

CHAPTER 14

A Girl Who Succeeded and How the School Helped Her: The Case of Roberta

The Girl and Her Family

ROBERTA'S FATHER was born in 1890 in Prairie City, and has never lived anywhere else. He has worked for the post office, first as a letter carrier and later as an office clerk. He is a medium-sized man, wears glasses, and looks older than his real age. He and his daughter have spent a good deal of time together, especially while she was in the last years of grammar school. Mrs. R. said of her husband:

They both love to listen to the radio. They're great for talking over scores of games and she'll tell him about the games at school. Once he took her up to Chicago to a ball game. But the other things—no, I think she talks to me more about her other affairs. Of course, he never punishes her or even scolds her much. I don't believe he's ever spanked her. If he thinks something she's done isn't right, he'll tell me about it. He's always sort of expected me to take care of that, but then he always tells me whatever he thinks about different things. Only we never talk about those things when she's around—he doesn't approve of that at all. Why, even if he hasn't liked something I've told her he'd never say a word until we're alone.

Mrs. R. is five years younger than her husband. She came to Prairie City from a neighboring small town upon graduating from high school and took a job in an office, which she held for ten years until she married Roberta's father. Mrs. R. had eight brothers and sisters, who are now scattered over the state, but they visit one another frequently. She wishes that she had more children, but Roberta is the only one.

Mrs. R. is gray-haired, short, plump, and pleasant-looking. Both she and her husband give the appearance of being older than they actually are. They are a settled pair, having lived in their present home all their married life. Their house is a five-room bungalow on a quiet street that has not changed much in the years since their marriage. Mrs. R. told about buying the house.

Dad has always lived on this street. When we were about to be married, I quit my job a month early to get ready for the wedding and to find a house we could buy. I'd come home after tramping the streets all day and say, "Now, I've found a nice house on the West Side," and Dad would say, "No, I don't think I'd ever care to live on the West Side." Then I'd find a house across the railroad tracks and he'd say, "No, I don't think I care to live across the tracks." Finally, I said, "What you mean is you don't want to live any place but on this street, don't you?" and he said, "Yes," he guessed that's what he did mean. So we bought this house and have lived here ever since.

Although the house is old, they have kept it well repaired and added the new laborsaving devices. The fieldworker described the house as follows:

Before I left, Mrs. R. showed me around the entire house, showing the closets, the drawer space which she has, the kitchen with a view, the basement where she has laundry facilities, where the oil burner is and where there is a large room where Roberta can entertain her friends. Afterwards we went outside and she showed me the various evergreens and shrubs which they have planted. She seems to be very proud of her home and interested in it. She spends a good deal of time in its care, although she apologized for not yet having done her spring housecleaning. Her closets are extremely orderly, everything is neatly packed and labeled and put away for the spring and summer months. Roberta's room is bright, and cheerful, and attractive. Apparently her mother lets Roberta arrange her own room. She has several stuffed toys and dolls around the bed. Around the frame of her mirror are small photographs of various special friends. There is also a doll, which her mother says she makes dresses for frequently. This is an unusually modern, attractive, pleasant home.

Mr. R. belongs to the American Legion and to the Moose, and goes occasionally to the Baptist Church. His wife said of her club activities:

I used to do a good deal more, but I don't care much for clubs. I joined the Eastern Stars a long time ago, but my, they gave too many parties. It just got too expensive. They started doing things so elaborately, and I just couldn't keep up. I belong to the Auxiliary of the American Legion, but that's mostly for Dad's sake. I don't go so much. I'm just not much for most club activities.

The fieldworker described the mother's attitude toward Roberta:

Mrs. R. seems to have a great deal of affection for Roberta without in any way being unable to see faults in her. She spoke quite frankly about Roberta's faults and her special abilities. This seems to be a very happy, normal family. The parents seem to have put a great deal of thought and care into Roberta's upbringing. Not only in strictness but also their concern for her mental growth, her recreation, her companions, etc. They have made a pleasant home atmosphere for her. They apparently do not expect a great deal from her in the way of home duties. Mrs. R. twice remarked that she didn't feel a child should have to work unless there is a need for it in the family, and "anyway their schoolwork takes so much time I hardly think we should give them any more to do. They have so many things they belong to." She also mentioned that she spends a lot of time getting Roberta ready for things, performances and things in which she's going to appear, but she feels that this is very important for her child. She said: "We always used to read to Roberta all the time when she was small, from the time she was an infant, and she has always enjoyed reading herself. I think she should be out and around other children a lot of the time. She has no brothers and sisters, and then too, she's always away in the summer, so I like her to be with other children when she's here and when she's at school."

Of Roberta's training, Mrs. R. said:

When she was a baby I had her on a very strict schedule. When she went to bed she'd go right to sleep and sleep all night. She still does that. I was always very careful of her when she was a baby, pretty strict about her diet and her habits, because that's important for children. As far as her going away from home now, if I were to go some place with her and leave her, she wouldn't stay, but if I send her on the bus, as I have been able to do the last couple of years, or her relatives come and get her, well, then it's all right. Once though, when she was in the country she came home after three days. She said, "Mother, I have sort of a lump in my throat and I thought that was homesickness so I came home." So I let her stay and then she wanted to go back. Well, I told her, "Honey, it's all right but you have to make up your mind to go back or stay here." And she said she wanted to go back, that she thought she'd gotten over it, so of course I let her and she's never said any more about it since that one time when she complained of homesickness. I don't know what it was, but just something she felt that one time. But you know it's dreadful for people who are never apart from each other. They don't know how to behave. Why, my husband and I have often been separated. If he could do something and I couldn't or he could go and I couldn't, all right. After all, you have to get used to things like that because if you don't it's too hard if you ever do get separated or lose someone. Of course, it's hard with a child to make them understand that you want to let them go and, at the same time, you don't want to send them away. It's a real problem so that they'll know that you'll let them be free but still feel affectionate about them.

Roberta has never had much work to do around the home, and neither has she been given much spending money. Mrs. R. said:

I'd say some children are given too much. They don't know how to handle it. For instance, children can't budget money. It's foolish to expect it. On the other hand, other children have to do too much and are given nothing. That's not right either. Maybe I'm wrong, but when I was little I had to do dishes every single day of my life. I think Roberta will learn when it's time. Dad sometimes says, "Will she ever learn?" but I think she can use her time more valuably some other way. I'd rather have her practice her piano if she has any time.

ROBERTA AS A TEN-YEAR-OLD

Roberta was an average-appearing girl, slender but not small. She was lively, active, popular. On a sociometric test she received high scores from her age-mates as "everybody seems to like her," "unusually able and dependable," "does not argue with or tease other children."

Teachers agreed with the children in rating her very favorably. They ranked her at the very top on honesty and moral courage and only slightly below the top on responsibility and loyalty.

She ranked second in her class in school marks. Her intelligence quotient was 130 to 140, depending on the particular test. Her reading scores were especially high, but she was generally high in all types of ability.

Roberta Writes about Herself

The following essays and questionnaires were written by Roberta when she was in fifth and sixth grades:

THE PERSON I WOULD LIKE TO BE LIKE

If I could go into the future about eleven years from now, I might see myself as a dancer. I would be twenty-one with light brown hair and dark brown eyes with long eye lashes. My height would be five feet three and my weight would be 120. As I see myself in the movies dancing with a famous dancer, I would be wearing a white dress with net over it. I would have a lovely personality.

IF I WERE SIXTEEN

It is seven-thirty on a Saturday morning and I am still in bed. Suddenly the alarm clock rings and at the same time the door bell rings. I jump out of bed, put on my robe and go to the door. My mother opens it and brings in a large box. She hands it to me saying, "Your things are home." After examining the box I take it to my room. With trembling hands I take out a white formal with red satin ribbons. It is my spring prom formal. I spend the morning running up town to get my shoes, get thread for Mother to fix my dress and to get ribbons for my hair.

In the afternoon I go play tennis with another girl. I have blue shorts, shirt with my initial on the pocket. At four I leave and help mother until supper time.

At 7:00 my boy friend calls for me and I go to the prom in a convertible coop. I have a lovely time after the prom. A bunch of us go to a restaurant and have lunch. I have had a lovely time all day.

Good Things To Do	*Who Would Praise You?*
1. Study in school	Parents and teachers
2. Get good grades	Parents
3. Know how to do things	Parents, friends, relatives
4. Let your mother and father go out nights	Parents
5. Be willing to do things right away	Parents
6. Obey school rules	Teachers
7. Play with children	Mothers and children
8. Help little children build things	Mothers and children
9. Help your country	Your government and parents and boys fighting all over the world

Bad Things To Do	*Who Would Blame You?*
1. Talking back to teachers	Parents and teachers
2. Acting silly in school	Teachers
3. Not obeying your patrolman	Teachers
4. Teasing little children	Mothers
5. Using things and not returning them	Neighbors
6. Saying "Just a minute, Mother" and not coming at all	Mothers
7. Annoying others	Teachers and parents
8. Not doing homework when you are supposed to	Teachers and mothers
9. Thinking your smart	Everybody

I was happy:

When I got my white shoe ice-skates.
The First grade school picnic.
When I heard I was going to see a ship launched.

I was sad:

When I got sick and couldn't go to the launching.
When the ice had air holes and I couldn't go skating.

I was afraid:

One night I had to turn off the radio because the program of Sherlock Holmes told about a snake strangling a girl and there was a lamp that was throwing a shadow and I didn't know what it was.

Our neighbor has a cat and it chased me one night. Now I hardly like to go out at night.

I was angry:

When a girl told me she was going to give me a may basket if I'd give her one so I did but she didn't give me one.

I was ashamed:

When I called Ruth a baby when I was mad at her baby talk. She talks queer but she can't help it, because she was born like that. Her sister talks that way too.

The *Best Thing* that could happen to me is:

I could get to be a real good figure skater.

The *Worst Thing* that could happen to me is:

If I was blind.

Responding to a questionnaire on family relations when she was eleven years old, Roberta answered "very often" to the following questions:

Do you get a square deal at home?
Are you allowed to select your own clothes?
Do your parents take your wishes into consideration when planning a family trip or vacation?
May you spend the money you earn (or your allowance) as you please?
Do you feel happy and contented when at home with the family?
Do you feel that your parents understand your problems and worries?

She answered "almost never" to the following questions:

Are you worried about what your parents think of you?
Do your parents ever whip you?
Do your parents ever compare you unfavorably with other children?
Do you feel your friends have happier homes than you do?
Do you fool around uptown with your friends on school nights?

ROBERTA AT THIRTEEN YEARS OLD

A young woman described Roberta at thirteen as tall, slim, well-groomed, simply but tastefully dressed, with poise and self-assurance. Though never beautiful, Roberta was definitely attractive. She was beginning to show a feminine figure, and she reached the menarche almost on her thirteenth birthday.

She and two or three girl friends of hers were the leaders of their eighth-grade class. She was a cheerleader, she sang in the chorus, and she was editor of the school newspaper.

Roberta was quite close to her mother, and the two of them maintained an affectionate, though matter-of-fact, relationship. One observer reported:

> There's a very easy and free give-and-take between Roberta and her mother in all conversation. She seems perfectly at ease with her mother, and another elder person, and although some of her remarks sound very breezy, the manner in which they are made is not at all smart. She is unusually attractive and speaks very well. Apparently her family have encouraged her in an adult fashion. She never gives the impression that she's just a child trying to show off for company.

Another fieldworker reported the following comment by Mrs. R.

> We always talk over more things than lots of girls do with their mothers. I think you do with an only child—you can't help it. I suppose if there were a half a dozen children around, you just wouldn't have so much time to pay attention to any one of them. I know when Roberta has her friends over and they're talking things over, I can always hear them, too. Some of them don't say so much at home. Now, the other day they were talking about something or other and Roberta said to Patsy: "What did your mother say?" and Patsy said, "Oh, I never tell my mother stuff like that." But Roberta always has. And she's always been such an affectionate child. If anything came up between us during the day, she couldn't go to bed until she'd said, "Say, mother, let's forget all about this, can we?"

Mrs. R. approved Roberta's friends and trusted her judgment in picking friends. She said that Roberta liked to go roller skating, but did not care to go to a certain skating rink "because lots of boys and girls go downstairs or on the sidewalk and fool around."

As Adults Saw Her

The generally high esteem in which Roberta was held by her teachers persisted. They rated her as follows:

Very high on: Loyalty, Honesty, Moral Courage, Responsibility, Kindliness, Ambitiousness, Strength of Conscience, Optimism, Creativity, Self-confidence, Self-sufficiency, General Health.
Above average on: Emotional Stability, Self-control, Energy Output
Below average on: Hostility
Very low on: Self-centeredness

Her school grades continued to be good, though not the very highest. In this connection, her mother reported her saying:

Mother, you know I don't want to pat myself on the back or anything, but I just realized kids don't like you so well if you get too good grades. All the other boys and girls seem to think you're trying to show theirs up, and it just doesn't help much.

At this time she took the test of primary mental abilities and got close to the highest possible scores in Number Ability, Vocabulary, Spatial Imagery, Reasoning, and Memory. On Word Fluency she was not quite at the top.

In a test of educational achievement she scored at the level of the average sixteen-year-old in Reading, Arithmetic, Language, Literature, Social Studies, and Science. Only in Spelling was she down from the top.

About Roberta's reading, her mother said:

We always used to read to Roberta all the time when she was small, from the time she was an infant, and she has always enjoyed reading herself. I buy her lots of books and I always try to buy her good books and then she gets books for Christmas and her birthday all the time for presents, but she buys them herself, too. And then she has one aunt who's always giving her books. She says she doesn't know what else she'd like as well. Roberta likes to read them and she likes to read things like *National Geographic*. She also likes to read *Reader's Digest* but sometimes there are articles in it that I don't think are too good for her. So sometimes I go over it first to see what's in it because I don't think every kind of article is just right for her yet. She doesn't read just stories either. She likes pretty deep books, some that are pretty hard for her. She loves ancient history. She'll sit down with a history book any time and read. It seems to be the thing she likes best. She never takes a book that's easy; but I encourage her to go out a lot, too.

Artistic Talent

Roberta's artistic talent was noticed quite early by her mother, who said:

She draws on everything she can get hold of. When she was a small child she began using a pencil when she was probably not more than six months old. People were always saying, "Oh, that child will stick the pencil in her eye," but she never did. She loved to draw. She just loved a pencil and she still covers a scrap of paper with pencil drawing. Here, I'll show you some: (Mrs. R. got out some sheets of paper from a magazine. Roberta had made several drawings of girls and then had made 2 or 3 drawings which looked like fashion advertisements, one of shoes and one of a series of hats. Mrs. R. went on:) I find these all over, in all my magazines, stuck into books and everywhere. I really think that Roberta has a knack for this. You know Mrs. Axford, of course; well, she helped Roberta with drawing. She has her for art this year. Roberta did a sketch of the view across the river and Mrs. Axford thought it was very good and took it up to Chicago to show to some friends of hers. Of course, Roberta is interested in dress designing, too. That's what she likes. She has a doll and she's always cutting out and designing clothes for it. She just pins them on to get the design. I don't usually let her use the sewing machine because it's too hard to run a sewing machine for such small clothes. But she loves to do that, and I sort of think that if she still likes to when she's older and out of high school, there's no reason why she shouldn't go on and study art if that's what she wants to do.

(Mrs. R. took up a small seed catalogue on which Roberta had animated all the fruits and vegetables, adding faces, legs, and arms and naming them Carl Carrot, Tillie Tomato, etc.) She's doing something like this all the time—sort of doodling. Though sometimes it's just a little bit irritating to pick up a brand new magazine and see it all drawn up. But she really does some fine work. I ought to have some of it around. Let me see—I've kept so much since she was little. Wait a minute. (Mrs. R. went into the kitchen and returned with two sketches of girls in spring suits—quite attractive in detail. She went on to describe the patterns Roberta had worked out for tea towels three years ago, the beautiful calla lily she had drawn last year, other school posters, and how her friends were always asking her to design formals and dresses for their mothers to make.)

I don't know if she'll want to go on to school after high school. If she wants some special training in something, that's all right. But if it's just to spend four years away at college playing around, I can't see much point in that. Our money has come too hard to spend it that way, I tell her. Of course, we haven't really thought that far, but if she should want to take up designing or learn something special she needed, that would be important, I think. I've told her, though, "I do wish you would take typing in high school." "But mother," she says, "I'm sure I never want to be a stenographer. I couldn't stand that."

As Her Peers Saw Her

With her age-mates Roberta got extremely high ratings on: Honesty, Loyalty, Responsibility, Kindliness, Moral Courage, and Self-Control. On a sociometric test she received the highest score from her classmates on the item "Nice to be near" and on "Enthusiastic," and she was next to the highest on "Leader" and on "Well-liked; stimulates fun." She did, however, get an average score for "Bossy," which indicates that some children saw her as one who manipulates other people.

In her own peer relationships she was just ahead of the crowd, always moving in advance of them but never so far ahead as to lose touch with them. For example, she and her friends started to talk about boys when they were twelve years old, and to go to parties with boys when they were thirteen. She began to like a boy in her class, and he would walk home with her from parties. Her mother described the following incident:

Their class was going to have a hay-ride. Well, Roberta was awfully fond of Ray Johnson. Really, he was the best-looking, curly-headed youngster I've seen. He was the first one on the hayrack. Then another little girl got on, and she just curled up right beside Ray and stayed there the rest of the ride. He and Roberta never did get together. Well, that evening when Roberta came home she just came in and went to her room. I called to her, "Did you have a nice time?" "Oh, yes," she answered, but she never did come out. "What's the matter with that girl—something wrong?" her dad said. "Oh, probably she didn't have as much fun as she expected," I replied. Well, then Roberta called out a little later, "Mother, will you come and open the window for me before I go to sleep?" So I went in, and she said, "Oh, Mother, that Barbara sat right beside Ray and I never had a chance to be near him all evening." She just cried and cried. I said, "Well, honey, that's all right. You're so young still to worry so about that. Just try to lie down and sleep. You're tired and in the morning it won't seem nearly so bad. Just try to sleep, honey." In the morning I said to her, "Well, how are you feeling now?" She said, "I feel all right now. I slept fine last night, except I couldn't go to sleep for a long time. But I don't think I care so much today. Ray's just another boy after all." Well, that was her first heartbreak. But right now—I don't know. Roberta will go out with some boys once and that's all there is to it.

Roberta Writes about Herself

In a test of moral judgment, Roberta made an above-average score, and she showed a high average ability to evaluate moral behavior objectively. On a self-report (The California Personality Test) she scored high average on personal and social adjustment.

The Person I Would Like To Be Like

I think that I would like to be like Madam Curie in a way. She was brave and was a scientist. There is the wish of mine that I could fly. I would join the WAAFS and ferry planes across. I'd be about 25 years old with brown hair and eyes. For sports there would be ice-skating, boating, and archery. I would also like to be a dress designer.

If I Were Sixteen

If I could suddenly become sixteen for a day and leave the rest of my room behind in age I would only want to be this for a day so that I could grow up with the rest. I'd probably wake up in the same room, eat the same things for breakfast and leave the same way as now only earlier. I would be in the Junior Class in High School, taking typing, Latin, English, and in study hall I might sit by Jim Morgan, Maud

Long, and Esther Innis. Afternoon would be about the same but afterwards I would probably go down to The Drug Store with Jim and the rest. At night I might have a date or maybe a slumber party. This is what I would call an ideal day for a sixteen-year-old.

I was happy:

> When my cousin came home on leave.
> When I went for some ice skates of my cousin thinking they were black and they turned out to be white figure skates.

I was sad:

> When my grandmother died.
> When it rained for our hay-ride.

I was afraid:

> When a cat jumped out at me at night.
> When a ventilator fell out of the window one night.

I was angry:

> When rain comes to spoil parties.

I was ashamed:

> I hardly ever am.

The *Best Thing* that could happen to me is:

> To have Ray Brown my own age.

The *Worst Thing* that could happen to me is:

> To lose the war.

ROBERTA AT SIXTEEN-SEVENTEEN

As a junior and senior in high school Roberta was a leader in extracurricular activities, while she coasted along in her academic work, easily holding a position in the top tenth of her class. She played basketball and tennis on the girls' teams, took part in class plays, was on the staff of the school paper and the class annual, and was president of a club of girls which more or less dominated the social life of the school.

As Seen by Adults

Teachers' ratings of Roberta were high, but not as high as when she was thirteen. Her highest rating was on responsibility, and she was also high—though down slightly from the thirteen-year-old ratings—in honesty, loyalty, and kindness. She was down to average rating on moral courage. Since her age-mates gave her high ratings on this trait, there is a difference of opinion between adults and age-mates which may be explained as follows: Roberta is now going along with her age-group in some things that adults do not quite approve. They interpret this as meaning that Roberta is not standing up for her principles as formerly. On self-control she is rated slightly lower than formerly by adults and age-mates.

Mr. and Mrs. R. had become somewhat uncertain about their attitudes toward some of the things Roberta did and said, as is indicated by the following report of a conversation between Mrs. R. and a fieldworker:

Mrs. R. made a number of comments about Roberta and other girls in high school with reference to dating and their conversations about boys. She said, "You know, there are ten of the girls that have a society and they get together and talk things over, and honestly you'd be surprised to hear them. You wouldn't think they were girls at all. You'd think they were adults, the things they talk about and the ideas they have. And the way they figure things out. That bothers my husband. He thinks they ought to be just little girls yet. He just hates to see that. I think a father is likely to be that way, about his daughter especially."

The comment was made somewhere along the line about girls dating older boys and Mrs. R. said, "Yes, isn't that true? You know, I hadn't realized how much difference there was in the way boys and girls grow up. These girls don't like to go out with boys their own age. They say they're so icky and gooney and they don't know how to act, they're careless about dressing, and the girls want to go around with older boys who, as they put it, know what the score is.

"And many of these girls are very frank, too, in the way they talk. They'd just as soon talk to you about anything without holding anything back. I got so amused one morning with Roberta. I was concerned, too. She came down to breakfast and she said, 'Mother, there's something I want to ask you about. I hope you're going to approve.' I said, 'Well, Roberta, I probably will, but look at the time, it's getting a little bit late. You'd better get off to school.' Roberta said, 'Well, mother, it won't take but a minute, and I want you to know about it.' And she said, 'Mother, I'm thinking of going steady. Do you have any objections?' "

Mrs. R. said that she was at first amused about it and had a hard time keeping her face straight because Roberta was so serious and it just seemed so peculiar to have that coming out all of a sudden. "But she said, 'Well we talked it over last night and we just decided we'd like to go steady. That way I always know I've got a date, and when something comes up that's all settled and I know all about it, and I don't have to be wondering whether I'm going to get to go someplace or whether I'm going to have a date.' " Mrs. R. said she then remarked to Roberta, "Well, what do you suppose your father's going to think about this?" Roberta said, "Oh, mother, you know he'll hit the ceiling. Let's just postpone telling him for a while." Mrs. R. said that Roberta did tell her father shortly afterwards and he was quite put out about it. He said to Roberta, "I don't know what you kids are thinking of. Have you lost your minds? The idea of your going steady at your age." Roberta said to him, "Well, Dad, figure it out. There's somebody you like to go with and you have a good time with them, then you always know you've got a date for anything that's going to come up and if I don't like him and things don't work out I can always give him back his ring and that's all there is to it." Mrs. R. said that Roberta had been going out quite a bit, being up late several nights during the week, and she said that lately she had been a little bit concerned about it and asked Roberta if she didn't think her schoolwork was suffering. Roberta replied, "Well, no, mother, it's just the other way around. When you have somebody that you're going steady with and you've got a date you don't have to sit around worrying about that and wondering what's going to happen and whether you'll have a date when something comes up. So your mind's free to look after your studies and go ahead and do things the way they ought to be done." Mrs. R. laughed as she reported this. She seemed to be constantly puzzled and sort of overwhelmed by Roberta, and yet proud of the way she figured things out. She said, though, that the boy Roberta is going with will be going away to school this fall and she hopes then that maybe this will all die down.

With respect to her career plans, Roberta was undecided about going to art school. Her mother reports:

Until recently Roberta was sure she wanted to do something in the line of artwork. She's always been interested in that. Then last fall she decided she was going to take typing and her uncle was here at that time with my brother and he said that if she took typing she really ought to take at least a year of shorthand. Well, she didn't want to do that. She wasn't really interested in it. After he left she said, "Mother, I wish my relatives would stay at home and mind their own business," and I said to her, "Well, Roberta, he was just trying to help. After all, he's been a principal for thirty-seven years and he knows something about young people and he was trying to give you some good advice." Well, anyway, Roberta took shorthand and she did very well with it. She passed the 100-word-a-minute test, and Miss Bard says that is most unusual for a first-year student. Roberta likes it, too; she says that it's very easy, but some people say it's because of her artistic leanings that it's been easier for her. I know she comes home and says, "Oh, some of the kids just twist around trying to do it and if they'd just write it it'd be simple." It is easy for her, but obviously it isn't easy for everyone. Of course, I think Miss Bard is an awfully good teacher, too.

The interviewer asked if Roberta had had any specific training in art. Mrs. R. said:

"No, she's had just a very few lessons. That's all. But she says she didn't learn anything much from that. Oh, she says she learned a few things, but she said, 'Mother, I'm not interested in drawing landscapes and things like that. I'm interested in dress designing. If I were more interested in learning landscaping I could learn something from the teacher, but as it is I could teach her a few things about some of the stuff.' "

Mrs. R. went on to talk about Roberta's work in art. She said that since she was in the eighth grade she had been doing a lot of designing for things over at the high school, for example, the cheerleaders' costumes, and things of that sort. "They'll ask Roberta to figure out something and she'll sit down and think about it for a little bit and draw something right off, no telling what it'll be on—any old scrap of paper —but she'll come out with something and they've always used her designs. She started doing that when she was in the eighth grade, and then for the annual and things like that she's always drawing. Next year she's going to be editor of the annual and that will be a lot of work of course, but she'll enjoy it. Then she has a Sunday school class, you know, the little five-year-olds. She started out with eight children and she's built it up to twelve. She just loves that. You know, not many girls would be interested bothering with that, but she gets a big kick out of it. She always has liked children. They're always coming over here and wanting to know if Roberta can't come out and play with them. Children and dogs, she just loves them, but she doesn't have a dog. The children in Sunday school class always want her to draw and they'll say, 'Oh, Roberta, draw something for us to color!' And so she'll sit down and draw up a bunch of things before she goes to Sunday school and have them ready for the children to color and over Easter she made some little Easter bunnies. She boiled the eggs, fixed the eyes and put on cute little ears and so on for them, put them in little baskets. She fixed thirteen or fourteen of them. It was a good afternoon's work, but she stayed right at it. Got them fixed up and they were awfully cute, I thought."

As Seen by Herself

Roberta herself was uncertain about entering art school. At one time or another during this period, she spoke of going to each of three different art schools, and she finally did send in her application to a school for a course in commercial art. She said she did not plan to finish college, but only to take enough artwork to get a job in the field of dress designing. She also enjoyed music and studied piano for four years. She played the piano as an accompanist for the school chorus, and for a small school orchestra.

The fieldworker asked Roberta whether she could remember back to her childhood years and what she wanted to be when she grew up. Roberta answered:

Well, first I thought keeping house was nice, then I wanted to be a nurse and then a movie star and then I wanted to be a cowgirl. You know, all girls go through that stage of wanting to be a cowgirl right after they start going to the movies. And then you think of being on the stage or being a model but that isn't until after you start reading magazines. Then being a business or career girl comes later when you get in high school and you start thinking about having pretty clothes and having money.

The interviewer asked, "Do you ever think of being a schoolteacher?" Roberta replied:

No! I don't think anybody ever thinks of being a schoolteacher when they grow up.

THE PERSON I WOULD LIKE TO BE LIKE

I would like to be at the age of 28, a successful commercial artist or dress designer, married to a rather wealthy young business man. At that age I would like to have one child and live with my husband and child in a large home outside of New York, on Long Island perhaps and also have a large apartment in New York and have 2 or 3 large cars in which I could travel from one to the other. I wouldn't want to be any taller than I am now as I would want to wear the highest heels possible. By that time I would like to have my hair trained that I might wear it in any style that I pleased. I would like to give large parties in my homes.

WHEN I'M TWENTY-TWO

Here I am, twenty-two! How time flies—

It is morning in a small apartment (Small but very glorious) in Chicago or New York. A very beautiful girl (this is me in 5 years?) is getting ready to go to work. It's me!

I am the head fashion illustrator for Marshall Fields at the small salary of $500 a week! I am dying in poverty!

On my finger gleams a 1½ carat diamond. I am to be married in two months. I am marrying a guy I've been going with for the last five years. (I know our friends weren't supposed to grow but I had to drag him along.)

I have two cars—a Cadillac limousine and a Lincoln convertible—

Well, now we've had fun dreaming—maybe I'll be married with ten kids (well one anyway), maybe I'll be working my life away (this is improbable) and who knows I may still be in High School!

A GOOD KIND OF PERSON IN OUR COMMUNITY IS

A good kind of person to have in our community is a teacher like Mr. Allen, our music teacher here at school.

He has enlarged the interest in music both in the students and in the community. In the department of vocal music we have an a capella choir, a girls' glee club, boys' quartette, a first year chorus class, and a madrigal group. He has started these and, besides being the director of them, finds time to give private lessons, teach a speech and dramatics class, a business English class, direct community choirs at various things, sing in his own choir, promote dramatic interest, and sponsor the dramatic club. He directed both the junior and senior plays this year and will direct the senior style show.

He accomplishes all this because the students like and respect him. He's one teacher that you feel free to talk with. You're relaxed when he's around.

This is his first year in Prairie City. We had singing groups before he came but he has enlarged and improved them immensely.

As Judged by Clinical Psychologists

Roberta was studied thoroughly at age thirteen and again at age sixteen-seventeen by a clinical team. Recognizing her outstanding intellectual and artistic abilities, they studied closely her emotional balance, trying to find out whether she would become a happy, warm-hearted person. A summary of their conclusions when she was thirteen follows:

High creativity and high ambition in the intellectual area (Rorschach —1946).

Impulse acceptance rather low. Excellent social techniques give impression of more impulse acceptance than is really present.

Age 13—not yet adjusting on a mature level. Infantile patterns of adjustment. Some conflict over this.

Self-centered and basically introverted pattern of adjustment.

It was felt that she would always sacrifice her impulsivity to set social standards with a minimum of anxiety, which is an example of a very highly incorporated superego.

Conceives of herself as a person with moral principles.

Her security depends on her being somewhat detached from other persons.

Well-structured but somewhat isolated ego, which functions effectively on the societal level.

Ego-ideals—Curie, Henie, Hepburn, Madame Chiang Kai-shek. Interpreted to mean achievement through techniques and impulse denial.

Summary: She sees herself as a non-loving, competent, and achieving person and the outer world as something you can conquer by techniques. Question whether close affectional ties are a threat to her, or does she simply lack experience in this area as yet? Will she achieve the biological task of accepting her sex-role? The problem area is in terms of her affectional relations.

In discussing Roberta at the age of thirteen, two members of the clinical conference group raised a question about whether she was growing sufficiently toward independence from her parents.

Tryon felt that we must not overlook the fact of apparent absence of rebellion on the part of the child. She felt that some rebellion might be a good thing here. Henry pointed out that the family hardly ever ties Roberta down or censures her for her activities, in fact they permissively encourage them. This he felt is the reason for her lack of rebellion and her ability to integrate so effectively.

The clinical conference group that studied Roberta at the age of sixteen-seventeen carried on this discussion as follows:

As though Roberta and her family had read this and cooperated in revising it, the succession of evidence since age thirteen has brought into better balance the entire picture. Father (TAT's, Interviews, Anecdotes) has become more harsh and controlling. Roberta cooperates by becoming more rebellious against parents and adults (See shift in Moral Courage and Self-Control scores.) We note that she is moving from rigidity of controls to flexibility, from repression of impulses to greater awareness and integrated expression of impulses. These factors seem to answer the question concerning how much it costs her to maintain tight intellective control. She is becoming a more "human" sort of person, feeling and expressing hostility, turning good-humored criticism against herself and others, and allowing some emotions about others to gain awareness.

In spite of all these positive signs of emotional maturing, it must be emphasized that Roberta is predominantly an intellectual individual. The entire area of affective interrelations is underdeveloped. She has avoided heavily the establishment of any love relations, feeling these would be dangerous and uncontrollable.

We can predict she will never be the sort of person who enters warm, personal situations and in this respect her life will lack richness and depth. She can hardly overcome the long years when she had little experience in nor enjoyment of such relations. In terms of her goals of status, security, achievement, and appropriate group recognition, this picture assures her of attaining her own desires.

The latest information about Roberta was obtained during the summer after she graduated from high school. She applied for entrance to an art school and was all ready to leave home for school in September. But the boy with whom she had been "going steady" returned to Prairie City after a year away at college and decided to stay out of school and go to work.

Roberta then changed her plans, and got a job in an office in Prairie City.

RATINGS ON DEVELOPMENTAL TASKS

The clinical conference group studied all the available data about Roberta at ages ten, thirteen, and sixteen, and made the following ratings on a scale from 1 to 10, comparing her with American children generally, of these ages.

Getting Along with Age-Mates:

Age	Average Rating
10	9.5
13	9.4
16	9.5

This was the highest rating given to anybody in the group. Roberta's combination of creative ability with her sensitivity to the wants and feelings of other people made her popular and accepted as a leader by all kinds of boys and girls.

Achieving a Feminine Social Role

Age	Average Rating
10	9.4
13	8.6
16	8.6

Roberta was everything a little girl is supposed to be in America at the age of ten. At the later ages she falls a shade under the highest rating because of a lack of warmth and a trace of manipulative tendency in her relations with people.

Achieving Emotional Independence of Parents and Other Adults

Age	Average Rating
10	7.2
13	7.9
16	8.6

In the minds of the clinical conference members, Roberta was a little more dependent upon her mother as a ten-year-old than some girls, though more independent than the average girl. The rating for the later ages rise, because Roberta displayed greater independence, and by the time she was sixteen she was quite mature for a girl her age in handling and governing herself.

Developing Conscience and a Scale of Values

Age	Average Rating
10	9.4
13	9.4
16	9.4

These are extremely high ratings, reflecting the judgment of the clinicians that Roberta had formed a coherent and rational scale of values, governed by a strong and rational conscience, far in advance of most children of her years.

Analysis of This Case

The principal characteristics of this outstandingly competent and gifted girl are:

1. Very high intellectual ability. She is in the upper 2 or 3 per cent of the population.

2. A fair degree of talent. Roberta's artistic talent is not easily evaluated, because no one with good judgment about childrens' art saw her work. However, the fact that her desire to draw appeared so early and that it persisted without training for so long indicates that she probably had a talent in this area.

3. A friendly, outgoing, and responsible personality. This commended her to all kinds of people. She was generally trusted and liked. Possibly she was not as warm and affectionate as some people would like the ideal woman to be. Perhaps she was somewhat cool and manipulative in her relationships with people.

4. Leadership. Roberta played the role of clarifier for her age-group. Securely at the head of them in social and personal development but not too far ahead to be out of touch with them, she was able to foresee the path of development and to clarify the problems of growing up for her age-mates.

5. An orderly, affectionate home experience. The father and mother both treated Roberta consistently, disciplined her if they thought it necessary, and gave her sufficient love. From this experience she inferred that the world would reward her with respect and love if she gave a constructive performance. Her stability of character seems to have been an outgrowth of the stable, consistent, and fairly affectionate experience she had in the home of her early childhood.

Nevertheless, there were some shadows on the nearly perfect personality of Roberta, at least as seen by certain observers.

One shortcoming in the eyes of some of her teachers and some other adults was Roberta's lack of "ambition." She did not wish for a college education. If she went beyond high school at all, it would be to an art school for a practical course in dress designing or commercial art. Although she could dream dreams of luxury and personal comfort, these dreams did not include a high level of artistic performance. Some people would feel that she fell short, in this respect, of the heights she should have reached, or at least have sought after.

Another shortcoming, as seen perhaps by another group of observers, was a certain manipulative quality in her relations with people. Although this made her an effective leader, it meant that she lacked warmth in relation to others, that she used intellect more than empathy in her approach to people.

How the School Helped Roberta

The ordinary American school seems to have been made for Roberta. It gave her a stage on which to practice and to play the success roles of American youth. She could do very well on practically everything in the curriculum and in the sphere of extracurricular activities. Her talent combined with her personal quality and mental ability earned approval from everybody in school, and she gave the school in return the gifts of responsible and stimulating leadership.

The school taught her a set of middle-class values that were supplementary to those taught in her home and her church. And the school gave her a useful vocational skill—stenography—which she could use until her marriage.

Some persons will want to ask whether the school did not fail Roberta when it failed to encourage in her a "divine discontent." Instead of merely providing her a stage for a brilliant performance of the ordinary developmental tasks of youth, why did not the school stimulate ambition in Roberta to become an artist or a musician, or to get a liberal education and enter a career of leadership? Did not the school abet the family and the peer group in denying society the gifts Roberta might have brought to it had she been better trained and more ambitious? Or will society gain sufficiently through Roberta's future life as a wife, mother, church worker, clubworker, and citizen in her home community? What is the responsibility of the school to the gifted child?

CHAPTER 15

A Girl Who Failed and What The School Might Have Done To Help Her: The Case of Elsie

Family Background

ELSIE COMES from a family of nine children. She has two older sisters and two older brothers besides four younger sisters and brothers. Elsie was a "depression baby," born in 1933.

The family is considered to be in the lower socioeconomic class. It has no reputation for immorality as a family although the father is said to have drunk too much. The father has held a series of unskilled jobs and has been on relief many times. The mother, too, has worked at many unskilled jobs to help support the family. There has been some improvement of living conditions over the years, as the children grew up and contributed to the family income.

The Parents

The father was born in 1901 in this country. He is a small man standing only five feet four inches. After a fourth-grade education, he tried various unskilled occupations. At one time he worked with relatives in a market garden business. In Prairie City he worked at the paper mill but quit this job because he "didn't like to work around so many people." During the depression he was working on WPA as a laborer. At the time of the last contact with the family he was a kind of straw boss on a railroad section gang. According to the mother's report, he liked this work because it was among fewer men and kept him out of doors more than did the job at the paper mill.

An official at the Prairie City Relief Office said the father "is a long-time (relief) case. He gets a lot of help and has received it through every agency." Another social worker said, "It is a big family. They beg for all they can get." The father was also described as "a typical WPA worker."

The mother was born in 1906 in this country and lived in a town near Prairie City until she was seventeen, at which time she was married. She had an eighth-grade education. She met her husband in a community near Chicago, married him shortly after. Since their marriage she has worked most of the time when she was not pregnant or confined at home with a small baby.

In Prairie City she has held several jobs. At one time she worked as a dishwasher at a restaurant at noon and held another dishwashing job at a tavern-restaurant in the evenings. Earlier she held a job in a defense industry and followed this with work as a laundrywoman in the hospital.

The mother was described by an interviewer as being "a very drab-looking woman. Her figure is now quite shapeless. She is not attractive, but she does speak with some animation." Another interviewer said the mother was "five feet one inch tall and weighed ninety pounds as a younger woman, but she has grown heavier."

Mr. and Mrs. E. seldom did things together. When she was home in the evening, she usually patched clothes while her husband enjoyed the radio program. They did go to the movies together. Describing their relationship, the mother said, "Me and my husband don't even see each other very much because I'm always gone when he's here, and when I get home after nine, then he's ready to go to bed."

Home Accommodations

During the years when the children were coming the family lived in the one big room of an old store building, on a side street in the business district. The fieldworker reported, "The family consists of eleven people who live in this one room. They can have no privacy and no place to put their belongings. There is no yard for the children to play in. They have their sleeping space curtained off from their cooking and eating space."

When the older girls were able to earn money the family fortunes improved, and they moved into a larger store-front room, which they remodeled, putting in partitions, wallpapering, etc., until they literally constructed for themselves a pleasant four-room house. The front third of the house was a large living room containing a studio couch, a slip-covered davenport and chair, smaller furniture, and a coal heater. The floor was linoleum-covered throughout the house. The middle third of the space was a kitchen-dining room, brightly wallpapered and decorated in red and white. A small cot stood in one corner of this room. A small space off this room had been partitioned off as a bedroom for the two oldest girls and contained a double bed and two dressers. The back third of the house was a large bedroom, almost giving the appearance of a dormitory. In it were two double beds, a crib, and a bassinette. A lavatory was partitioned off in one corner, and a closet in another. At the end of the room stood a sink, where dishes were washed, clothes laundered. It also served as a bath.

These were the accommodations for the father and mother and their nine children ranging in age from twenty-one years down to four months.

Community Participation

The family belonged to the Methodist Church, but the children seldom attended except at Christmastime, when they went to the Christmas party and got a bag of candy and an orange. There was no further evidence of organized community participation. Mrs. E. said that she had no time to go out and see people because she didn't have time to do more than go to work and come home to take care of her family. However, she had numerous relatives in the neighboring towns, and she often saw them on holidays.

The Children

The oldest girl, Lucile, was born in 1924. She acquired an eighth-grade education. She worked for a time at housework and then got a job in a factory where she has been ever since.

Mary was born in 1927. She is the only one who finished the twelfth grade. She did housework while still in school, earning $1.50 per week. Also while she was in school, she took care of the family housework, prepared meals, and worked as a clerk in the 5 and 10 cent store. The mother, who was working at the time, commented that Mary knew as much about the children's care as she did.

Earl, the oldest brother, was born in 1929. He was the tallest member of the family, standing five feet six inches when he reached his growth. He did not finish the eighth grade. He spent a good deal of time at an aunt's, helping her on the farm. One of the interviewers said of him:

> Earl left school at the age of sixteen, before finishing the eighth grade to stay at home and take care of the children under school age. The parents, of course, had to sign an affidavit in order to have him released from further school attendance. The mother had to work and said she could not get satisfactory help to care for the children.

John was born in 1931. He, too, quit school when he reached sixteen, and worked for a lumber yard.

Elsie was born in 1933. Joseph was born in 1936. Mrs. E. had a miscarriage between 1937 and 1939.

Esther, born in 1939, was the last of the children to be born at home. Clara, born in 1942, and Henry, born in 1944, both were hospital babies.

The mother reported, I had never had a baby in a hospital before. I wasn't so keen on the idea. But the older girls both said, 'Now mother, you're going to have that baby in the hospital. It's too hot for you to be here at home.' And, of course, it was; the baby was born in August. Then too, there wasn't much privacy here what with us all being in that same room, and so forth. So I had the baby up at the hospital. It really wasn't bad, what with my working there and all. It was quite cozy and then the two girls used to come home and change their clothes and come to the hospital at seven and stay until nine. So it really wasn't bad. And you know, that child hasn't ever been sick at all. In fact, I think she's the healthiest one in the bunch!"

The interviewer reported that Clara was much plumper and had a better color than the other children. The mother, however, had actually expected it to be dangerous to have a baby in the hospital.

The family is often referred to as having many children. One person said, "They have a baby every moon." In an interview with this person the following things were said of the family: "This is a large family. Much too large. And they recently had another new baby. The children are all emaciated and undernourished."

In a very early contact the interviewer described the family as follows:

> The mother said that the tallest of the children is the boy, "and he's five foot three." This is a rather unattractive-looking group of children. But Mary is quite pretty and blonde and has a pleasant smile. A picture of the older girl, Lucile, indicated that she and the girls, Elsie, Esther, and Clara, strongly resemble each other. None of them was at all attractive. They have straight, lanky hair, rather expressionless faces and do not look very well. Their color is bad and their teeth look uncared for.

The impressions of another interviewer were as follows:

> All are physically more attractive than Elsie, and dressed more becomingly. Elsie looks more like a child of ten or eleven (rather than the fourteen-year-old that she is). The two youngest children are well-developed for their age and are very good-looking, healthy youngsters. Esther is less so, and an unhappy appearing and acting child. She cried a good deal while I was there. The two older girls are really quite attractive. Half of them are blonde, and half are brunette. Elsie is the only one I saw who wore glasses, and also the only one with quite poorly fitted clothes.

Parent-Children Relationships

In a talk with the mother, one of the interviewers gained the impression that Elsie was a less attractive member of a large group, an "in-between" child in age and in the family constellation who is ignored or perhaps even rejected. This same interviewer reported:

> I had great difficulty in getting the mother to talk about Elsie for any length of time. Whenever I asked a pointed question about Elsie, she answered it briefly and led back to something about the other children. She told me a good deal about the rest—about her own sisters, nieces, and nephews, how they were brought up, her early married life, how much the children weighed to the exact ounce, her miscarriage—in short, anything and everything but Elsie.

When asked whether she ever found time to do much of anything with Elsie, she replied, "Oh yes, I take her along to the stores with me sometimes." Elsie is not allowed to go often to the movies on school nights, but she had gone "the night before because she complained that she was the only one who didn't get to go Sunday."

At one point the interviewer asked a direct question of the mother regarding how Elsie compared with her brothers and sisters in general. The interviewer detected a fleeting expression of disturbance on the mother's face. She answered that "Elsie isn't much for the house, nor for any of the interests of the older girls. She just likes to be outdoors playing ball or riding a bicycle. She and Joseph are the closest; they play outdoors more."

On the other hand, the mother did find time to go to the movies with her husband and with the older girls, but not with Elsie. Mary and the mother seem to have had an especially close relationship. Mary commented to the interviewer how much she and her mother loved to go walking and mentioned the fact that they had gone for a long walk the night before. Mary also said that when she earned some extra money, she and her mother were going to go to Chicago to buy a dress for the Junior-Senior Banquet and Prom. Mother would pay for part, but Mary didn't think she should pay for all of it since that would cost too much.

The mother did not display much affection for Elsie, although she seemed kindly enough disposed toward the littler ones, especially Clara. In describing the mother's attitude toward Clara, the interviewer said:

Clara was fussing and begging for candy during the afternoon. "I guess she's just been spoiled," commented the mother. "Everyone was giving her so much for a while, and then you know how they get." Clara was unhappy when refused candy and produced a forced cry, stalking away in a comical stride to indicate her distress—"A habit she learned from Esther," her mother said.

The baby wasn't on any regular feeding schedule "now," the mother informed the interviewer, "but he seems to eat just about the same amount anyway." When he was hungry, or when he cried, he was given a bottle.

The interviewer reported that the children played around the house together a good deal. Esther and Clara played with dolls much of the time, although there were frequent spats. Clara was much distressed at such times until peace was re-established, but Esther withdrew and said she didn't love her sister any more.

When asked what she did when they quarreled, Mrs. E. said, "Oh! Nothing much. Just separate them and put them in different parts of the house."

In the evening everyone settled down pretty much to playing games or doing puzzles or coloring pictures. The father sat in the front room and the mother, too, if she was at home. "Sometimes, of course," reported the mother, "we have to settle Joseph and Elsie down (in bed). But there's not much other trouble."

The children rarely brought friends home. There was neither room nor money to spare for parties. In the summertime the children played with a few of the neighborhood playmates.

ELSIE AT AGE TEN

There is little information on Elsie as a ten-year-old. She was retarded in school by one year and was therefore not in the class of youngsters on whom scientific data were collected.

How Her Peers Saw Her

Being overlooked seems to describe pretty well the way Elsie was treated in school generally at age ten. When her classmates were given a chance to rate each other, including Elsie, on a series of personal and social characteristics, this is the way Elsie lined up:

1. She received the lowest number of mentions in the group as being a person who would cooperate well in a group project of the class, who would work well with a leader, and not try to boss others around. She received the lowest number of mentions as being a person who was unusually able and dependable. She was also lowest in the group on being kind, patient, waiting her turn, and not showing off.

2. Elsie received next to the lowest number of mentions on the following items: being liked by most of the other children, working

well in a group, very much at home in school, not quarrelsome or a tease. She was rated low on bashfulness, shyness, and quietness—or perhaps she was overlooked by her classmates on this item.

3. Elsie never was given a large number of mentions on any characteristic. For her, the items on which she received most mentions by her classmates were items that described characteristics that were undesirable: selfishness, showing off, bothering children near her and quarreling with them, not taking responsibility well, not being liked by children or being wanted on their teams.

4. Even on the items on which she was mentioned most often, Elsie never received a high score in the class, nor anywhere near it. She simply was not noticed by her classmates; she was invisible to them.

A general impression one gets is that Elsie did not interact much with her age-mates or her classmates. Her position in the group was one of quite complete isolation. One of the investigators commented: "At school, few children play with Elsie. She usually seems to find ways of amusing herself, and does not seem to be unhappy." The same investigator mentioned: "She plays with the girl next door, and with her brother (Joseph). They prowl around on the streets all hours of the day and night. At school few children play with Elsie."

Elsie did not appear to be very much aware of her isolation from her age-mates and did not strive for a place in the group. Apparently she found other satisfactions and somehow adjusted herself to her status. She did make some effort to get attention from her peers, however, as is evidenced by the fact that she bothered them, showed off, would not wait her turn. These efforts, however, were rather feeble.

Elsie in School

Elsie started school in 1939, at age six. When asked by an interviewer whether she had gone through each grade year by year, she replied, "Well, in the second, see, I passed into the third grade, and I couldn't read so well for a while and I had to be put back into the second grade. I didn't fail, though." In another place she said that she did not get her glasses until the "third or fourth grade—I couldn't read the board." The school nurse said that all of Elsie's brothers and sisters had been retarded at school.

As Her Teachers Saw Her

Although her teachers did not pay much attention to her either, they tended to regard her unfavorably. They rated her very low on loyalty and responsibility, and low on honesty, moral courage, and friendliness.

Her Physical Make-up

Elsie was the smallest of the ten-year-old children studied in the schools of Prairie City. She had never been regular in school attendance. She was bothered by bad tonsils and eyes. Her tonsils had not been taken out. Her glasses were changed later, when she was twelve, but there is no report that they had been changed before that. She got headaches and colds about as often as other children. Her throat was often sore from bad tonsils. She had chicken pox before she started school. In the second grade she had the mumps. She also had the measles.

There is no information on Elsie's energy output, her growth pattern, or her motor pattern at this age. However, one cannot mention Elsie's physical growth and health without also looking at the family background in relation to her health. There is considerable evidence of malnutrition. Her diet was probably most inadequate during the depression. The school nurse reported that "the children are all emaciated and undernourished." Another interviewer reported: "All the children in the family have suffered from malnutrition. . . . The younger children look like little old men and women."

Another interviewer said: "I suspect that their diet is not too adequate. . . . Mrs. E. said they all were small eaters. According to her, the two older girls and the husband didn't care for any breakfast, 'maybe a cup of coffee or so' . . . The family has only a lunch at noon. For their main meal the evening of the day I visited, the main dish was lima bean soup. . . . Then, in the evening, about eight or nine o'clock, someone goes into the kitchen and fixes something. Pretty soon they all gather around and 'lunch.' "

One informant thought that "Elsie has more spunk than the other children. She seemed healthier and some of the neighbors thought that she got more to eat than the other children did. She is more aggressive than the other children." This same interviewer, in describing Elsie as a ten-year-old, stated, "In spite of poor home conditions, I would say that Elsie is well adjusted, probably with a delayed development pattern." This opinion was questioned by other fieldworkers, however.

Family Life

Elsie was growing up in a clanlike family that was just living on the margin, economically. The family lived an irregular life, in a barnlike atmosphere, without much regulation, and with the mother working at mealtimes. There was a strong element of neglect coupled with a kind of emotional malnutrition as well as physical.

Elsie is described as being more aggressive than her brothers and sisters. She got along quite well with her brothers and sisters at this age. She played a lot with John and Joseph. The children seemed to have a "nice attitude toward each other," according to an interviewer. They seldom quarreled and often talked approvingly about the others.

Elsie's own picture of her family, as revealed in a family-relations questionnaire, was confused and inconsistent. There was some regularity and some irregularity in the home. Meals were served at irregular hours, but she went to bed at a regular hour and was never allowed to fool around uptown with her friends on school nights.

Her relationships with her parents were not very good as revealed in this questionnaire. She answered that she was fairly often worried about what her parents thought of her. Her parents seldom praised her. They very seldom had confidence in her. She answered "very seldom" to the following questions:

Do you ever talk over your problems and worries with your parents?
Do your parents show an interest in your work?

She answered "almost never" to the following questions:

Do you get a square deal at home?

Can you refuse to do what your parents say without causing an argument?

Are you allowed to select your own clothes?

Are you allowed to spend your allowance as you please?

On the other hand Elsie's answers indicated some satisfactory parent-child relationships. She said that her parents very seldom cheated her, that they almost never showed that they like one of the other siblings better than her. We might conclude from her answers that neither parent took much interest in her as an individual.

There was very little information on the personal development of Elsie at age ten. The only information on her mental functioning are two IQ scores: An IQ rating of 79 on one test (Stanford-Binet) and an 88 on another (Otis). On her emotional adjustment there was the following report of an interviewer:

> Elsie is a rather nervous child—she chews her fingernails, etc. She usually accepts a "no" from her parents without objection. She sleeps well, is full of life, has no temper spells, likes to play, color, draw, look at funnies and papers, work puzzles, and knit a little. Tag and hide-and-go-seek are her favorites.

ELSIE AT AGE THIRTEEN

Elsie received even less notice from her peer group at this age than she did as a ten-year-old. She was almost entirely ignored on items on a "Guess Who Test" that describes participation, cheerfulness, friendliness, helpfulness, and temper. There was a tendency for Elsie to receive a little more attention on items concerned with character, particularly those describing lack of responsibility and lack of courage to stand up to leaders and teachers for what she believed was right. She was rarely mentioned on items concerned with honesty.

For example, the characteristics on which her peers mentioned her most often were the following: sometimes lets friends persuade her to do something that she believes is wrong; sometimes takes things that don't belong to her; careless, and does not do her share; tells many lies, cheats in games, doesn't play fair. The characteristics on which Elsie did not get many mentions by her classmates were the following: plans and finishes work before going out to play; always tells the truth even if it gets her in trouble; is nice to anyone; will help a friend; never lets a friend persuade her to do something that is wrong; always controls her temper; will share with others; likes people; never takes anything not belonging to her.

On a self-report test Elsie indicated that she felt less of a sense of "belonging" than did perhaps any other child. This is illustrated by her answering "no" to the following questions.

Do your friends seem to want to be with you?
Do people at school usually pay attention to your ideas?
Do most people seem to enjoy talking to you?
Do members of the opposite sex seem to like you as well as they do your friends?

and "yes" to such questions as:

Do you find it hard to get acquainted with new students?

She also answered "no" to the following questions involving relations with peers:

Do you often visit at the homes of other boys and girls in your neighborhood?
Do you have good times with the boys and girls near your home?
Do you like most of the boys and girls in your neighborhood?
Do you sometimes go to neighborhood parties where both boys and girls are present?

She indicated some anti social feelings in her relationships with her peers as evidenced by the affirmative answers to the following questions:

Do people often treat you so mean that you call them names?
Have you found that telling falsehoods is one of the easiest ways for people to get out of trouble?
Is it all right for you to laugh at people with foolish beliefs?

However, she felt it was wrong to push smaller boys and girls around, that one should obey teachers and parents even when they are unfair, and that it is wrong to take things even when one has been unfairly denied them.

She harbored some suspicions of the outside world as indicated by answering "yes" to the following questions:

Have you noticed that people often say and do mean things?
Does it seem to you that people cheat whenever they can?

The results of this test were summarized by an investigator as follows:

Elsie's social adjustment in relation to her peers . . . seems to be rather poor. She exhibits withdrawing tendencies with some signs of aggression. Her friendships with peers seem insecure, and her social standards and social skills are both low. From this we should expect that Elsie would be an unpopular member of the peer group, more because she is ignored than because she is disliked.

For her thirteenth birthday she invited twelve girls to a party, the first birthday party she had ever had. Commenting on it later, she said, "It rained, and only a few came."

Nobody in class chose her as his or her best friend. Seventeen said they would not want her as their best friend. Nineteen said she was not liked and not noticed; only one said she was liked and one said she was nice to be near. She was avoided with distaste, and as being uninteresting by eight ("makes one feel uncomfortable"). No one said she was well groomed, and twenty-seven mentioned that she was unkempt.

One of the investigators noted that "Elsie seems to operate on a momentary, superficial level without continuing pervasive unhappiness at her social rejection. She is aware of her rejection but seems not to feel any strong personal threat in it."

She did not strive hard to find a place in the group. One of the persons who was studying Elsie said of her: "She does not attack much or make overt demands . . . is existing on the fringes, accepting submissively her excluded position."

Elsie in School

In school, Elsie was still doing quite poor work. Her average grade in the sixth grade was a D. Her best grades were in spelling and language (C); her worst, in arithmetic (F). She was still one year retarded, and ranked the eighth from the bottom in a group of sixty-eight children. Her "educational age" was three and one-half years behind her chronological age.

Adults Describe Her

Her teachers rated Elsie on a list of behavior items. Her average rating for the total of all the items was very low. Only on the undesirable characteristics of self-centeredness and covert hostility was she placed above the average for her classmates. The teachers placed her on about the class average on overt hostility. She was below average on ambitiousness, strength of conscience, physical courage, optimism, and emotional stability. She was rated low on introspectiveness, creativity, self-confidence, self-sufficiency, general health, and energy output.

Elsie's Mental Functioning

All the tests that were administered to Elsie indicate that she had a low-average mental capacity, but that she was functioning somewhat below her capacity. This evidenced itself as retardation in school. She had no redeeming intellectual gifts except for high-average memorizing ability. From the Rorschach test, the investigator reported:

Imagination and creativity are both very constricted, and may be very low even as potential qualities.

Her Physical Make-up

At age thirteen years, Elsie presented an unattractive, uncared-for appearance. She was of medium body build, underweight and undersized, having light blond, thin, and straggly hair that appeared unkempt but not filthy. An interviewer said: "Her clothes were usually poor, usually showing torn places, and the fabrics were always cotton, often faded and soiled . . . with her large metal-rimmed glasses she succeeded in looking like a little gnome."

Elsie is described as being "the least attractive child in her family —poorly dressed and cared for. She has an uncared-for appearance, both in the quality and fit of her clothing and in cleanliness." A marked body odor was noted by the person giving her the physical examination, indicating rather low sanitary standards. Another interviewer mentioned that Elsie was the only one in the family who wore glasses. The same interviewer mentioned that Elsie was one of the smallest girls in the study and that she looked "more like a child of ten or eleven."

Talking to a friendly interviewer about herself, Elsie was at first very shy, and then she began to talk more freely. "I'm the smallest one in the class," she volunteered. "I've always been the smallest." She wrote quietly on a questionnaire for a few minutes, and then said, "They've all gone to the game." She went on to explain that all her classmates had gone to a neighboring town for a football game. She did not seem to complain, but merely mentioned it in passing, though with a slightly regretful tone of voice.

Miss Montague, the English teacher, said she felt sorry for Elsie. In small, pitifully comic ways she tried to get some attention. At times she would switch the lights on and off in the room, and play similar inane tricks. But no one paid any attention to her.

Personal Development

Elsie was asked to write about herself in answer to questions about what made her happy, sad, fearful, angry, ashamed, the best thing that could happen to her, and the worst.

Happy—"Go to potluck; to go away; go to a show." The home seemed to hold no positive attraction for her, since none of the things that made her happy happened in the home.

Sad—"When I couldn't live on a farm; one day I wanted to go to my aunts, and I couldn't; one day when I could not go to the show." Her sadness arose from restrictions placed on her by other people.

Fearful—"I am afraid of a train; I am afraid of a horse; and one time I nearly got run over by a car, and was I ever afraid."

Anger—"When I had to do dishes, and I did want to go to the store; and not to take care of the baby."

Ashamed—"I was ashame to do the dishes; and to take care of the baby; to take care of my two little sister." It seems that Elsie is here describing things that make her angry rather than ashamed.

The *best thing* that could happen to her was to "get a wrist watch for my birthday or graduation." The *worst thing* that could happen "is that I'll die."

Elsie was asked to name things that she should do that were approved by others and to name who was the person who approved of them. Her mother was named most frequently by Elsie (33 per cent of the time) as the person who would approve of her. The kinds of behaviors that the mother would approve of were: "having lots of exercise; going to the show at least three times a week; . . . obeying your mother." The father was mentioned (about one-fourth of the time) as a source of approval. He approved of Elsie when she, to use Elsie's words, "do[es] what your father tells you to do." He also says she "should stay at home." Other children, she said, approve of her when she plays in the yard and obeys her mother. She mentioned children's approval of her behavior one-quarter of the time. Her brothers and the nurse each get one mention as being sources of approval. Her brothers approve when she goes "to a potluck once in awhile." The nurse is mentioned as approving of "playing outdoors a lot."

Elsie was also asked to tell the kinds of things she did that got disapproval, and who it was that disapproved. Mother and father were mentioned most often; the mother (33 per cent of the time), the father (33 per cent); brothers, sisters, father, and mother together (11 per cent of the time for each). The kind of behavior her mother disapproved of was "go[ing] to the show anytime you feel like it; you should not go any place you feel like it; cut[ting] up paper or tear[ing] the curtain." Brothers disapproved of "play[ing] by the railroad tracks; hit[ting] a boy not your size; talk[ing] back to your mother or father." Sisters disapproved of her when she "break[s] any dishes." Father disapproved of her when she "play[s] in the street." She mentioned both parents in connection with "you should not be bad."

When asked to name three persons whom she wished to be like, Elsie named three girls who were in the seventh grade with her.

The interviewer who gave the tests to Elsie reported: "Elsie was so happy to do the tests and seemed to enjoy immensely the relationship with and the attention given her by a friendly adult. She filled the questionnaires quite rapidly and often appeared not to have understood the directions well."

When she was fourteen, and in the eighth grade, Elsie wrote in response to some questions:

Who are your friends?

"My best friends are Jean Carlton and Bernice Kamp. We go to the show together." (These girls were eleven years old and in the sixth grade.)

How are things at home?

"I think my mother will let me go to high school. She would not let Earl because she said he had to be home to look after the kids. She was out working. At home I have to do dishes and take care of Henry. I am not allowed to leave home when I am supposed to take care of Henry. I think Lucile and Mary could take care of Henry more."

How are things in school?

"I would like to get good grades in Reading. We had to memorize 2 stanzas of Evangeline. I didn't get it. That's how I do everything, I can say it to myself, but not out loud, I could have written it down. I get scared."

Family Life

Elsie answered a questionnaire on the relationships within her family. Her answers showed that her family was especially low in areas dealing with common participation and in parental attitudes toward peer activities. She wrote that "very seldom" is she allowed to invite her friends into her home, or do her parents approve of her friends, or do her parents seem proud of her activities. She said that her parents "almost never" visit with the parents of her friends.

She said that the meals are "occasionally" served at regular hours. She answered "very seldom" to the following questions:

Do you go to bed at a regular hour on school nights?
Are things always in their proper places at home?
If you are unavoidably detained when expected home, do you try to let your parents know about it?

Apparently, Elsie's tie with her parents was very slight, both on the active and on the verbal level. This is shown by her answer of "almost never" to the following questions:

Do you go to games with your parents?
Do you have a hobby that one or both parents share with you?
When you are in trouble at school, do you tell your parents about it?

and "very seldom" to the following questions:

Do you go to the movies with your parents?
Do you run errands or do little chores for your folks without complaining?
Do you talk to your parents about your problems and worries?
Do your folks discuss family problems with you?

Elsie did not give evidence of anxiety over her parents' relationship to her. She was "almost never" worried about what her parents thought of her, and she felt that their criticism of her was fair.

ELSIE AT AGE SIXTEEN-SEVENTEEN

Elsie entered ninth grade when she was fifteen, still a year behind her age-group. Talking to the fieldworker in the middle of this year, she said she liked home economics. She had sewing the first semester, and made an apron. Now she was studying cooking. She had joined the Home Ec Club, the only club she ever belonged to. The fieldworker asked which of her classes was the hardest. Elsie replied, "I don't know. All the rest of them seem hardest to me. Home economics is the only one I like in the whole school." As for sports, she said she liked to watch basketball, but didn't like to play any games. This was partly because of her poor eyesight. She said she did not know how to dance (social dancing), but she had learned a few square dance elements.

During this year, and the two or three years preceding, Elsie's mother was working at noon and in the evening, and Elsie had to hurry home from school to fix the meals and look after the younger children. Her two older sisters were both working full time, and she was the next oldest girl. Consequently, the burden of housekeeping fell upon her. She had no chance to stay around school after classes and talk to schoolmates or teachers. She never went to the drugstore in the afternoon to gossip with friends. The one social interest she had was roller skating, where she went once a week with a younger girl friend.

In the summer at the close of this school year, when Elsie was just sixteen, the fieldworker called on Mrs. E. The family had just moved into a large frame house—they were now out of the cramped quarters of the store-front where they had lived for so long. They could afford this now, for the two oldest girls and the two oldest boys were all working, and all helping to support the family.

The fieldworker reported:

Elsie came to the door and stated that her mother was not there but to come into the living room. She took the interviewer through the dining room which had a dining-room table and two chairs but no other furniture, through a double doorway through a large hall which held the landing of the open stairway, and was also the place for the telephone but held no other furniture. We went through another double doorway to the living room which is a large room but very sparsely furnished. The rose-colored rug on the floor was of the twist variety, new but obviously not expensive. A mulberry-color davenport and two overstuffed chairs to match constituted the only furniture in the room.

When Mrs. E. arrived she was dressed in an attractive cotton print and wore good-looking nylon hose and well-cared-for shoes. She is an energetic and very pleasant woman, easy to meet, and sounds and looks much younger than she probably is.

Mrs. E.: I had to go to the studio to pick the proofs for the pictures. They took numbers out of the phone book and mine was one that was called so we had a picture taken of our little girl and we can get a big one free, so I had to pick out which one I wanted but you know it was hard to pick because she wrinkled up her little nose on all of them. I don't have much time to do anything because I am only off from two to five.

Interviewer: That must keep you very busy. Where do you work?

Mrs. E.: I work out at Jimmie's Tavern. I've been working there for two years but now I'm trying to get in at the mill. I know somebody who is out there and some of the people I used to work with are out there and I'd like to work there too.

And I think now that they've started work and with this friend helping me maybe I can get in. I'll only have to work forty hours a week, only five days a week. I work where I am from eleven to two and then I go out again from five to nine. But if I worked at the mill I would work from seven to three-thirty and then I'd be through and I'd have all day Saturday and Sunday off. Now I work every day in the week except on Monday. Saturday and Sunday I have to work until one in the morning.

Interviewer: How do you manage your household and a job like that, too?

Mrs. E.: Well, my husband gets up in the morning and gets his own breakfast because he only drinks coffee so I sleep later and then I get up and take care of the children and get to work by eleven and when I come home between two and five there are always a lot of things to do, so my husband always has to get his own lunch, he comes home for lunch and the children's too and they have to get their own dinner. Then on Mondays when I'm off I always wash and clean my house. I can never do much in the two hours in the afternoon. Elsie takes care of the children, she always has. They look to her for everything and when little Henry wakes up at night sometimes and wants a drink of water, he always wants Elsie to get it for him. All of the children are with her all of the time and look up to her and she can manage them I think better than I can. Sometimes I plan to give her some time so that she can go to some basketball games at school and to a show sometimes or something like that. Now there's a young couple moved into the place where we lived, they moved right in when we left and sometimes Elsie stays with their baby and then she makes a little money, and sometimes she takes care of other children. She is good with children and they always like her.

I've always worked. I've worked for three and one-half years over at the hospital, and that was before I went to work over here. I used to walk to the hospital from here, even when the snow was way up over my hips. I enjoyed the walk and I felt better I think. I always liked to get out and work with other people, I think it is so much more fun. I enjoy visiting with my people, but where I am now it has its drawback, but I like to work with others. I think it will be nice to get into the mill because I have so many friends around and we have a good time visiting. I don't visit otherwise.

Interviewer: Then you don't get to see too much of the children either?

Mrs. E.: No, my daughter takes care of them. Except when she's in school.

Interviewer: Elsie likes school, doesn't she?

Mrs. E.: Yes, I guess it's mainly just to get away though, when she gets to school she is away from taking care of the children all the time and I think that's what she really likes.

Interviewer: Then school is recreation for her.

Mrs. E.: Yes, well, she doesn't have so many friends but she stays with the girls. It's funny none of *r y* children have cared for dates and so on. Oh, my girls have had dates sometimes, they just love to dance, but they don't care much about going out with boys, they say that the boys always want to take them to a tavern and if they don't take them there, then they always have their own bottle along and the girls don't care for that. None of my girls was ever boy crazy.

When September came, Mrs. E. decided that Elsie was needed at home, and so Elsie quit school. From this time she had no more contact with her age-mates at school. She was friendly with another girl her age who had also quit school, and she occasionally went to the movies with some younger girls. She had no dates with boys.

How Adults Saw Elsie

On *sociability*, the majority of adults rated her quite low. She "has few friends and seems not to want any." A few thought she "is as sociable as the general run of children."

On *loyalty* there was much disagreement about Elsie, one person seeing her as "a good supporter of all organizations to which she belongs," whereas two others said, that she "takes no pride in belonging to any club or organization."

On *honesty*, one adult saw her as "dishonest in places where it is easy to be dishonest."

On *moral courage*, two saw her as above average, and two below.

On *responsibility*, three judges described Elsie as "need(ing) frequent 'reminding' to get her to complete her duties." Two others were more lenient toward her.

On *kindness*, there was some disagreement spreading from "considerably more courteous and thoughtful than most children" to "is sometimes thoughtless and indifferent toward those with whom she is not especially friendly."

On *self-control,* most adults saw her as either "immature and childish in her way of meeting problems and crises" or "has somewhat less control of her feelings than most children."

Elsie Looks into the Future

As a fifteen-year-old Elsie wanted to be:

1. Telephone operator.
2. Waitress.
3. Keep House.

As a seventeen-year-old she wanted to be:

1. Bookkeeper.
2. Waitress.
3. Take care of children.

"WHEN I'M TWENTY-TWO," Elsie wrote, "I would like to have a job by then and go on a long vacation and have an apartment for myself. I would like to go to difference places that I had never seen before and then go dancing if I wanted to go. Have more fun going places."

Elsie wrote about THE PERSON I WOULD LIKE TO BE LIKE, as follows: "I would like to be like Barbara Jackson. She is fifteen years ole and she has good appearance. She take care of kids a lot of times and she plays baseball and tennis. She is a Girl Scout and she does a lot of sports that she like to do. She is a real person."

A GOOD KIND OF PERSON IN OUR COMMUNITY IS . . . "To have a nurse and doctor because they can do a lot to help people and save them from terrible disease that they may have or other things that they can catch from other people like polio or T.B. Even in the crowd you might catch something."

Physical Make-up

An interviewer gave the following description of Elsie when she was not quite sixteen:

She is about four feet nine inches tall and weighs only about eighty pounds. She has not started having monthly periods but states that she sometimes has cramps in her stomach especially if she walks too fast on her way to school.

Elsie is small-boned but is well proportioned and is just now beginning to show signs of body maturity. She has straight blonde hair cut in a long bob, parted on the side with the part never straight. As she took off the head scarf she pulled her comb from her pocket and ran it through her hair to tidy it but did not get near the regular part. Elsie's hair seems somewhat coarse in texture and not too heavy. Her skin is light in color but seems very dry and she has unusually deep wrinkles across the top of her forehead and suggestions of wrinkles in her cheeks and around her eyes. However, her hands are well-proportioned and do not seem to have the dryness of her face. Her fingers are long and the nails of her fingers have been chewed down about one-third of the way. She is always well-dressed in simple but neat garments.

Elsie Talks about Herself

When she was just seventeen and had been out of school and keeping house at home for a year, Elsie responded to some questions about herself.

Question: Describe some conditions or situations in which you had a lot of unpleasantness or disappointment.

Elsie: Taking care of kids all the time. I have to take care of my four brothers and sisters all the time. Seems like it is easier to take care of somebody else's children than it is them.

Q.: Describe some conditions or situations in which you had a lot of fun and enjoyed yourself.

Elsie: I have fun at the skating rink. I go with my girl friend.

Q.: If you could change your situation—your school, your job, yourself, anything—what changes would you make?

Elsie: Not to take care of the kids.

Q.: What would you like to do?

Elsie: I don't know. I'd like to take care of somebody else's kids, but not our own.

ELSIE'S ACCOMPLISHMENT OF DEVELOPMENTAL TASKS

The research staff compared Elsie's success in accomplishing the developmental tasks in relation to the success of other American youth. This they did by rating Elsie on a scale from 1 to 10, where a score of 10 means she was very successful in accomplishing the task, and a score of 1 means she was unsuccessful. She was rated at ages 10–11, 13–14, 16–17.

Getting Along with Age Mates

Age	Average Rating
10	1.7
13	1.0
16	2.0

Learning a Feminine Social Role

Age	Average Rating
10	1.7
13	1.6
16	1.4

Achieving Emotional Independence from Parents and Other Adults

Age	Average Rating
10	3.0
13	2.6
16	2.4

Developing Conscience Morality, and a Scale of Values

Age	Average Rating
10	3.3
13	3.2
16	3.2

Elsie's ratings on each of these developmental tasks indicate that she was far behind other children of her age. She was not successfully achieving her developmental tasks.

Elsie had not learned to be a member of her own age group. Her unkempt appearance, immature ways of demanding attention, and inability to respond on the same emotional level as her age-mates prevented her from enjoying their friendship.

As for learning her feminine role, Elsie was very far behind. Physically, she matured slowly. She did not date boys or display interest in the opposite sex.

Elsie was always tied to adults. She depended on them for approval and satisfaction. She was quite unable to become independent of her mother, who unconsciously exploited Elsie for the benefit of herself and the rest of the family.

Her highest ratings were in development of conscience and moral values. But here, too, she was much below average.

Elsie's Inner Life

Elsie was asked to tell stories about each of a number of pictures on cards that were presented to her one by one. At another time she was also asked to tell what she imagined she saw in some ink-blots of various shapes and colors that were presented to her. Her responses to these tests revealed much of her inner life when analyzed by expert research workers who had been trained to work with these kinds of tests. The analysis agrees with what has been written in previous sections, and also gives some additional information about Elsie. According to the analysis, the following picture can be drawn of Elsie's inner life:

1. She had a strong need to receive affection, and attention, but could not give the same at an equal level. She was much like an infant in this respect.

2. She was starved for parental affection.

3. She was operating intellectually at almost the borderline of feeble-mindedness, but she probably could do better if her emotional disturbance did not interfere with her intellectual functioning.

4. Her imagination seemed stunned and non-operative. She used no original concepts in these tests.

5. Her emotional attitude was one of conformity to the will of others and denial of her own. She showed clear signs of anxiety and of hostility to her mother.

6. Her chief methods of adjusting to life's situations were described as "crawling into empty isolation," and as stereotyped conformity and submission.

Elsie Explains Herself

If she could have expressed herself as clearly as the research workers could after they had studied her, she would probably have explained herself somewhat as follows:

I only live from day to day, but dimly I see that it would be nice for me to get away from Prairie City into something that might be more stimulating and interesting for me. Perhaps if I were somewhere else, everything would be different—I would be loved, cared for, given the opportunity to blossom into the woman I know I could be and should be. All I have been able to learn here is that people are no good, they really don't care about me, don't help me—and, once in awhile, I become so bitter about them that I really hate people, just people, anyone, everyone. Of course, I can't let any of that kind of feeling out.

I'm too weak, for one thing. And if I did, others would turn on me and almost tear me apart, I think. So, I try to be the good girl, obedient and quiet all the time, taking things as they come. But since people don't respond to me even then, it makes me mad inside, and my hostile feelings do have to come out. The way I let them out is by picking on, teasing the few friends I have. That is too bad, because it serves then to drive even that little comfort away from me.

So I try to do the work, not make a fuss, be a good girl by not doing anything.

What the School Might Have Done

By the time she was ten years old Elsie had made it plain to anybody that she was failing in all of her developmental tasks. She lacked physical skills and health habits, she was getting along very poorly with her age-mates and was learning only the least satisfying elements of a feminine social role. She was failing to become an independent, morally autonomous person, her conscience and scale of values were not developing, she had only the most childish of social attitudes, and she was very poor at her tasks of mental development.

Perhaps Elsie was failing partly because she was "poor stock"— that is, because she inherited small stature, poor eyes, and low intelligence. But no expert in genetics would say that she was constitutionally incapable of doing better than she actually did. Her performance on her developmental tasks depended partly upon her environment and partly upon her inherited endowment. Since environment was obviously poor in her case, there was hope for great improvement if her environment could be improved.

There was something of Cinderella in Elsie, slaving away at home and waiting for some magic to transform her into a princess. Only there could be no magic other than what could be performed by wise teachers, social workers, and church workers.

Analysis of Elsie's Strengths and Weaknesses

At the age of ten, Elsie was obedient to authority, colorless, and almost invisible to those around her. When they did notice her, they saw an undesirable child, who was quarrelsome, selfish, and did foolish little things to attract attention. Looking beneath the surface, they would have discovered a deep unmet need for affectionate attention, and an intellectual dullness due not so much to poor quality of brain cells as to emotional conflict that prevented her from putting her mental abilities to use.

Looking at the family, observers would have seen heavy demands made on Elsie with nothing to repay her for her slavery. The two older sisters had served their terms and were now relatively free. They had jobs of their own and could give their mother some of their earnings, but they would no longer be tied down to domestic servitude in the home. It fell on Elsie to "look after the kids" for a long term of years, from about the age of ten. Her mother was a gregarious person wanting to be near people, and so she did not take the financial assistance she might have gotten from the Community Welfare Office in order to stay home and look after her children; but instead she worked at mean, ill-paying jobs which had the saving grace of giving her companionship. "I always liked to get out and work with other people, I think it is so much more fun," she said. Thus Elsie's mother exploited her, unconsciously to be sure, by forcing her to take the mother's role with respect to the younger children so that the mother could lead a more enjoyable life outside the house.

How Could Elsie Have Been Helped?

The things Elsie needed desperately might have been given her by a motherly, affectionate teacher, club leader, or church worker. Such a person could have helped her to learn how to groom herself and how to play with people her own age. The self-confidence Elsie would have obtained from knowing that such a person loved and respected her would have released her own energies for constructive solution of her social problems. Furthermore, she would have imitated such a person and thus have learned values and social attitudes at a more mature level.

The school could also have worked with Elsie's mother. A visiting teacher could have helped the mother to see how she was robbing Elsie of a chance to be part of the peer group by tying her down to being a little mother to the younger children long before she was ready for such a heavy burden.

If the school had had a hot lunch program Elsie would have been a healthier youngster. She could almost surely have been heavier and perhaps taller. She could have had more energy for play and work.

A home economics teacher might have opened the way to satisfying womanhood for Elsie. Through her own example, through what she could teach in the way of knowledge and skills, and through giving the affection that Elsie did not get from her mother, such a teacher could have helped Elsie move her performance on all her developmental tasks at least up to the level of average satisfaction. Even the intellectual task of developing concepts and mental skills would have been accomplished much better by Elsie with this kind of help from the school.

PART FOUR

Adulthood and Old Age

CHAPTER 16

Developmental Tasks of Early Adulthood

OF ALL THE PERIODS OF LIFE, early adulthood is the fullest of teachable moments and the emptiest of efforts to teach. It is a time of special sensitivity and unusual readiness of the person to learn. Early adulthood, the period from eighteen to thirty, usually contains marriage, the first pregnancy, the first serious full-time job, the first illnesses of children, the first experience of furnishing or buying or building a house, and the first venturing of the child off to school. If ever people are motivated to learn and to learn quickly, it is at times such as these.

Yet the amount of educative effort expended by society on people is probably less during this period than during any other period except old age—if we make the proper exception of college and university education, which are really an extension of the schools, and seldom deal with the developmental tasks and problems of young adults.

It makes one wonder what education is about, after all, if it is not directly concerned with helping the individual to meet such problems as these. One possible answer to this question is that the developmental tasks of early adulthood are the goals toward which all the earlier education has been aiming—that these tasks are really the final examinations which come at the close of the course and test the pupils' learning. These tasks must therefore be met without coaching by teachers, so as to make it a fair examination. But only a person completely without human sympathy could argue for this view if he saw young men and women suffering unhappiness and defeat in life for lack of the help they could get from educational and other agencies. If people need help with their developmental tasks in early adulthood, and if educational and social agencies can give them what they need, let them have it.

Early adulthood is the most individualistic period of life and the loneliest one, in the sense that the individual, or, at the most, two individuals, must proceed with a minimum of social attention and assistance to tackle the most important tasks of life.

This loneliness and egocentricity of early adulthood was expressed in a halting way by a high-school senior who was trying to explain why young people seemed to be without interest in religion during this period, until they achieved some of their tasks and found places in the religious and other institutions of adult society. This person said: "I think a person between the last two years in high school till they are twenty-five isn't so religious because they have no responsibility. All they do is think about themselves and worry about themselves. When they get married, they get on a different track. Then they're parents and they start their children that way and they get back to a religious life."

Early adulthood seems, then, to be a period of storm and stress in America, and especially in the middle-class part of American society. The basic reason for this, when expressed in sociological terms, is that this is a relatively unorganized period in life which marks a transition from an age-graded to a social status-graded society. During childhood and adolescence one climbs the age ladder, getting new privileges and taking on new responsibilities with each step up the ladder. The ten-year-old has such and such privileges and such and such responsibilities, which enable him to look down on the eight-year-old, but also cause him to look up to the twelve-year-old. He climbs the age ladder, rung by rung, year by year, knowing that each step up gives him more prestige, along with new tasks and pleasures.

This simple age-grading stops in our culture somewhere around sixteen to twenty. It is like reaching the end of the ladder and stepping off onto a new, strange cloud-land with giants and witches to be circumvented and the goose that lays the golden eggs to be captured if only one can discover the know-how.

In the adult society prestige and power depend not so much on age as on skill and strength and wisdom, and family connections. Achieving the goals of life is not nearly so much a matter of waiting until one grows up to them as it was in the earlier years. There must be a strategy, based on an understanding of the new terrain, which can only be got by scouting around and getting the lay of the land for a few years. This is what young people do, and it often takes several years to learn how to get about efficiently and to go where one wants to go in the adult society in America.

1. SELECTING A MATE

Until it is accomplished, the task of finding a marriage partner is at once the most interesting and the most disturbing of the tasks of early adulthood. It is carried out by an elaborate process of courtship in the American culture, that may last for several years. The rules of the courting process vary from one social class to another, as does the degree of involvement of parents and other relatives.

This task is considered to be primarily the responsibility of the young man or woman, in middle-class and lower-class circles, and there is little attempt by parents and others to "interfere." However, some assistance is given with this task through courses in marriage and family life in high school and college, and agencies for premarital counseling.

2. LEARNING TO LIVE WITH A MARRIAGE PARTNER

After the wedding there comes a period of learning how to fit two lives together. In the main this consists of learning to express and control one's feelings—anger, joy, disgust, love—so that one can live intimately and happily with one's spouse.

Biological satisfaction from sex relations tends to make this task easier, while emotional dependence upon parents makes it more difficult. The culture affects the task, by providing conflicting roles for the young woman—those of wife and of career woman. If she wants to play both roles, the young wife has a more difficult time with this task than if she accepts fully the role of wife.

Success with the tasks of emotional maturing in childhood and adolescence is the best preparation for the task of learning to live with a marriage partner. But often help is needed with this specific task. Such help is probably best given by counseling that leads to understanding and acceptance of oneself and others.

3. STARTING A FAMILY [1]

Nature of the Task. To have a first child successfully.

Biological Basis. Childbearing is a biological process; but the task of bearing the first child is both a biological and a psychological one. Assuming that the mother and father are fit and that there are no accidents, the biological part of the task takes care of itself.

Psychological Basis. Psychologically, both the woman and the man have a task to achieve in becoming a mother and a father, respectively.

For the woman, there is the question of acceptance or rejection of pregnancy. If she is scared, or disgusted, at the thought of pregnancy, the task will be hard for her. But if she regards motherhood with pleasure as the fulfillment of her sex role, the task will be relatively easy. For the husband, too, there is a problem of accepting or rejecting the idea of his wife's pregnancy.

Then there is the question of confidence in the doctor. For both wife and husband, the choice of a doctor in whom they can have confidence is of major importance.

Sex relations during pregnancy are an aspect of this task. Some women experience little desire for sexual intercourse during pregnancy, while others have increased feelings of sexual desire. The husband's sex behavior is affected also by the pregnancy, and he must find a way of adjusting to his wife's feelings about the matter as well as to the actual necessity of reduced intercourse with her.

Women worry over possible failure to have a normal baby. They are afraid of miscarriage, neonatal death of the baby, or of having a baby which is deformed. It may be a deep sense of pride that is involved here, for the woman "makes" the baby. In any case, women are full of concern on this point, and are easy prey to superstitions about prenatal influence.

The question of breast feeding is a worrisome one for many women. Shall they accept the idea readily, accept with resistance,

[1] The writer is indebted to Dr. David B. Treat, Director of the Clara Elizabeth Fund for Maternal Health, Flint, Michigan, for the material dealing with this task.

or reject the idea? The husband also has his concerns on this point. Will breast feeding tie his wife down, so that she cannot go out with him on social occasions? Will it spoil her figure?

Finally, there is the matter of reactions of relatives and friends to the pregnancy. Will they be pleased or vexed? In particular, what will the in-laws think?

Cultural Basis. The problem of first pregnancy as it has just been stated in psychological terms is mainly a middle-class problem. Upper-class people seem to take the first pregnancy more "in their stride." Lower-class people do, also. In fact, a large number of lower-class marriages are the result, rather than the cause, of the first pregnancy.

Social class differences extend to the amount of medical attention the pregnant woman gets, the amount of preparation made for the new baby, and the kind of regime the wife follows.

When women are working, whether middle or lower class, there is a question when to quit the job during the pregnancy, whether to shift to another kind of work, and when to resume work after the baby's coming.

In general, the American culture has moved toward making the task of starting a family less a task involving the young couple's parents, and more a task worked out by the young couple with the aid of doctors, hospitals, and educational agencies. The young mother gets her information out of a book or a course more often than she gets it from her own mother. She goes to a hospital rather than to her mother's home to have her first baby.

Social and Educational Implications. Success in this task requires certain kinds of knowledge for the wife and husband, and attitudes favorable to having children.

The knowledge is increasingly being given through books for young parents and through educational courses for prospective mothers and fathers. The husband needs to learn about medical services for pregnancy and childbirth, the care of the pregnant mother and the newborn child, and the kind of financial provisions, through insurance and otherwise, that are necessary to meet the needs of this period. The wife needs to understand the physical and mental hygiene of pregnancy.

Such courses can be given in city school systems in their adult education programs, and by agencies especially concerned with family life education.

The attitudes which make for success or failure with this task are probably learned in the home, from parents and brothers and sisters. If the attitudes are favorable, there is no need for anything beyond knowledge when the time comes to have children. But if the attitudes of wife or husband are unfavorable, extensive counseling and psychotherapy may be necessary. Counseling services should be available, through churches, schools, and social agencies, for young married couples.

4. REARING CHILDREN

With the gaining of children the young couple take over a responsibility far greater than any responsibility they have ever had before. Now they are responsible for human life that is not their own.

To meet this responsibility they must learn to meet the physical and emotional needs of young children. This means learning how to *manage* the child, and also learning to adapt their own daily and weekly schedules to the needs of growing children.

Much of the young parents' feelings about their child will be a reflection of their own peace of mind and harmonious adjustment or lack of it. The amount and kind of attention they give their child will tend to encourage his being warm, responsive, and outgoing or niggardly, fearful, and cold in his relations with others.

The rapidly growing parent education movement in this country is a reflection of the need young parents feel for help with this task.

5. MANAGING A HOME

Family life is built around a physical center, the home, and depends for its success greatly upon how well-managed this home is. Good home management is only partly a matter of keeping the house clean, the furniture and plumbing and lighting fixtures in repair, having meals well-cooked, and the like. It is these things and a great deal more.

While this task is more that of the wife than of the husband, the man has a necessary share in it. Not only must he arrange to finance the establishment of the home, he must also help to get furniture, help to set up a plan of expenditures, and work out the essential routines with his wife for making the home run smoothly.

The implications of this task are partly social, for inadequate physical housing makes this task a nightmare for many young couples, and only a socioeconomic government policy of low-cost housing can help very much.

6. GETTING STARTED IN AN OCCUPATION

This task takes an enormous amount of the young man's time and energy during young adulthood. Often he becomes so engrossed in this particular task that he neglects others. He may put off finding a wife altogether too long for his own happiness.

This task is much more difficult for middle-class than for upper- or lower-class men. For the middle-class man, success in an occupation is essential to holding his middle-class social position. He will usually subordinate all other tasks of life to this one, if it seems necessary in order to make a vocational success. Upper-class men are secure in their social position almost regardless of their vocational activity. Lower-class men, unless they have an ambition for mobility, get an earlier vocational start than do middle-class men, and reach their maximum earning capacity often before they are thirty.

7. TAKING ON CIVIC RESPONSIBILITY

Nature of the Task. To assume responsibility for the welfare of a group outside of the family—a neighborhood or community group or church or lodge or political organization.

Psychological Basis. The young adult's preoccupation with the tasks of finding a mate and getting a family started and getting started in an occupation causes him to postpone the task of taking on civic responsibility. He is too busy with his immediate personal concerns to attend to the wider civic concerns. Furthermore, he does not yet have the investments in the community that make him sensitive to community needs. Not until he has children growing up and property to care for does he begin to see that he has a stake in the quality of the civic, religious, and political life of the community.

Cultural Basis. The high geographic mobility of American young people makes it difficult for them to assume civic responsibility in early adulthood. Since so many of them start their careers in communities that are strange to them and move on quickly to new communities, they hardly have time to join churches and fraternal organizations, or to become absorbed in civic and political activities.

Morever, it takes time for them to learn how to participate in adult associations. Often they have had little or no experience in organizations and must learn what is expected of new members in lodges, church organizations, and social clubs.

For these various reasons, a young man or woman seldom comes into active participation in adult organizations before the age of twenty-five or thirty.

Social classes differ greatly in their performance of this task. Middle-class people go into it most vigorously, with a conviction that "civic" work or church work is a virtue in itself. They are sensitive to the quality of the community life, and they believe that much good can come from community action. Upper-class people are less sure of the importance of civic action, but they usually encourage their young people to go in for it, as a kind of apprenticeship for the leadership roles that will be theirs in middle age, when they work increasingly through middle-class people in their civic activities. For example, a young upper-class man may be encouraged by his older friends to run for the school board, or to accept the chairmanship of the board of a social agency. When he gets older he will not be so active, but it is thought to be good preparation for his later role of advising and using his influence in less formal ways.

Lower-class people have much less faith in the value of civic and community activities than do middle-class people. Their organizational participation is usually limited to labor unions, churches, and fraternal orders. The neighborhood, rather than the community, tends to be their scene of activity, and they prefer to operate through informal groups rather than through formal organizations. A collection to help pay the funeral expenses of a neighbor or a benefit to raise money for a playground are more to their liking than a community fund which is organized to meet such needs in an orderly fashion on a community-wide basis.

Studies of participation in organizations in relation to socioeconomic status [2] have shown that there is an increase in such participation as one moves up the socioeconomic scale, with people in the professions having the greatest organizational activity. One such study showed that 68 per cent of unskilled workers belonged to no organization at all (church excepted) while 40 per cent of the professional workers belonged to seven or more organizations.

There is also an increase of participation with increasing age from early adulthood to middle age, for middle-class people.

Social and Educational Implications. If the social welfare really depends upon a large number of people participating in churches, civic organizations, and political organizations, as middle-class people believe, there is reason to be disturbed at the way this task is met in America. The working class pretty largely ignores this task, except for labor union activity, while middle-class people take it up late and often listlessly. It is common to compare the citizenship interests and qualities of present-day America disparagingly with early New England, ancient Athens, and modern Denmark.

Encouragement of more widespread and more informal participation in civic affairs might take place by three methods:

(1) by organizations such as churches, political organizations, and community organizations making a special effort to interest young men and women and finding jobs for these young people to do;

(2) by high schools and colleges encouraging students to par-

[2] Mirra Komarovsky, "The Voluntary Associations of Urban Dwellers," *Amer. Sociol. Review*, 11 (1946), 686–98.

William G. Mather, "Income and Social Participation," *Amer. Sociol. Review*, 6 (1941), 380–83.

A. A. Kaplan, "Socio-Economic Circumstances and Adult Participation in Cultural and Educational Activities," *Teachers College* (Columbia University) *Contributions to Education*, #889 (1943).

ticipate in local community activities and in national civic and political activities;

(3) by giving more social assistance to young people in their tasks of getting a family started and getting started in an occupation, and thus freeing them earlier from preoccupation with these tasks so that they will have more time for civic activities and at the same time giving them a stake in the successful working of civic organizations.

8. FINDING A CONGENIAL SOCIAL GROUP

Marriage often involves the breaking of social ties for one or both young people, and the forming of new friendships. Either the man or the woman is apt to move away from former friends. In any case, whether old friendships are interrupted by distance or not, the young couple faces something of a new task in forming a leisure-time pattern and finding others to share it with. The young man loses interest in some of his former bachelor activities, and his wife drops out of some of her purely feminine associations.

Together they look for new friends, people about their own age, who have similar interests, and with whom they can develop a new kind of social life that may last for forty years.

Considerations of social status enter into the accomplishment of this task for young couples who have a social position to gain or to hold. Invitations may come to join a young couples' organization in a church, and to join the country club, and to participate in an informal group of eight or ten couples who play cards and have refreshments once a week in rotation at their respective homes. The young couple may feel that they must choose among these three social groups, not having time or money to participate in more than one group. Which group will give the best "contacts" to the husband? Which group will give the highest social prestige to the wife? With the children of which group would the young couple like their own children to associate?

Success in the task of finding a congenial social group will go a long way toward making the wife feel that she is being rewarded for some of the things she gave up to get married. Failure may cause them to look for another community.

This is a task for which direct education is probably of little value, but it can be made easier and achievement can be improved if the institutions of the community, such as churches, and fraternal organizations are alert to this need of the young adults and attempt to provide a number and variety of social groups to suit various tastes and temperaments.

CHAPTER 17

Developmental Tasks of Middle Age

IN THE MIDDLE YEARS, from about thirty to about fifty-five, men and women reach the peak of their influence upon society, and at the same time the society makes its maximum demands upon them for social and civic responsibility. It is the period of life to which they have looked forward during their adolescence and early adulthood. And the time passes so quickly during these full and active middle years that most people arrive at the end of middle age and the beginning of later maturity with surprise and a sense of having finished the journey while they were still preparing to commence it.

The biological changes of ageing, which commence unseen and unfelt during the twenties, make themselves known during the middle years. Especially for the woman, the latter years of middle age are full of profound physiologically-based psychological change.

The developmental tasks of the middle years arise from changes within the organism, from environmental pressures, and above all from demands or obligations laid upon the individual by his own values and aspirations.

Since most middle-aged people are members of families, with teen-age children, it is useful to look at the tasks of husband, wife, and children as these people live and grow in relation to one another. Each family member has several functions or roles.[1]

The Man of the Family	*The Woman of the Family*	*The Teen-Ager*
a man	a woman	a person
a husband	a wife	a family mem-
a provider	a homemaker and	ber
a homemaker	family manager	
a father	a mother	

[1] This formulation and a good deal of the discussion of the developmental tasks of this age-period are taken from the Committee Report prepared by Leland H. Stott, Chairman, on *The Family with Teen-Agers* for the National Conference on Family Life. Other material in the following pages is taken from the Committee Report prepared by Ruth Shonle Cavan, Chairman, on *The Family in the Later Years*. These were subcommittees of the Committee on *Dynamics of Family Interaction* with Evelyn Millis Duvall and Reuben Hill as co-chairmen.

Unless the man performs well as a provider, it will be difficult for the woman to perform well as a homemaker. Unless the woman performs well as a mother, it will be difficult for the teen-age child to meet the tasks of adolescence. The developmental tasks of family members, then, are *reciprocal*; they react upon one another.

1. ACHIEVING ADULT CIVIC AND SOCIAL RESPONSIBILITY

The obligations of citizenship lie most heavily upon middle-aged people. Since they are at their peak of influence and still possessed of great energy, they are the natural leaders in the civic life of the community.

Men often find this task irksome because they are so engrossed in making money or seeking professional success that they have no time for civic responsibilities. Or they may have the attitude that "politics is rotten," and that government is hopelessly monopolized by incompetent and irresponsible individuals.

On the other hand, many men find real pleasure in working for the civic welfare. They enjoy keeping "up to date" on economic and political events and are glad to spend the necessary time studying and working with other people.

For women whose children are growing up and leaving the home, there is a gain in developing new social and civic interests at this time of life, so as to fill the void left by disappearing children. Such women become active in civic organizations, furnish most of the rank and file of civic reform movements, and give time to the serious study of foreign affairs.

There are wide differences between the various social classes in America in their definition of and acceptance of this task. Working-class men are usually less interested in the broader social and political problems, and more concerned with the issues that affect their labor unions and their own immediate neighborhoods. Working-class women usually pay very little attention to the social-civic life of the community. Upper-class men and women show much the same variety of interest in social and civic problems that middle-class people show.

Since the civic health of a democracy depends upon responsible and informed citizenship, this task is of such great social importance that it has become one of the principal concerns of adult education in America.

2. ESTABLISHING AND MAINTAINING AN ECONOMIC STANDARD OF LIVING

Income and the cost of maintaining the average family rise together during the early adult years, and then the cost continues to mount during the middle years while income, of the great majority of families, ceases to rise and may even commence to drop.

The American standard of living includes a number of expensive elements. The wife is expected to operate the home as a separate establishment for feeding and housing people—a very inefficient procedure from a purely economic point of view. There is strong social pressure, especially in middle-class families, to maintain a high economic standard of living due to advertising, home economics education, mass production, and the "democratic" social philosophy which teaches that everyone should have access to all the material goods of life.

This puts the larger families in the United States at a disadvantage, since they tend to be the families with smaller incomes. The economic resources of the country are definitely *not* invested in the larger families.

For the successful achievement of the task of maintaining a satisfactory economic standard of living, the great majority of middle-aged men and women must learn to plan their expenditures and investments more carefully, and they must make the task one in which the children also participate. The man must learn to place economic security for his family ahead of his desires to speculate and venture, and he must learn to enlist the participation of the rest of the family in making decisions concerning finances. The wife and mother must learn to manage the family budget efficiently and to bring the children into the task of keeping up the home with a minimum of unnecessary expense.

3. ASSISTING TEEN-AGE CHILDREN TO BECOME RESPONSIBLE AND HAPPY ADULTS

Just as adolescence is a time for boys and girls to become emotionally independent of their parents and to become emotionally mature people, middle age is a time for parents to cooperate with adolescent children in this task.

Perhaps the most useful and important thing the father or mother can do is to provide a worthy pattern for the adolescent to follow— a pattern of the good father or mother, the good husband or wife, the good homemaker, and the good citizen. The adolescent is still going to follow the example of his parents, through the ingrained unconscious habit of imitating them which he formed as a young child.

Parents should also get enough insight into their own emotional reactions to their children to be able to give their children the freedom as well as the guidance they need. The mother should understand herself well enough to avoid projecting the problems of her own adolescence onto her daughter and therefore being oversolicitous, or overpunitive. Similarly with the father in relation to his son.

This task is made more difficult by the changing conditions under which children grow to maturity, from one generation to the next. Thus, what the adolescent child needs in the way of guidance may bear little relationship to the kind of treatment the parents received when they were young.

4. DEVELOPING ADULT LEISURE-TIME ACTIVITIES

With the coming of middle age the demands of a growing family are lessened, the pressure for "getting ahead" in the business or professional world is often reduced, and people find themselves with more leisure than they have known for two or three decades. Some of this leisure is taken up with civic activities, but there is also time for fun.

The new leisure comes at a time when old leisure-time habits are becoming inappropriate. The leisure activities of early adulthood— strenuous games, courting, social dancing, auto-riding, and indiscriminate movie-going—usually lose their attractiveness to middle-aged people. What they want are leisure-time activities that give a measured satisfaction, and that can be developed into central sources of interest and pleasure during the years to come, when there will be ten or twelve hours of leisure every day.

In addition, middle age gives the last opportunity to achieve certain lifelong ambitions—the trip abroad, or the purchase of a motion-picture camera, or the fishing trip to the north woods.

5. RELATING ONESELF TO ONE'S SPOUSE AS A PERSON

With the relinquishment of the satisfactions of motherhood, the woman in the middle years may resume the role of wife, a role often of secondary significance to herself and her husband during the years of childbearing and rearing.

During the years that have intervened since courtship and marriage the husband has become absorbed in his work, finding his vocational niche and putting forth his greatest productive effort. He, too, is usually ready by middle age to resume the role of husband. Often he needs desperately the encouragement and appreciation he received from his wife in the early days, for he may have to face the realization that he can never reach the peak of his ambitions, and that younger men will take the lead away from him.

The husband may need to understand the special needs of his wife as she goes through the psychological difficulties of the menopause. He may also need to reinforce his own habits of grooming, and of outward courtesy and attentiveness to his wife.

The wife, for her part, may need to give new attention to her husband as a man, to meet his needs for affection, understanding, or solitude. She may need to take care to maintain her own personal attractiveness and charm.

6. ACCEPTING AND ADJUSTING TO THE PHYSIOLOGICAL CHANGES OF MIDDLE AGE

Nature of the Task. For men and women there is a decline in physical capacity, and for women there is a profound physiological change, during the middle years. Everyone must adjust his way of living to these changes, and accept them with as good grace as possible.

Biological Basis. Ageing of the body tissues has been going on, mostly unnoticed, since early adulthood. Muscular strength has been diminishing, neuromuscular skills have been fading, and the body has been slowing down. Some of the physical symptoms of ageing are:

Growth of stiff hair in the nose, ears, and eyelashes of men.

Growth of hair on the upper lip of women.

Drying and wrinkling of the skin.

Deposition of fat around the middle.

Presbyopia—loss of accommodative power of the lens of the eye. The elasticity of the lens decreases steadily from childhood to old age, and by the age of seventy-five the lens is ordinarily completely inelastic, making it impossible for the eye to adjust itself unaided to the task of focusing on objects at varying distances.

Between ages forty and fifty, accommodative power usually ceases to suffice for ordinary close work, and bifocals or reading glasses become necessary.

The menopause, or climacterium, occurs in women over a period of several years, usually between forty-five and fifty-five. First, the Graafian follicles cease to open and the mucous membrane of the uterus is no longer periodically replaced. Menstruation gradually ceases and the ovaries become mere masses of connective tissue. With the cessation of ovarian activity, the delicate balance of the endocrine system is disturbed. Physical symptoms may take the form of hot and cold flashes, dizziness, sweating, insomnia, and excitability.

Psychological Basis. For the man, adjustment to the physical changes of middle age is usually smooth enough. There may be a few flurries, such as an argument with the doctor about giving up tennis, or a period of denying the manifest need of reading glasses, but generally the man slows down on the more strenuous forms of physical activity, conserves his energy if he is a manual worker, and counts on experience and skill to enable him to hold his own with younger, more active men. Sexual activity and interest decrease slowly in men, but continue far into the period of old age. Some men seek new sexual stimulation with younger women at this period of life.

For the women, there may be a premenopausal "thrust of activity" in which the woman seems to try to make up for lost time. This may take the form of having another child "before it is too late" or of picking up old social and civic interests which had been abandoned with the coming of children. With some women there is a period of increased sexual excitability just before the menopause, which has gained for this period a name, "The Dangerous Age." The woman may resume earlier habits of grooming and dressing "to appear young again" and she may make friends with people of dubious reputation, who pay court to her.

The menopause itself may be accompanied by a period of psychological depression. Almost every woman goes through a shorter or longer depression while her body is readjusting to a changed endocrine balance.

Cultural Basis. The extent to which the period of middle age, especially for women, is a period of psychological stress and strain probably varies greatly from one culture to another, but the comparative anthropological data dealing with this topic are not plentiful. Within the American society, there seems to be variation among the several social classes. Middle-class and upper-class women appear to have more psychological disturbance during this period than do working-class women, though the latter appear to have fully as much physical difficulty.

Educational Implications. To a limited extent, knowledge about the physiology of ageing would probably help people to adjust to the changes which their bodies are undergoing. Therefore this topic might be treated in courses for adults.

More important, as far as education is concerned, is the task of assisting middle-aged people to develop the new interests and activities that are appropriate to their biological and psychological capacities. This means the development of courses dealing with civic and political problems, and the offering of instruction in arts and crafts, gardening, dramatics, and other leisure-time activities that will survive as the person grows older.

7. ADJUSTING TO AGEING PARENTS

Nature of the Task. To meet the responsibility for the needs of ageing parents, in such ways as to make for a satisfying old age for the parents and also to promote the happiness of the middle-aged generation.

Biological Basis. None.

Psychological Basis. During middle age, a person is usually a member of a three-generation family. The older generation is from fifty-five to seventy-five years old while the middle generation is thirty to fifty years old and the younger generation is five to twenty-five. Thus, as the children grow to maturity and leave the home, the grandparents become older and may become a charge on the home.

The ageing parents may need financial help or physical care. They may be passing through a crisis of loss of employment and reduced income. The death of one of the old people may leave the other to adjust to the break-up of a forty-year partnership.

In spite of the general feeling of obligation on the part of grown-up children for their ageing parents, it often happens that neither generation wants to live with the other. Yet there may be real advantages for a couple with growing children to having grandparents living with them. The grandparents can look after the children if the parents want to leave home for a while. When domestic help is hard to get, the grandmother may be an invaluable aid to her married daughter.

When neither generation wants to live with the other, it is partly due to a desire for privacy and to the desire to avoid overcrowding, but very often there is an added factor of a parent-child relationship that was not altogether satisfactory, which one or the other generation does not wish to revive.

Cultural Basis. There are many variant relationships of middle-aged people to their ageing parents among the societies of the world. In some societies the older generation retain power and property until they die, and their grown children live with them in *their* habitation. Other societies pass on property and power to the middle-aged generation, which, however, looks after the older generation carefully. Still other societies leave the older generation to care for itself, and expect old people to go quietly off and die when they can no longer take care of themselves.

Within the American society there is a considerable difference among the social classes in the ways they have of meeting this task.

The older generation in the upper class usually retain their high status until the end, and live comfortably by themselves. They keep an interest in civic and business affairs through their middle-aged children, but do not become dependent on them.

In middle-class families, there is often a good deal of conflict and tension between the two generations. The conflict is seldom over finances, since both generations are usually able to support themselves. Usually the conflict results from an unresolved parent-child conflict that is reactivated whenever the two generations try to live together.

In lower-class families, there seems to be a reasonably good relation between middle-aged children and their parents. Often the two generations live under the same roof, together with grandchildren. The grandparents are often helpful in looking after the children and in keeping house, while the middle-aged children support them. There is probably less hostility between generations in lower-class than in middle-class families.

Social and Educational Implications. With the increasing numbers of old people in the population, the numbers of three-generation families are increasing, and the problem of the relations between grown children and their parents is growing. From the educational point of view, it appears that conflict and tensions between the generations had best be handled by counseling rather than by trying to teach a solution to the problem in adult classes.

Because the two generations frequently need each other, there appears to be a good chance that ways will be worked out of achieving this task better than it is done now. For example, houses may be designed for three generations, with a small apartment on the ground floor for the grandparents, who can thus have privacy while living with their children.

CHAPTER 18

Developmental Tasks of Later Maturity

THE FACT that man learns his way through life is made radically clear by consideration of the learning tasks of older people. They still have new experiences ahead of them, and new situations to meet. At age sixty-five when a man often retires from his occupation, his chances are better than even of living another ten years. During this time the man or his wife very likely will experience several of the following things: decreased income, moving to a smaller house, loss of spouse by death, a crippling illness or accident, a turn in the business cycle with a consequent change of the cost of living. After any of these events the situation may be so changed that the old person must learn new ways of living.

The developmental tasks of later maturity differ in only one fundamental respect from those of other ages. They involve more of a defensive strategy—of holding on to life rather than of seizing more of it. In the physical, mental, and economic spheres the limitations become especially evident; the older person must work hard to hold onto what he already has. In the social sphere there is a fair chance of offsetting the narrowing of certain social contacts and interests by the broadening of others. In the spiritual sphere there is perhaps no necessary shrinking of the boundaries, and perhaps there is even a widening of them.

1. ADJUSTING TO DECREASING PHYSICAL STRENGTH AND HEALTH

The human body does age, in almost every one of its cells and cellular systems. The cells pile up useless or poisonous materials which they cannot get rid of. They gradually slow down in their nutritional processes. They gradually lose their self-repairing properties.

Thus, if a person has been spared from the things which might take his life at any age, such as accidents, and germ diseases, his body will eventually wear out and give way. The ageing process finds the old person's weakest places in the cardiovascular system, the kidneys, and the joints. Of all people who live to be over fifty, half die of heart disease or its complications. This would constitute no adjustment problem if it was a matter of sudden death, but heart disease usually comes on slowly and makes an invalid out of a person before it kills him. Hence a large proportion of older people must adjust to invalidism due to heart disease; and another considerable group must adjust to invalidism due to arthritis or other diseases of the joints.

Fully half of the people who live to be seventy-five or over must adapt themselves to a period of invalidism before they die.

2. ADJUSTMENT TO RETIREMENT AND REDUCED INCOME

In the American society a job is the axis of life for most men and for many women. If the occupation goes, the individual feels that he does not count, that he is not a worthy member of society. Yet the occupation must be abandoned by the great majority of people, whether they be professional or manual workers, sometime between sixty and seventy.

Some people fill up the vacuum created by retirement in their lives with a useful and interesting leisure-time activity; others find a part-time job which keeps them busy and happy; too many fret and mope over their forced inactivity.

When retirement also means a serious reduction in income another adjustment problem appears—that of reducing expenditures —which often means a narrowing of contacts. For instance, an elderly lady feels that she must drop out of the Church Ladies' Circle because she cannot pay her dues. An old man must drop out of his club or his lodge just at a time when he has increased leisure.

This task is at present needlessly difficult for people, because of the rigid retirement rules in certain professions, and because business and industry reject older people and retire their employees relatively young. Hence it is a matter for study and action by social institutions as well as for adjustment by individuals.

3. ADJUSTING TO DEATH OF SPOUSE

After a man and a woman have lived together for forty years, it is hard for one to get along without the other. Yet death separates nearly every married man and woman. Women lose their husbands more often than men lose their wives, because women are longer-lived than men. There are about twice as many widows as widowers in the average community. By the later sixties as many women are widows as are living with their husbands. Among women eighty-five years of age and over, 85 per cent are widows.

If a woman loses her husband, she may have to move from her house to a smaller place, she may have to learn about business matters, and above all she has to learn to be alone. A man has the same adjustment to make to loneliness, and he may have to learn to cook, to keep house, and to keep his clothes in order.

The solutions of this task run through the range of living on alone in the old home, moving into a small home, living in a rooming house, moving in with brothers or sisters, living with children, remarrying, going to an old people's home. Every solution requires unlearning of old ways and learning of new ways, at a time when learning comes harder than it did in earlier years.

4. ESTABLISHING AN EXPLICIT AFFILIATION WITH ONE'S AGE GROUP

Nature of the Task. To accept one's status as a member of the elders of the society and to become a constructive participant in one's age group.

Biological Basis. Physiological ageing slows down the organism and makes it increasingly difficult for older people to keep up the tempo of life which they followed in middle age. Hence, they tend to drop out of the activities of the middle-aged group.

Psychological Basis. It is useful to look at the rewards and punishments involved in participation by a person turning sixty-five in (a) the group just younger than he (later middle age) and (b) the group just older than he (early old age).

Rewards in Continued Participation in the Middle-Age Group. Feeling of achievement—something is going on all the time. Satisfaction from the wielding of economic and social power. Satisfactio from the repetition of behavior patterns already well learned.

Punishments in Continued Participation in the Middle-Age Group. Fatigue due to the "rapid" tempo of life in this group.

Older persons are increasingly ignored by this group, or perhaps unintentionally insulted by references to their age and declining powers.

Embarrassment at decrease of income and occupational responsibility—making it difficult to "keep up" with the middle-age group.

Rewards in Participation in the Old-Age Group. Tempo of life is slower and more comfortable.

Companionship is easily found; people have more leisure time. Prestige positions are available in organizations of older people, and no longer available in organizations of middle-aged people.

Punishments Involved in Participation in the Old-Age Group. The tacit admission that one has become "old."

The general loss of status connected with "ageing" in U.S.A. Difficulty of learning to participate in new groups.

For thirty or forty years the individual, now growing old, has participated in occupational, social, and religious groups in which age-grading was at a minimum, and status was achieved on the basis of social position, economic power, talent, and other things that were largely independent of age. The ageing person must now learn once more to participate in an age-graded group. The ease or difficulty of this task depends on the relative magnitudes of the rewards and punishments which have been suggested above.

Sociological Basis. There are several types of age-graded groups for older people.

The Political or Economic Action Group, such as the Townsend Clubs: This kind of group emphasizes political and economic action, but also has a certain amount of social and recreational activity. The future of this kind of group probably depends upon the economic status of old people. If they feel themselves deprived, they will undoubtedly organize to improve their economic status.

The Social or Recreational Group:

A. Based on occupation or economic status.

For example—associations of retired teachers or retired Y.M.C.A. secretaries. Such groups make fellowship and recreation their primary purpose, although they may also work for their economic welfare.

B. Based on recreational or cultural interests.

For example—Borrowed Time Club, Three-Quarter Century Club; a University Half-Century Club, which takes on life as its members grow old, while they could hardly get together for a reunion once in ten years when they were in middle age.

Social and Educational Implications. With increasing numbers, old people will become a potent force politically if they organize on an age-graded basis. In any case, there is opportunity and obligation for adult education. Old people have time on their hands, they have new tasks to learn, yet they are generally "not interested" in existing adult education programs.

5. MEETING SOCIAL AND CIVIC OBLIGATIONS

Plato supposed that people were not fit to govern in a democracy until they were past fifty, and then only if they studied philosophy. Whether he was right or not, the increasing numbers of older people in the U.S.A. are becoming increasingly responsible for the conduct of civic and political affairs, both as citizens and as office holders. Studies of the ages of holders of important offices show that the average age of such people has increased during the past century.

If old people are to have greater civic and political power, and to use it wisely, they must add knowledge continually to their wisdom. They must "keep abreast" of current affairs. For this task they must create agencies for study and they must participate increasingly in adult education programs.

6. ESTABLISHING SATISFACTORY PHYSICAL LIVING ARRANGEMENTS

Nature of the Task. To find the kind of living quarters that are most comfortable and convenient.

Biological Basis. The high incidence of heart disease and "rheumatism" in older people makes physical exertion difficult or dangerous for many of them, and argues against stair-climbing and heavy housework. There is increasing danger from falls, due to the increasing brittleness of bones and their slow mending rates. A decreasing ability to masticate foods, with an increasing need for a good diet, makes good food-preparing and selecting necessary. Decreasing metabolic ability of the body makes it difficult for older people to "keep warm" and requires good heating facilities.

Psychological Basis. The principal values that older people look for in housing, according to studies of this matter, are:

(1) quiet,
(2) privacy,
(3) independence of action,
(4) nearness to relatives and friends,
(5) residence among own cultural group,
(6) cheapness,
(7) closeness to transportation lines and communal institutions —libraries, shops, movies, churches, etc.

These values vary for different people. Most older people tend to cling to established housing arrangements until they become very unsatisfactory. Yet residential mobility is high, especially among the very old.

Sociological Basis. Most older people live in homes not much different from those they were accustomed to in middle age. Seventy-eight per cent of men over sixty lived in private households as heads of families in 1940, 38 per cent of women lived in private households as wives of the heads of the home, and 30 per cent of women lived in private households as heads of families.

Of those who do not live in their own homes, women live mostly with children (18 per cent) and men live about equally often with children (8 per cent) and in private homes as lodgers (5 per cent). Only 4.5 per cent of men and 3.3 per cent of women over sixty live in old people's homes, hotels, and lodging houses. The proportion who live in old people's homes is limited by the scarcity of such homes, most of which have waiting lists.

Practical Applications. The following types of housing arrangements seem best for older people in the U.S.A.

1. Small villages in warm climates, specifically planned for old people. These villages should have movie, library, restaurant, and church facilities.

2. Housing units specially designed for older people in all parts of the city, with heating, cooking, light, and laundry facilities planned for their use.

3. Dwelling units (small apartments) in single-family residences, designed for three-generation families. The grandparents have a small apartment of their own, which gives them quiet and privacy, and yet they are in the same house with the rest of the family and can help and be helped as need arises.

4. Cooperative housing projects for older people with communal eating, laundry, and other facilities.

5. Old people's homes, best for people with limited ability to care for themselves physically. Interesting experiments could be made in such homes for more active and vigorous people.

PART FIVE

*An Empirical Study of Developmental Tasks
in Middle Childhood and Adolescence*

CHAPTER 19

Purposes and Methods of the Developmental Task Study[1]

WHILE THE NOTION of developmental tasks is useful in thinking about boys and girls and their education, the validity of the concept as a scientific one has had very little testing. Some of the questions a critical scientist asks are: Can achievement of developmental tasks be measured? If so, how much interrelationship exists between the several tasks? To what extent can we predict achievement of a developmental task in the future by knowing how well a person is achieving his developmental tasks now?

In order to answer these questions a study was made of a group of boys and girls, all the same age and living in a small midwestern city. They were studied intensively for six years, from the age of ten to sixteen. A plan of study, both broad and intensive, was carried through on these children by means of: interviews with children and their parents; sociometric tests; projective tests (the Rorschach Test, given twice, the Thematic Apperception Test, given three times, and a Sentence Completion Test); ratings and observational reports by teachers, employers, and other adults;

[1] The writer wishes to express his appreciation and debt to the work of Dr. Aileen Schoeppe in this study. Miss Schoeppe made an exhaustive study of performance on developmental tasks, which is described in her Ph.D. dissertation, "A Study of Factors Related to the Achievement of Five Developmental Tasks of Adolescence." Library of the Department of Education, The University of Chicago, 1951.

See also: Aileen Schoeppe and Robert J. Havighurst, "A Validation of Development and Adjustment Hypotheses of Adolescence," *Journal of Ed. Psychol.* 43 (1952) 339–53.

Aileen Schoeppe, Ernest A. Haggard, and Robert J. Havighurst, "Some Factors Affecting Sixteen-Year-Olds' Success in Five Developmental Tasks," *Journal of Abnormal and Social Psychol.* 48 (1953) 42–52.

essays and check lists and questionnaires written by the children; tests of intelligence and aptitudes; physical growth measurements; analyses of data by a clinical conference; and ratings on personality, character, and developmental tasks by a research staff of eight people.

These children were all residents of "Prairie City," a midwestern county seat of about 7,000 inhabitants. They were all born in the year 1933; all were studied from 1943 to 1950. Prairie City is one of 110 cities between 5,000 and 10,000 in the twelve midwestern states, which are the largest cities in counties with a mixed agricultural-industrial economy. In such a county between 25 and 50 per cent of the gainfully employed men are engaged in agriculture, and the remainder are in business, industry, and other non-agricultural occupations. This is the most common type of small city in the Middle West, and Prairie City is close to the average of these cities in a number of census characteristics.

There are four primary schools in Prairie City, but the children all come together in one school building at the fifth grade, which was the grade in which the study started. About ninety children became ten years old during 1943, and the entire age-group was studied. Then, when the children were about thirteen years old, a special group of thirty were selected for more intensive study. These thirty were followed for another three years. They were selected because at the age of thirteen most of them seemed to be either quite well adusted or quite poorly adjusted, with only a few from the average-adjusted middle group. This was done so as to make it easier to study the things that make for success or failure of children. However, it developed on further study that some of the so-called "well-adjusted" group were not so happy and healthy and successful as seemed at first to be the case; and consequently the group proved to be more nearly a representative sample than might have been supposed. Thus the sample included a wide variety of boys and girls (but all white and all native-born), and appears to be a good one for the kind of study that was made on them.

There were fifteen boys and fifteen girls in the group. Using Warner's scheme of social classes, one boy was upper-middle class, twelve boys and thirteen girls were either lower-middle or upper-lower class, and two of each sex were lower-lower class. The near absence of upper-middle class children was due to the fact that only two of the total age group were of this class (no one from an upper-class family), and only one upper-middle class child happened to be selected for the intensive study group.

The thirty children had an average Binet IQ of 113 at age fourteen, compared with 106 for the entire age-group in the community. The range in the special group was 75–145.

In 1950, the collection of data on these children was stopped, when they were sixteen or seventeen years old. Then a research staff varying in number from eight to twelve spent two years analyzing the data, with the major aim of understanding the development of moral character in the group.[2] As a by-product of the study of moral character, this study of developmental tasks was carried on by the same research group.

The method of study was to define the developmental tasks in terms of the behavior of boys and girls, and then to rate each child in the special group on his achievement of each task at the ages of ten, thirteen, and sixteen.

The Hypotheses To Be Tested

With the ratings on achievement of the various developmental tasks, the following hypotheses were tested:

1. Good achievement on a developmental task at one age is followed by good achievement on similar tasks at subsequent ages.
2. Good achievement on a developmental task tends to be associated with good achievement on other tasks at the same age.
3. In a minority of cases good achievement on one developmental task may be used to compensate for poor achievement on other tasks.

Since an intensive personality study was made on these children, it was also possible to explore the relations between personality

[2] Robert F. Peck, Douglas M. More, Robert J. Havighurst, Jesse Lilienthal, and Ruth I. Cooper, *The Psychology of Moral Character.* To be published in 1955.

characteristics and achievement of developmental tasks. Consequently, the following hypothesis was tested:

4. There are personality characteristics that are significantly related to success or failure in the achievement of developmental tasks.

The Method of Rating

For the purposes of this study five developmental tasks were selected, for which achievement could be readily defined and rated at the ages of ten, thirteen, and sixteen. The five tasks were:

1. Learning an appropriate sex role.
2. Achieving emotional independence of parents and other adults.
3. Developing conscience, morality, and a set of values.
4. Getting along with age-mates.
5. Developing intellectual skills.

Each of the first four tasks was then analyzed, by defining success and failure in terms of behavior of boys and girls of ages ten, thirteen, and sixteen. When this had been accomplished, and the definitions had been discussed and agreed upon by the research staff, a rating scale for each task was devised. The rating scales were discussed, tried out on one or two cases and revised, and finally emerged in the form given on the following pages.

The research staff rated each child against the entire group of American children of that age as the research staff knew children. Top rating (10) was given to a child who performed as well as the top one-tenth of American children of that age. Bottom rating (1) was given to a child who performed no better than the bottom one-tenth of American children of that age. In theory, the ratings on a representative group of children would spread evenly over the ten-point scale. In practice the ratings on the Prairie City group spread unevenly over the scale, as would be expected of a group that was not a cross-section and contained unusually large proportions of children who showed signs of very good or very poor adjustment.[3]

[3] The lowest mean was 4.8 (Conscience and Moral Values, ages ten and sixteen) and the highest was 6.5 (Intellectual Skills, age thirteen). Standard deviations ranged from 2.26 to 3.12.

The lack of a normal distribution of scores makes the computation of product-moment correlation coefficients somewhat questionable, but not enough so to cast serious doubt on the results of the correlation analysis.

Definitions and Rating Scales

For each of the following developmental tasks, the task will first be defined in terms of success or failure (at the age of 10–11; definitions will not be given for the other ages, since they are implied in the rating scales), and then the rating scales will be given for three ages.

GETTING ALONG WITH AGE-MATES

Operational Description of Success and Failure in this Task at Age 10–11

SUCCESS

Boy. Is a member of a group of boys his age, who form a loose-knit play-group. Spends most of his free time with this group. Is accepted by this group, and has one or more acceptable roles in it. Has one or more mutual friends, as shown in a sociometric test. Has the reputation of being a good loser, is reasonably "daring," not thought of as unduly "bossy." On the whole has a favorable reputation on a Guess-Who test. Will fight on occasion, though not reputed to be quarrelsome.

Girl. Has a small group of friends her own age, with whom she spends spare time. Has one or more acceptable roles in this group. Is invited to parties by members of this group. Gives parties and invites her friends to them. Has one or more mutual friends. Has them stay with her overnight and stays with them overnight once every month or two. Has reputation of being ladylike, clean, friendly.

FAILURE

Boy or *Girl.* Usually spends spare time alone. Is not a firm member of any small group. Is a scapegoat. Is either a "fraidy-cat" or a bully. Tries to dominate, when in a group, or stays on the fringe.

Has no accepted role in a group. No mutual choices in a sociometric test. Many rejections. Unfavorable reputation on a Guess-Who test.

Rating Scale on Getting Along with Age-Mates—Age 10–11

SCALE VALUE 10 (HIGH)

Has two or more mutual friends. Has a small group or "gang" in which he feels secure. High score on "popular" items in a Guess-Who test. High score on social adjustment in California Personality Inventory. High score on sociability in Interest Inventory. Observers report excellent social adjustment with age-mates.

SCALE VALUE 9

Much the same as 10, but at least one piece of evidence indicating something less than excellence in this area.

SCALE VALUE 7–8

Above average scores on sociometric tests for items indicating sociability and popularity. Has one or more mutual friends and is a member of a clique. Thought of as a constructive member of a group. Quite well known to age-mates.

SCALE VALUE 5–6

Has a mutual friend. Plays occasionally in groups and can be identified as a group member. Average scores on Guess-Who, California Personality Inventory (social adjustment), sociability category of Interest Inventory.

SCALE VALUE 3–4

Tends to be overlooked by others. Mutual friendships temporary, if present. May be mildly disliked, because of quarrelsomeness or other evidence of aggression. Generally low scores on Guess-Who, California Inventory (social adjustment), sociability category of Interest Inventory.

SCALE VALUE 2

Solitary person. No mutual friends. Some dislike manifested by others, but not universal. At least one piece of evidence indicating something less than unrelieved social rejection.

SCALE VALUE 1 (LOW)

No mutual friends. Heartily disliked. Scapegoat. Very low score, indicating rejection, on Guess-Who. Low score on California Inventory (social adjustment) and sociability category of Interest Inventory. Observers report very poor social adjustment. Evidence of hostility to others, generally.

Rating Scale on Getting Along with Age-Mates—Age 13–14

SCALE VALUE 10 (HIGH)

Has two or more mutual friends. Has small group or "gang" in which he feels secure. Has a high score for popular attributes on Guess-Who. If a girl, shows some interest in boys, but is not necessarily dating. If a boy, may not show much interest in girls. High score on sociability in Interest Inventory. Observers report excellent adjustment with age-mates. Has social skills.

SCALE VALUE 9

Almost up to value 10, but falls below in one or two respects, or evidence is lacking in one or two respects.

SCALE VALUE 7–8

One or more mutual friends and is in a friendship group. If a girl, shows some interest in boys, but may not be dating. If a boy, is not dating more than rarely. Better than average score for popularity items on Guess-Who, and for sociability on Interest Inventory. Better than average score for social adjustment on Personality Inventory. Well-known to age-mates.

SCALE VALUE 5–6

Is definitely a member of a group, but may not have a mutual friend. Average score on Guess-Who, sociability category of Interest Inventory, and social adjustment on California Personality Inventory. If a girl, shows interest in boys. If a boy, shows no interest in girls.

SCALE VALUE 3–4

Overlooked by others. Something of a fringer on sociometric tests. Below average score on popularity items of Guess-Who, sociability category of Interest Inventory, and social adjustment score on California Personality. No show of interest in opposite sex. Lacks social skills.

SCALE VALUE 2

Solitary person, but may be actively rejected by peer group or mutual friends. At least one piece of evidence showing something less than unrelieved social rejection.

SCALE VALUE 1 (LOW)

Socially rejected. Scapegoat. Low score on sociability category of Interest Inventory, on popularity items of Guess-Who. Observers report very poor social adjustment.

Rating Scale on Good Adjustment to Age-Mates of Both Sexes— Age 16–17

SCALE VALUE 10 (HIGH)

Has two or more mutual friends and is a solid member of a social clique. If a girl, has dates fairly often, and is thought of as a feminine person. If a boy, shows interest in girls. Has a high score for popular attributes on Guess-Who. Has been chosen by age-mates for responsible positions. High score on social adjustment in Adjustment Inventory.

SCALE VALUE 9

Almost up to Value 10, but falls below in one or two respects.

SCALE VALUE 7–8

One or more mutual friends and is in a friendship group. Has been selected by age-mates for positions of responsibility, if not of leadership. If a girl, has dates. If a boy, beginning to show interest in girls. Has a better than average score for items of sociability on the Guess-Who.

SCALE VALUE 5–6

Has a mutual friend. Can be identified as a group member, but is not conspicuous. Average scores on social adjustment in Adjustment Inventory and on sociability in Interest Inventory and Guess-Who. If a girl, has just become established with boys, not sure of herself yet. If a boy, very limited social contacts with girls.

SCALE VALUE 3–4

Inconspicuous socially. Friendships tend to be temporary, but may have one mutual friend. Thought of as immature, not "grown up." Below average scores on sociometric tests or Guess-Who for sociability and popularity, and on social adjustment in Adjustment Inventory. If a girl, very limited contacts with opposite sex. If a boy, no social contacts with girls. No offices in clubs.

SCALE VALUE 2

Solitary person. Just escapes being at scale value 1 because he is not at the bottom in everything.

SCALE VALUE 1 (LOW)

No mutual friends and no friendship group. An outcast, or completely invisible. Very low scores on sociometric or Guess-Who items indicating sociability and popularity. No contacts with opposite sex, or, if a girl, a reputation for extreme "looseness." Evidence of hostility toward other people, and self-justification.

LEARNING AN APPROPRIATE SEX-ROLE

Operational Description of Success and Failure in this Task at Age 10–11

SUCCESS

Boy. Plays with boys almost entirely. Plays active games. Male figures, regardless of their age, are important in the ego-ideal. Not concerned with cleanliness or with "dressing up."

Girl. Plays with girls almost entirely. Plays at least *some* girls' games. Female figures are important in the ego-ideal. Is neat, clean, and shows the "little lady" characteristics.

FAILURE

Boy. Plays alone or with girls. Interested in feminine activities. Reputation of being a sissy. Overly concerned with cleanliness and with being carefully dressed. Male figures not important in ego-ideal.

Girl. Plays alone or primarily with boys. Reputation of preferring boyish activities to those commonly liked by girls. Unkempt or refuses to wear feminine clothing when other girls normally wear such clothes. Female figures not important in ego-ideal.

Rating Scale on Learning an Appropriate Sex-Role—Age 10–11

SCALE VALUE 10 (HIGH)

Boy. Very active in games. Boisterous and unkempt. High score on sociometric test for active, daring. Much interest in sports. No observable interest in girls, though he may tease them. Essays show influence of masculine figures in ego-ideal. Interest and personality inventories show interest in same sex, games, and sports, and other masculine activities.

Girl. Rather quiet and sedate. Sociometric data indicate quietness, friendliness, and other "little lady" qualities. Plays girls' games. Seldom plays boys' games and seldom plays with boys if girls are available. Little show of interest in boys. Essays show influence of feminine figures on ego-ideal. Interest inventory and personality inventories show interest in same sex and in feminine activities. May show first signs of sexual maturation.

SCALE VALUE 9

Almost as high as level 10, but falls somewhat below in one or two respects, or information lacking in one or two respects.

SCALE VALUE 7–8

Boy. Likes sports and plays active games. Guess-Who test gives above-average score for daring, active, unkempt. Professes no interest in girls, though he may tease them. Essays show influence of masculine figures on ego-ideal. Interest and personality inventories show liking for same sex and masculine patterns of behavior. (In general, is different only quantitatively from scale value 9 and 10, not qualitatively.)

Girl. Little show of interest in boys or boys' games. Plays girls' games. Guess-Who and sociometric tests above average for "little lady" qualities. Essays show influence of feminine figures on ego-ideal. Interest and personality inventories show liking for same sex and feminine patterns of behavior. May show first signs of sexual maturation. (Difference from values 9 and 10 largely quantitative in nature. She just does not fill the feminine ten-year-old role so completely.)

SCALE VALUE 5–6

Boy. Fairly active in games and fairly interested in sports, but noticeably less so than many boys of this age. Average scores on Guess-Who for active, daring, and unkempt. Essays show influence of male figures on ego-ideal, but the males may not be strongly masculine. Interest and personality inventories show average likes for same sex and masculine behavior patterns.

Girl. Plays girls' games and boys' games with a liking for the more active games. Average scores on Guess-Who for "little lady" items. Professes no interest in boys. Essays show influence of female figures on ego-ideal, but they may be masculine females. Interest and personality inventories show average liking for same sex and for feminine patterns of behavior. (This is qualitatively different from ratings 7–10. There is now some feeling that she is not feminine, though also not at all masculine.)

SCALE VALUE 3–4

Boy. Rather passive personality. Interested in reading about sports, but unenthusiastic and unskilled in boys' games. Plays occasionally with girls, even though boys are available. Guess-Who scores are below average on daring, active, unkempt. Essays show weak influence of males on ego-ideals—male figures may be passive. Interest and personality inventories show below-average liking for same sex and for masculine behavior patterns.

Girl. Alternative patterns:

(a) Tomboy reputation. Sometimes plays boys' games with boys. No sexual interest in boys. Guess-Who scores below average on "little lady" items. Essays show little or no influence of feminine figures on ego-ideal; female figures below average on liking for same sex and feminine behavior patterns.

(b) Timid, shy, retiring. Plays little girls' games. Small for age. Guess-Who scores average or even higher for "little lady" items. No interest in boys. Essays may show ego-ideal related to mother or mother-surrogate. Interest and personality inventories show average interest in same sex and feminine behavior patterns.

SCALE VALUE 2

Not quite as low as level 1. Just above on one or two items, or evidence lacking on one or two items.

SCALE VALUE 1 (LOW)

Boy. Is a sissy. No active games, and little interest in sports. Reputation very low on daring, active, unkempt. May play with girls and have girlish interests. Essays show little or no influence of male figures on ego-ideal, unless they are father or father-surrogates. Interest and personality inventories show low liking for same sex and boyish behavior patterns.

Girl. Alternative patterns:

(a) Is a tomboy. Plays boys' games with boys, almost to exclusion of girls' games and of girls as companions. No sexual interest in boys. Guess-Who scores low on "little lady" items, and high (for a girl) on active, daring, unkempt. Wears boys' clothes whenever possible. Essays show influence of male figures on ego-ideal. Interest and personality inventories show low liking for same sex; and high liking for masculine behavior patterns.

(b) Very timid, "immature." Plays with dolls and with younger girls. Small for age. Guess-Who scores tend to overlook her, but may give average score for "little lady" items. No interest in boys. Essays show ego-ideal limited to mother or mother-surrogate. Interest and personality inventories show liking for "childish" behavior patterns.

Rating Scale on Learning an Appropriate Sex-Role—Age 13–14

SCALE VALUE 10 (HIGH)

Boy. Popular with boys because of active, aggressive qualities. Likes active games and sports. Boisterous and somewhat unkempt. At least average in pubertal growth cycle. Interest and personality inventories show strong interest in games and sports, and not much interest in opposite sex. Essays show strong influence of masculine figure, but some uncertainty about heterosexual activities.

Alternative pattern: Beginning to show interest in girls, with concomitant interest in grooming.

Girl. Definite evidence of interest in associating with boys, going beyond walking home with a boy from a party. At least average in pubertal growth cycle. Menarche is past. Careful of clothing. High reputation for sociability and friendliness. Essays show strong influence of females on ego-ideal, and acceptance of goal of marriage and motherhood, without strong guilt feelings over sexual impulses. Interest and personality inventories show interest in opposite sex.

SCALE VALUE 9

Almost up to 10, but falls short in one or two respects, or definite evidence is lacking in one or two respects.

SCALE VALUE 7–8

Boy. Likes active games and sports, and holds his own with other boys in competition, though he may not be outstanding. Is average or large for his age, not retarded in physical maturation. Boisterous and unkempt. Essays show strong influence of male figures on ego-ideal, but preadolescent sexual interests and attitudes. Interest and personality inventories show no interest in opposite sex. If he goes with girls at all, it is due to social pressure.

Girl. Some evidence of interest in boys, at least in mixed-group situations. Average in pubertal growth cycle. Menarche probably past. Concerned with grooming. Essays show influence of female figures on ego-ideal, though little interest in roles of marriage or motherhood, and guilt feelings over sexual impulses. Interest and personality inventories show some slight interest in opposite sex.

SCALE VALUE 5–6

Boy. Active in sports, though not very good in them. Unkempt and boisterous. Average in pubertal growth cycle. No interest in girls, singly or in groups. Essays show influence of male figures on ego-ideal, but no awareness of adult sexual attitudes. Interest and personality inventories show average or higher interests in sports and in same-sex activities, but no interest in opposite sex.

Girl. Physically at the average or slightly retarded. Menarche recent or not yet. Some interest in boys in mixed-group situations, but does not have dates. May take on active, almost masculine role in girls' groups. Essays show influence of female figures on ego-ideal, though they may be masculine females; no interest in wife or mother roles. Interest and personality inventories show more interest in same sex than in opposite sex.

SCALE VALUE 3–4

Boy. Rather passive personality. Only passive interest in sports. Does poorly in games. May have masculine hobbies such as photography. No interest in girls. Physically below average size, or retarded in pubertal growth cycle. Essays show influence of male figures on ego-ideal, but these may be weak male figures; no awareness of heterosexual problems and attitudes. Interest and personality inventories show no interest in opposite sex.

Girl. Physically retarded or, if advanced, then large and self-conscious. Menarche recent or not yet. No display of interest in boys. May have reputation of being a tomboy. Essays show influence of female figures on ego-ideal, though they may be masculine females; no interest in wife or mother roles and no awareness of adult sexuality. Interest and personality inventories low in interest in opposite sex.

SCALE VALUE 2

Almost as low as 1, but higher in one or two respects, or evidence lacking in these respects.

SCALE VALUE 1 (LOW)

Boy. Physically small, or retarded in sexual development. Is a sissy. Not interested in sports. Dresses fastidiously. Close overt attachment to mother and female relatives. Leisure time interests those of a girl. Essays show weak male figures influencing ego-ideal, and preadolescent sexual attitudes. Interest and personality inventories show no interests in masculine things.

Girl. Physically retarded, without menarche, or large and ungainly. Alternative patterns: (a) Quiet, "little lady," with no interest in sex or in adult feminine roles. Essays show immature attitudes. Interest and personality inventories show dependency and immaturity.

(b) Tomboy pattern. Likes rough, active games. Likes to play boys' games with boys and masculine girls, with no sexual connotation. Essays may show influence of male figures on ego-ideal, and no acceptance of roles of wife and mother, with preadolescent sexual attitudes. Interest and personality inventories show masculine patterns.

Rating Scale on Learning an Appropriate Sex-Role—Age 16–17

SCALE VALUE 10 (HIGH)

Boy. High rating on physical maturity. Active in sports. Enjoys group contacts with girls. Beginning to experiment with person-to-person relations with girls. Fairly careful grooming. On essays shows strong influence of male figures in ego-ideal and strong heterosexual interest and acceptance of heterosexual activity. Interest and personality inventories show interest in and liking for opposite sex. Masculine body build.

Girl. Physically mature. Interested in boys and successful with them. Dresses in feminine manner. On essays shows full acceptance of goal of marriage and motherhood; and female figures essential to ego-ideal. Interest and personality inventories show strong interest in opposite sex and good relations with boys.

SCALE VALUE 9

Almost, but not quite up to level 10. Drops off in one or two minor respects, or evidence unclear in one or two respects.

SCALE VALUE 7–8

Boy. Physically may not be mature, but shows definite masculine body build. Is passively or actively interested in sports. Enjoys group contacts with girls, but may not be dating. Fairly careful grooming. Essays show influence of male figures on ego-ideal, though they may also show some uncertainty about accepting heterosexual activity. Interest and personality inventories show more than average interest in opposite sex.

Girl. Physically mature. Dresses in feminine way. Interested in boys, but not the most successful with them. May engage in masculine games, and have masculine girls as friends. Essays show acceptance of goal of marriage and motherhood, though possibly some fear or uncertainty about the meaning of sex. Interest and personality inventories show more than average interest in opposite sex.

SCALE VALUE 5–6

Boy. Physically may or may not be mature. Passive interest in sports, but not much active participation. No effort to date girls, but is interested in mixed parties and will form part of a mixed sex group if given a chance. Grooming not attended to. Essays, while showing influence of male figures on ego-ideal, also show doubts and fears about sex. Interest and personality inventories show average interest in opposite sex.

Girl. Physically mature, but body build not especially feminine. Often wears boy's clothes. Engages in masculine sports with interest. Has masculine girls as friends. Has few or no dates, but interested in boys. Essays show feminine influence on ego-ideal, but some hesitation about accepting goals of motherhood and marriage, and definite fear or uncertainty about sex. Interest and personality inventories show less than average interest in opposite sex.

SCALE VALUE 3–4

Boy. Physically not mature. No dating. Slight interest in mixed-sex groups. No active participation in sports, and not much passive interest. Essays and projectives, while showing influence of male figures on ego-ideal, show little awareness of heterosexual relations and doubt and uncertainty, as far as there is awareness. Interest and personality inventories show less than average interest in opposite sex.

Girl. Somewhat retarded in physical development. Does not dress in feminine ways. If she has boy friends, they tend to be passive and feminine. Not much interest in boys. Essays show female influence on ego-ideal, but definite hesitation about accepting motherhood and marriage, and fear of sex. Interest and personality inventories show less than average interest in opposite sex.

SCALE VALUE 2

Almost as low as level 1, but one or two items seem slightly higher, or evidence is unclear on one or two items.

SCALE VALUE 1 (LOW)

Boy. Physically not mature. No interest in girls. Avoids mixed-sex groups. No active or passive interest in sports. Reputation as a sissy. Body build not definitely masculine. Essays show weak influence of males on ego-ideal, and preadolescent sexual attitudes. Interest and personality inventories show little interest in opposite sex.

Girl. Late maturing. May not have reached menarche. Appearance of a "little girl" in dress and body build. Essays show preadolescent sexual attitudes. Interest and personality inventories show little interest in opposite sex.

Alternative pattern: May be a tomboy, with masculine interests and masculine girl friends, and masculine habits and clothes. Essays may show influence of male figures on ego-ideal.

ACHIEVING EMOTIONAL INDEPENDENCE OF PARENTS AND OTHER ADULTS

Operational Description of Success and Failure in this Task at Age 10–11

SUCCESS

Prefers playing with age-mates to spending free time with parents. Ego-ideal shows influence of others besides parents. Shows interest in peer-group activities. Goes about the nearer sections of the community freely, unaccompanied by an adult. Is capable of enjoying at least one night away from home. Shows signs of resisting adult-imposed rules and restrictions and of wanting to structure more of his own life.

FAILURE

Ego-ideal is still limited to parents or, in their absence, parent-surrogates. Shows little interest in peer-group activities. Prefers playing at home with parents and younger siblings. Cannot enjoy spending a night away from them. Does not stray far from home unless accompanied by an adult. Is shy and timid with age-mates. Shows no outward rebellion toward adult rules, restrictions, and structuring of his life.

Rating Scale on Achieving Emotional Independence—Age 10–11

SCALE VALUE 10 (HIGH)

Ego-ideal is a fairly mature version of the glamorous adult type, or is possibly a visible, young adult whose behavior is attractive to the child. He rather often shows displeasure at the way one or both parents, teachers, and other authority figures structure his life. (This will be less apparent to the extent to which these people are unusually understanding and minimize opportunities for conflict by allowing considerable independent behavior on the part of the child.) Although overt rebellion may be much less than inner rebellion, overt rebellion frequently is expressed by such actions as disregarding commands and instructions, "sassing" or arguing with a parent or other adult, disobeying rules (against such activities as making noise in church, playing in forbidden places and with certain people, going out of the immediate neighborhood without reporting or seeking permission, raiding the neighbors' orchards and gardens, teasing siblings, loitering after school, "showing off" when expected to be on good behavior in front of adults). He is capable of spending at least one night away from the usual family circle without becoming homesick. His activities are peer-centered insofar as the parents and other adults permit. (This includes informal play groups in addition to the more structured Cub Scouts and Brownies, 4-H, church clubs.) Attempts are made by the child to structure his own life (particularly his leisure time). He wants and may earn money to spend as he chooses. He circulates freely about the community unaccompanied by an older person, particularly if he has a bicycle. He goes to the movies and to recreation areas alone. He may meet new situations with hesitation and caution but will not show timidity.

SCALE VALUE 9

Shows evidence of possessing most of the qualities listed at level 10 but *occasionally* displays *intermittent* "little boy" (or "little girl") behavior or has regressed to a less independent level of behavior for a short period during the year.

SCALE VALUE 7–8

Ego-ideal is a glamorous adult. Informal activity is with age-mates almost to the exclusion of parents or other adults. There is definite evidence of the child's ignoring or circumventing parental and other adult restrictions (e.g., doing any of the acts enumerated in level 10 description). The child is capable of spending a night away from home, especially if the hosts are relatives or close friends living not far away. He is somewhat less timid than the average ten-year-old.

SCALE VALUE 5–6

Ego-ideal is an *unrealistically* glamorous adult. The child plays with age-mates in preference to doing things with parents or other adults but enjoys adult structuring of a considerable portion of the activity time. He shows increasing evidence, however, of ignoring parental and teachers' restrictions regarding his mobility, friendships, interests, habits, tastes, etc. He is capable of staying away from home occasionally if a sibling or acquaintance near his own age is also present and the hosts are well-known to him. He has an average amount of timidity. (Activities are primarily within adult-structured situations, but there are increasing signs of a desire to range beyond it, with a tendency to be "led astray" by slightly more emotionally mature age-mates.)

SCALE VALUE 3–4

Ego-ideal may be limited to a parent, or in his or her absence, a parent-surrogate. The child plays with age-mates but goes home readily and enjoys just as much playing with younger siblings or doing things with a parent. He shows no evidence of preferring the peer standards of which he is aware to home standards. He will try to avoid staying away from home overnight and does not enjoy it when he has to do so unaccompanied by a parent. He is somewhat above average in timidity.

SCALE VALUE 2

Ego-ideal is exclusively a parent or, in his or her absence, a parent-surrogate. He shuns playing with age-mates unless it offers a means to please parents or teachers. He is unaware of those peer activities and codes that tend to draw a child away from parental "apron strings." He is *very* timid on most occasions. He habitually displays evidence of not wanting to be a ten-year-old behaviorally.

SCALE VALUE 1 (LOW)

Ego-ideal is exclusively a parent, or, in his or her absence, a parent-surrogate. The child not only has little self-direction but constantly demands the presence, attention, reassurance, and praise of a parent, teacher, or other adult to whom he is thoroughly accustomed. He prefers to play with or near adults. He accepts adult structuring and discipline, although he may protest the way it affects him by crying readily. He cries and complains to adults when activities with peers are not to his liking. He is *extremely* timid except with siblings and adults to whom he is completely accustomed. He never goes very far from home being accompanied by an older person and is terrified at the suggestion that he spend a night away from any of the family and familiar surroundings.

Rating Scale on Achievement of Emotional Independence—Age 13–14

SCALE VALUE 10 (HIGH)

Ego-ideal is at least a glamorized version of a young adult visible to the child. Regardless of pressures from parents and other adult authorities, the child makes a *sustained* effort to have his own decisions honored with respect to the type of clothing he wears, the food he eats, the activities in which he participates, the hobbies he pursues, the people with whom he associates, the books he reads and the movies he sees, the earning and spending or saving of money, and where he does and does not go. He welcomes the opportunity to visit away from the family for short periods and does not become homesick if surroundings prove congenial. He is not timid. He is peer-centered and at least pretends to prefer the peer pattern over the entire parental and adult code.

SCALE VALUE 9

Ego-ideal is influenced by a glamorized version of a young adult either visible or invisible to the child. He enjoys staying away from home overnight in congenial surroundings but may hesitate to go away for longer periods, although he usually enjoys it once he does it. He displays evidence of possessing the qualities of the level 10 child except for occasional episodes of *intermittent* lesser emotional independence.

SCALE VALUE 7–8

Ego-ideal may show some influence of adults in the community whose behavior is attractive to the child, but more prevalent is the influence of the glamorous invisible adult. The child often shows displeasure at the way one or both parents, teachers, and other authority figures structure his life, but his rebellion is largely confined to relatively minor misbehaviors, such as disregarding commands and instructions, "sassing" or arguing with a parent or other adult, making noise in church, playing in forbidden places with "forbidden" age-mates, going out of the immediate neighborhood for a brief time without reporting the fact to parents. His interests are definitely peer-centered and he constantly attempts to get his parents and other adults to let him substitute the peer pattern for the adult pattern, although he may be unsuccessful. He circulates freely about the community. He may meet new situations with hesitation and caution but will not show timidity.

SCALE VALUE 5–6

Definite evidence of rebelling against parents, though not of long standing. Sporadic efforts to structure his own life, falling back on parents for support. Peer-centered and not usually conforming to peer code. Enjoys a night or two away from home with people and surroundings he knows well. Ego-ideal of the glamorous adult type.

SCALE VALUE 3–4

Some slight evidence of attempts at planning and acting independent of parents, but generally continues to accept parental domination. Very little criticism of parents. Somewhat careless of parental rules and regulations about his play activities. Can stay away from home overnight with familiar people, but does not enjoy it. Ego-ideal limited to parents or to the unrealistic glamorous adult.

SCALE VALUE 2

Almost, but not quite, down to level 1. Evidence not clear or lacking on one or more areas.

SCALE VALUE 1 (LOW)

Child may play with age-mates at school or near his home but he prefers to be home-centered. Disinterested in or unaware of peer standards. No rebellion against parental restrictions. Incapable of being away from home overnight without becoming homesick. Extremely timid. Ego-ideal limited to parent or parent-surrogate.

Rating Scale on Achievement of Emotional Independence—Age 16–17

SCALE VALUE 10 (HIGH)

Ego-ideal is definitely influenced by young, visible adults in the community, or is a composite, realistic ideal that is the result of independent synthesis on the part of the adolescent. (May be mother, for girls). He has begun to build relationships with young adults. His pattern of resistance to parental and other adult authority is more discriminating as the result of applying rational thought to his own and others' experiences. If the parents warrant it, he accords respect and affection to the parents without believing it necessary to hide his feelings in order to present himself as an emotionally independent person. He makes his own decisions, although he probably seeks the advice and counsel of his parents and other adults. Absenting himself from home for considerable periods of time does not result in homesickness. When he has to oppose undue restrictions, he does so on rational grounds. He thinks of himself as an adult and wants to be considered one as often as possible.

SCALE VALUE 9

Adolescent shows evidence of possessing most of the qualities outlined in level 10 except for the fact that his recent development has been characterized by occasional episodes of *intermittent* lesser emotional independence.

SCALE VALUE 7–8

Ego-ideal shows some influence by young adults visible to the adolescent, who may also have begun to build relationships with some of these young adults. The adolescent's pattern of resistance to parental and other adult authority is showing signs of discriminating behavior based on the application of rational thought to his own and others' experiences. He tends as yet to be more successful in this respect with authority figures other than the parents. In times of stress, calling for objectivity of approach and discriminating behavior that takes into account the feelings of others, he still tends to disintegrate and behave rather crudely, although he appears quite self-sufficient, quite emotionally independent, during the process of ordinary living. He makes his own decisions, sometimes with a rather belligerent attitude, and often without taking advantage of the advice and counsel that parents or other adults could provide. Absenting himself from home does not cause him to become homesick, but it may cause him some anxiety over the state of his ties with the family circle. He is inclined to overstress the fact that he is on the threshold of adulthood in order to hide the feeling that he is not quite ready for this new stage of development. Has made his own choice of at least one of the following: employment, clothes, church, vacation activity.

SCALE VALUE 5–6

Ego-ideal is primarily a young adult visible to the child. Regardless of pressures from parents and other adult authorities, the adolescent makes a sustained effort to have his own decisions honored with respect to the type of clothing he wears, the food he eats, the activities in which he participates, the hobbies he pursues, the people with whom he associates, the books he reads and the movies he sees, the earning and saving and spending of money, and where he does and does not go. He welcomes the opportunity to visit away from the family for short periods and does not become homesick if surroundings prove congenial. He is not timid. He is peer-centered and at least pretends to substitute the entire peer pattern for the whole adult code. This may be a pretense because of real ambivalence concerning the desire to be emotionally independent. The rebellion he displays is irrational and undifferentiated, unless he happens to be living in a situation in which parents and other adults have considerable understanding of the emotional turmoil of adolescence and give ample opportunity for one to work through his own problems, all the while providing the essential support as unobtrusively as possible.

SCALE VALUE 3–4

Ego-ideal is often based on adults of the parental generation with frequently some influence of the glamorous adult being shown. The adolescent may show some attachment to a young adult in the community. Although the adolescent often shows displeasure at the way one or both parents, teachers, and other authority figures structure his life, his rebellion is largely confined to relatively minor misbehaviors, such as disregarding commands and instructions, "sassing" or arguing with a parent or other adult, making noise in church, playing in forbidden places with "forbidden" age-mates, loafing, going places without leaving word about where he can be found, destroying property, refusing to have anything to do with church activities. He *overtly* accepts parental structuring of his leisure-time activities, club memberships, choice of parttime jobs, expenditure of money earned or given him, absences from home, the food he eats, the clothes he wears, the books he reads, the movies he sees, and the special interest he pursues.

SCALE VALUE 2

Almost, but not quite down to level 1. Some evidence of intermittent attempts at independence.

SCALE VALUE 1 (LOW)

Ego-ideal is primarily a parent or parent-surrogate. The adolescent may or may not enjoy interacting with age-mates but definitely likes just as well spending his out-of-school time with his family. (However, if he does this because he has become an active member in a family business or is keeping house for his family, he should not be placed at this level.) He accepts the structuring of his life by one or both parents with little protest. He may or may not criticize his parents and other adults; he may or may not ignore or circumvent minor rules and restrictions laid down by them, but he will appear to be chronically unsuccessful at breaking away, or will show no signs of wanting to make the break toward independence. He is capable of staying away from home overnight if accompanied by a sibling, an acquaintance his own age, or a parent. He will appear definitely less emotionally independent than most thirteen-year-olds.

DEVELOPING CONSCIENCE, MORALITY, AND A SCALE OF VALUES

Operational Description of Success and Failure in this Task at Age 10–11

SUCCESS

Better than average rating on moral reputation. Examples well known of honesty, responsibility, loyalty, in the face of temptation. Above-average scores on test of moral judgment. Superior values indicated in behavior and in essays on ideals and ego-ideal. Flexible approach and constructive behavior in the peer-group on rules of games and controversies over group activities.

FAILURE

Low ratings on moral reputation. Examples well known of dishonesty, irresponsibility, disloyalty. Low score on test of moral judgment. Inferior values indicated in behavior and in essays on ideals and ego-ideal. Dependent on external authority in games where peers govern themselves; or dishonest and unfair in such games.

Rating Scale on Achievement of Task of Developing Conscience and Morality—Age 10–11

SCALE VALUE 10 (HIGH)

Upper quartile in character reputation. Flexible approach to peer games. Takes the lead in adjusting rules to the needs of the peer group, and lives up to the rules himself. Integrity never questioned by peers. Highly responsible. High discrimination of values. High concern over principles of what is fair, right, etc., in concrete situations. Highly consistent. Considerate of the feelings and privileges of age-mates even to own discomfort, if necessary. Always willing to accept obligations toward others. As obedient in the absence of authority as in the presence of authority; disobedience, if it should occur, would be accompanied by strong guilt feelings.

SCALE VALUE 9

Similar to level 10, except that subject falls below in one or two of the criteria considered essential to a rating of 10.

SCALE VALUE 7–8

Above average on character reputation. Above average in abiding by the rules of the game. Better than average discrimination of values. Generally somewhat concerned over moral value judgments in concrete situations: fairness-unfairness, right-wrong, etc. Usually considerate of the feelings and privileges of age-mates. Usually willing to accept obligations toward others. Usually obedient in the absence of authority; disobedience followed by considerable guilt.

SCALE VALUE 5–6

In second or third quartiles on measures of reputation. About average in abiding by the rules, i.e., subject's behavior would be questioned by his peers at slight provocation. Essays show about average development of values and consistency. Concern, under some situational prodding only, over what is fair, etc. Observations and interviews leave a neutral impression. Occasionally says things to hurt age-mates' feelings, but generally considerate. Accepts obligations toward others with some hesitancy. About average obedience in absence of authority; some guilt follows disobedience.

SCALE VALUE 3–4

Below average on character reputation. Below average in mastery of game and behavioral peer rules; inconsistent in obeying the rules known; integrity is openly questioned by peers. Development of values below average and somewhat inconsistent. Below average in concern over what is fair, right, etc. Inconsiderate more often than considerate of the feelings and privileges of age-mates. Accepts obligations toward others unwillingly, and then only if some pressure is exerted from the outside. Below average obedience to rules in the absence of authority; slight guilt follows disobedience. Behavior ratings by teachers below average.

SCALE VALUE 2

Similar to level 1, except that subject is higher on one or two of the criteria considered essential to a rating of 1.

SCALE VALUE 1 (LOW)

Lowest quartile on character reputation. Has either a) an over-rigid respect for rules as they are handed down by authority; or b) little feeling and little respect for rules. Evidence of lying, cheating, or of being irresponsible in general. Evidence, from observation or interviews, of poor value discrimination. Value system markedly inconsistent. Shows little or no concern over what is fair-unfair, right-wrong, etc.; has little or no feeling one way or the other. Ruled by impulse. Highly inconsiderate of the feelings and privileges of age-mates. Accepts obligations toward others only under duress. Usually does not "obey" in the absence of authority, and feels very little guilt for disobedience. Behavior ratings by teachers low. Essays show low or immature values in choosing the ego-ideal.

Rating Scale on Achievement of Task of Developing Conscience and Morality—Age 13–14

SCALE VALUE 10 (HIGH)

Upper quartile on character reputation. Above average on moral judgment test. Shows flexible discrimination in the moral sphere. Essays show altruism and service motives present and well integrated with lower-order values. Observation leaves strong positive impression of moral behavior. Evidence of guilt feelings and superego control over behavior and impulse. This person differs from those with lower ratings chiefly through his more *rational* control and order to his moral behavior and beliefs.

SCALE VALUE 9

Almost up to level 10, but evidence lacking or unclear on one or two points.

SCALE VALUE 7–8

Above average and may be very high on character reputation. Above average or very high on moral judgment test. Essays show fair consistency of values, with altruism and service motives clearly present. Observation leaves positive impression about moral behavior. Evidence of guilt and superego control over behavior and impulses. Controls over behavior and impulses tend to be rigid and nonrational. Moral judgment is accurate in ordinary situations, but not flexible enough to fit unusual situations.

SCALE VALUE 5–6

In second or third quartile on character reputation and moral judgment. Essays show some feeling for altruism and service values, though immature and inconsistent. Observation leaves neutral impression about moral behavior. No explicit incident of flagrant dishonesty or irresponsibility. Evidence of guilt over infraction of moral rules, or over impulses. (This person *may* still be quite heteronomous, in Piaget's sense, and in that case will show fairly high moral values with great dependence on adult authority.) Tends to be a conformer in moral matters.

SCALE VALUE 3–4

Below average on character reputation. Average or below on moral judgment test. Lack of moral discrimination shown on essays. Behavior ratings by teachers below average on moral traits. In playing games with peers, cannot be counted on to abide by the rules, though he may have helped frame them. Obeys ordinary rules of morality when adults are present to enforce them, but cannot be counted on to obey these rules of his own accord. Regarded as behaving morally mainly for expedient reasons.

SCALE VALUE 2

About as low as 1. Evidence doubtful on one or two points.

SCALE VALUE 1 (LOW)

Lowest quartile on character reputation. Lowest quartile on moral judgment test. Essays show values on a low or indiscriminating level. Values in behavior markedly inconsistent. Subject gets in trouble with authority and with peers. Behavior ratings by teachers very low on moral traits. Instances known of dishonesty, irresponsibility. Shows no feeling of respect for rules, regardless of their source.

Rating Scale on Achievement of Task of Developing Conscience and Morality—Age 16–17

SCALE VALUE 10 (HIGH)

Upper quartile on character reputation. Above average on test of moral judgment. Essays show a well-organized set of values with altruism or service values in the ascendant. Observation leaves strong positive impression of moral behavior. Can be counted on to obey rules of games without enforcement by a referee or judge.

Evidence of guilt feelings over behavior and impulse, with superego control. This person differs from those with lower ratings primarily through having a set of rational moral principles that he applies intelligently, and through having his conscience open to modification by reason.

SCALE VALUE 9

Almost up to level 10, but evidence lacking or uncertain in one or two respects.

SCALE VALUE 7–8

Above average and may be very high on character reputation. Above average in tests on values or moral beliefs. Essays show altruism and service motives integrated fairly well, though values lower on a moral scale may also be present. Observation leaves positive impression about moral behavior. Evidence of guilt feelings, and of superego control over behavior and impulse. Controls over impulse and behavior tend to be rigid and nonrational. Moral judgment not flexible enough to fit the unusual moral situation.

SCALE VALUE 5–6

In second or third quartile on character reputation. Above average on self-reports on moral beliefs. Essays show at least some feeling for altruism and service values, though perhaps immature and inconsistent. Observation of subject leaves neutral impression about moral behavior. No definite recent incidents of flagrant dishonesty or irresponsibility. Some evidence of guilt feelings over impulses or overt behavior. Tends to be a conformer in moral matters.

SCALE VALUE 3–4

Below average on character reputation. On essays shows materialistic values, or values that lack discrimination. Behavior not expressly hostile to public values, but often inconsistent. Cheats in games unless watched by referee, and takes advantage of situations when no one is around to enforce rules. In other words, does not have a consistent self-regulating moral code. Distinguished from ratings 1 and 2 mostly through being passively immoral and lacking "moral fiber" rather than actively and defiantly immoral.

SCALE VALUE 2

Almost as low as 1, but evidence not available or doubtful on one or two points.

SCALE VALUE 1 (LOW)

Lowest quartile on character reputation. Essays show values to be largely materialistic, and to lack discrimination. Behavior is highly inconsistent with respect to moral values; or if consistent at all, is consistently hostile, aggressive, and dishonest. Subject gets into trouble with authorities and with peers. Instances known of flagrant dishonesty or irresponsibility. No evidence of feelings of guilt over behavior or impulse.

DEVELOPING ESSENTIAL INTELLECTUAL SKILLS AND CONCEPTS

Operational Description of Success and Failure in this Task at Age 10–11

SUCCESS

Average or above in verbal ability, reading ability, arithmetic ability, as measured by achievement and aptitude tests. Ability to express self in writing and speaking average or above.

FAILURE

Below average in abilities and performances in the skills and concepts cited above.

Rating Scale on Achievement of Task of Developing Intellectual Skills and Concepts

Scores on a standard set of School Achievement Tests were averaged with school marks to secure ratings on the children at ages ten and thirteen. For age sixteen–seventeen, achievement scores were not available, and school grades alone were used. At this latter age several subjects had dropped out of school. They were rated at the level they held in school marks when they dropped out.

Reliability of the Ratings

Since the ratings (with the exception of those on Intellectual Skills) were made by judges on the basis of a variety of data, both quantitative and nonquantitative, it is important to know how reliable these ratings are. Reliability of the ratings was determined by computing the product-moment correlation coefficients for each pair of judges on all thirty subjects for each of the four developmental tasks.

TABLE I

Data on Reliability of Developmental Task Ratings

Developmental Tasks				
	AM	SR	EI	CMV
Average *r* of 6 interjudge correlations......	.82	.67	.67	.78
Highest interjudge *r*	.92	.75	.86	.86
Lowest interjudge *r*	.74	.61	.59	.71
Reliability of the average ratings of 8 judges (Spearman-Brown formula).............	.98	.94	.94	.97

Although there were eight judges, the reliability study was confined to four of these, so as to save work. This was considered to be justified, since an exhaustive reliability study of the ratings on personality variables had already been made for all eight judges, and it had been found that the average ratings of any one set of four judges had nearly the same reliability as the average ratings of any other set of four judges.

For each of the four developmental tasks rated by four judges, there were six interjudge correlations. Each coefficient of correlation represented the degree of agreement between two judges in their ratings of thirty children on a given developmental task at the ages of ten, thirteen, and sixteen. The average interjudge correlation and the high and low interjudge correlation coefficient are given for each of the four tasks in Table I.

These correlations were computed from the ratings *made before discussion of the cases*. Some ratings were modified as a result of discussion in the clinical conference, in the direction of greater agreement among judges.

Since there were eight judges doing the rating, the average of their ratings is more reliable than the rating of any one judge. Using the Spearman-Brown prophecy formula, we have computed the reliability of the pooled ratings, with results shown in the table. This level of reliability is as high as that of a good "objective" test. It is probably as high as the reliability of the ratings for achievement of intellectual skills, which depended in part upon the grades teachers gave to the children.

These data on the reliability of the ratings on achievement of developmental tasks show that we may proceed confidently to a study of the intercorrelations of the several developmental tasks.

CHAPTER 20

Interrelations of Developmental Tasks

WE HAVE PREDICTED that good or poor achievement of one developmental task will go together with good or poor achievement of other tasks. We can put this proposition to the test by studying the relationships between performance on the developmental tasks in the Prairie City group.

The simplest way to do this is to compute the product-moment correlation coefficients for each pair of developmental tasks at each age level. Table II shows the results of these computations. This table shows that there is a relation between every pair of tasks, and that this relation is much higher in some pairs than in others. Any coefficient of .6 or above will be called a "high" relationship. Five pairs of tasks show a consistently high relationship. Three pairs of tasks show a consistent relationship that is positive but low (.37 to .51). Two pairs are strongly related, but the degree of relationship varies from age to age.

The age-mates task is most highly related to the others. It is notable that getting along with age-mates is very highly related with the development of conscience, morality, and a scale of values. This task is also highly related to the development of intellectual skills.

The development of conscience, morality, and scale of values is also rather highly related to the other tasks. The lowest relationships, though they are still positive and undeniably present, are between emotional independence and the other tasks.

A second prediction was that good performance on a task at one age will be followed by good performance on this or similar tasks at later ages. This can be tested by computing the product-moment correlations between ratings on the tasks for ages ten and thirteen and ages thirteen and sixteen. Results of this computation are shown in Table III. Close relationships exist between performance at different age levels on a given task. The one task on which the relationship is not extremely high is that of learning an appropriate sex role, where correlations of performance at age ten with later ages are only fairly high.

TABLE II

Summary Table of Correlations of Tasks at Various Ages *

Correlations Consistently High from Age to Age	Age		
	10	13	16
Sex Role Task with Emotional Independence Task......	.68	.83	.79
Sex Role Task with Age-Mates Task................	.68	.82	.73
Emotional Independence Task with Age-Mates Task....	.57	.64	.63
Conscience, Morality, Values Task with Age-Mates Task	.80	.68	.78
Intellectual Skills Task with Age-Mates Task..........	.62	.63	.69
Correlations Consistently Low from Age to Age			
Sex Role Task with Intellectual Skills Task............	.45	.49	.42
Emotional Independence Task with Conscience, Morality, Values Task	.43	.38	.51
Emotional Independence Task with Intellectual Skills Task	.37	.45	.49
Correlations Inconsistent from Age to Age			
Sex Role Task with Conscience, Morality, Values Task..	.70	.53	.53
Conscience, Morality, Values Task with Intellectual Skills Task	.57	.78	.78

* For thirty subjects, an *r* of .36 is reliable at the .05 level, while an *r* of .46 is reliable at the .01 level.

TABLE III

Intercorrelations of Ratings of Thirty Subjects on Developmental Tasks at Each Age Level with the Other Two Age Levels

Age Levels	Sex Role Task	Emotional Independence Task	Conscience, Morality Values Task	Age-Mates Task	Intellectual Skills Task	Average r
r 10–13	.61	.83	.80	.75	.92	.78
r 13–16	.84	.95	.98	.94	.91	.92
r 10–16	.42	.79	.78	.71	.78	.70

A striking finding arising from Table III is that the relationships are closer between ages thirteen and sixteen than between ages ten and thirteen. This may be taken to mean that the level of achievement on these tasks is practically fixed by age thirteen, while there is a noticeable amount of fluctuation of performance on these tasks between ages ten and thirteen.

A third prediction was that some individuals use good achievement on one task to compensate for poor achievement on another. This hypothesis can be tested in a limited way by reference to Table II, since a very high intercorrelation between any two tasks would negate the hypothesis. The correlation coefficients of Table I are high, but not so high as to rule out a small amount of compensation. In other words, the number of people who are using good achievement in one task to compensate for poor achievement in another must be quite small.

To make a more careful test of this prediction, the number of individuals was counted who appear simultaneously in the top quarter on one or more tasks and in the lowest quarter on one or more tasks. Five out of thirty children did compensate, by this criterion. Only one of these five appears in the extreme quarters at all three ages, ten, thirteen, and sixteen. Thus the factor of compensation does not appear to be an important one in more than a very small number of cases. Furthermore, the kind of compensation that one might expect does not occur—namely, a high development of intellectual skills to compensate for low achievement on getting along with age-mates. The person who shows the most consistent compensation is high on intellectual skills and on conscience, morality, and values, and low on emotional independence and on learning an appropriate sex role. This pattern of compensation "makes sense" but it occurs in only one of the other four cases, and in that case only at age sixteen.

Developmental Tasks and Personality

The self, or the personality of the individual, is related to developmental tasks in two ways. For one thing, the self, together with society and the biological organism, defines and poses the developmental tasks for an individual. Thus the importance or urgency of a given developmental task depends to some extent upon the personality of the individual. For instance, getting along with age-mates may be an extremely important task for one child while another child may view this task with relative indifference. One child may succeed very well in the task and yet count it of little value; another child may succeed very poorly and also count it of no significance.

Beyond this, however, the personality of the individual is casually related to the level of his performance of one or another task. For example, the personality trait of a positive or friendly attitude toward the opposite sex should enable a boy or girl to get along better with his age-mates than he will if his attitude toward the opposite sex is negative or indifferent.

In order to find out what personality characteristics were definitely related to performance on the several developmental tasks, we studied the ratings of the special study group on forty-seven characteristics of personality at age sixteen. These personality ratings were made by the same clinical conference group that rated the children on their developmental tasks. While the total list of personality traits will not be repeated here, the tables that follow will give a good idea of the nature of these personality ratings.

The following procedure was used for studying the relations between developmental tasks and personality traits. Boys and girls were studied separately. By means of the chi-square test the hypothesis that there was more than a chance relation between high and low scores on a developmental task and high and low scores on each of the personality traits was put to the test. By this method it was found that certain traits were related consistently with certain developmental tasks.

Table IV shows the personality characteristics that are significantly related to the task of getting along with age-mates, for boys and for girls at age sixteen. The table shows how sure the relationship is, by citing three levels of probability. When P is .05, there are about five chances in a hundred that this relationship could have appeared in the data by chance. When P is .001, there is about one chance in a thousand that this relationship could have appeared by chance. We may be quite sure that all of the variables listed in Tables IV–VIII are certainly related to the developmental tasks, for the group of boys and girls under consideration.

Table IV shows that four characteristics are common to both boys and girls who have good peer relations. These are: acute, accurate observation of human behavior; rationality of behavior; a friendly feeling-tone toward the same-sex peers; and moral autonomy or self-direction. In addition there are certain factors unique to successful boys in this task. They are: a sociocentric concern or tendency to cooperate well in group activities and to sacrifice for group goals;

TABLE IV

Personality Traits Significantly Related to Age-Mates Task *

Personality Trait	Male	Female
Autonomy	***	**
Acute, accurate observation of human behavior	**	**
Attitude toward same-sex peers—Positive outer feeling-tone	**	**
Rationality of behavior	**	**
Sociocentric concern—Identifies with group goals	**	
Realistic assignment of responsibility for behavior of self and others	**	
Realistic, balanced self-perception	**	
Introspectiveness (inner)	**	
Attitude toward opposite-sex peers—Positive outer feeling-tone		**
Internal consistency of values (inner)		**
Trustfulness (outer)		**
Optimism (mainly inner)		**
Creativity (outer)		**
Functioning intelligence		*
Insight		*

* P-value of .05
** P-value of .01
*** P-value of .001

* Some of the traits are described as "outer" and some as "inner." When "outer" is used, it means that the trait is visible in behavior and the individual is conscious of it; when "inner" is used, it means that the trait is not readily visible, and can only be discerned by using projective tests or other methods of getting beneath the surface of behavior.

introspectiveness; a realistic view of self and others and accurate perception of the motives and behavior of oneself and of others. These suggest that the boy who succeeds well in this task is sincerely altruistic and fair in his dealings with others and understands and controls his own self.

Factors unique for the girl are of somewhat different nature. The girl, rather than the boy, has a positive and friendly feeling-tone toward the opposite sex. She has consistent life-aims and values and expresses them creatively and optimistically. She approaches people in a trustful way, at the same time with insight into their behavior.

Table IV, as well as the other tables, points to the very interesting fact that it takes different things in boys and in girls to make for success in the same developmental task.[1] Boys, it seems, are expected to show more freedom in expression of their feelings, and at the same time to understand and accept themselves realistically as well as to approach other people in the same way. Girls, however, are expected to be uniformly friendly, trusting of people, emotionally well-balanced, and more conforming than boys.

For the boys it seems quite important to have a strong primary identification with the father. (Several of the boys lacked this and were generally lower in achievement of the developmental tasks. All of the girls showed a strong primary attachment to the mother, and consequently it was not possible to observe the effect of a lack of this kind of relationship in girls.)

On all the tasks, emotional features, self-directed rational behavior, and understanding of self and others are more closely related to good performance than is intelligence. Even the task of achieving intellectual skills has a strong relation to emotional factors, particularly among girls.

Conclusions

The several developmental tasks *do* seem to be highly interrelated. Good achievement on one task tends to go with good achievement on other tasks. Poor achievement on one task presages poor achievement on other tasks. Good achievement at one age

[1] For a further development of this topic, see: Aileen Schoeppe, "Sex Differences in Adolescent Socialization," *Journal of Soc. Psychol.* 38 (1953) 175–185

tends to go with good achievement at later ages. The relationships are strong and undeniable, but not so strict as to rule out any possibility of improvement on the part of a poor performer as he grows older.

Together with the major theme of concordance among the tasks is a very minor theme of compensation. A very few children do well on some tasks and poorly on others. Only one out of thirty showed this pattern of compensation consistently at ages ten, thirteen, and sixteen. Four more showed it briefly and then fell into line with the general trend of consistency of performance from one task to another and from one age to another.

Performance on developmental tasks is related to personality primarily through emotional rather than intellectual factors. That is, attitudes toward people and certain other qualities of personality that are emotional in nature appear to be most firmly associated with developmental task performance. Boys differ from girls considerably in the personal characteristics that are connected with achievement of developmental tasks.

TABLE V

Personality Traits Significantly Related to Emotional Independence Task

Personality Trait	Male	Female
Insight	**	*
Sources of morality system—Same-sex parent	***	
Primary identification—Same-sex parent	**	
Attitude toward father as authority—Positive inner feeling	**	
Situationally-appropriate emotional reactivity (inner)	**	
Acute, accurate observation of human behavior		**
Attitude toward same-sex peers—Friendly outer feeling-tone		**
Attitude toward opposite-sex peers—Friendly outer feeling-tone		**
Autonomy		**
Rationality of behavior		**
Internal consistency of values (inner)		**
Trustfulness (outer)		**
Optimism (mainly inner)		**
Creativity (outer)		**
Functioning intelligence		*

TABLE VI

Personality Traits Significant for Sex Role Task

Personality Trait	Male	Female
Situationally-appropriate emotional reactivity (inner)....	**	
Primary identification—Same-sex parent................	**	
Sources of morality system—Same-sex parent..........	*	
Attitude toward opposite-sex peers—Outer feeling-tone....		***
Attitude toward mother as authority—Positive inner feeling		**

TABLE VII

Personality Traits Significantly Related to Conscience, Morality, Values Task

Personality Trait	Male	Female
Realistic assignment of responsibility for behavior of self and others	**	**
Realistic balanced self-perception......................	**	**
Emotional stability (outer)	**	**
Acute, accurate observation of human behavior..........	**	
Sociocentric locus of concern—Identifies with group goals..	**	
Autonomy	**	
Introspectiveness (inner)	**	
Conformity to external code		***
Potential intelligence		**
Superego strength (inner)............................		**
Functioning intelligence.............................		*
Insight		*

TABLE VIII

Personality Traits Significantly Related to Achievement of Intellectual Skills Task

Personality Trait	Male	Female
Functioning intelligence	**	*
Potential intelligence	**	
Internal consistency of values (inner)..................	**	
Creativity (outer)	**	
Optimism (mainly inner).............................	*	
Attitude toward same-sex peers—Positive outer feeling-tone		**
Emotional stability (outer)...........................		**

Case History of a Concept

I FIRST HEARD the term "developmental task" probably from the lips of Lawrence K. Frank about 1935. It was in one of many meetings of the staff of the "Adolescent Study" of the Progressive Education Association, a study of adolescent boys and girls carried on under the direction of Caroline Zachry in order to throw light on the problems and goals of secondary education.

Frank and Zachry probably got the kernel of the idea from Frankwood Williams, whose essays on the developmental problems of adolescence [1] were stressing the view that the most important things for an adolescent boy or girl to do are (1) to become emotionally independent of the family and (2) to achieve a good relationship with age-mates of the opposite sex.

Through intensive study and interpretation of the lives of adolescent youth Dr. Zachry and her colleagues came increasingly to see adolescence as a period of life when certain essential tasks must be mastered in socially acceptable ways by the boy or girl if he is to be happy and comfortable as an adolescent and later as an adult. Peter Blos, a member of the Adolescent Study Staff, was probably the first to refer to these problems of adjustment as "tasks" in print, in his book, *The Adolescent Personality*.[2] He did not use it as a key concept, but more as a useful illustrative term, and so it remained during the period of its use by the Adolescent Study group.

At about the same time, Dr. Erik Homburger Erikson, then at the Yale Institute of Human Relations, developed a very similar concept in his study of the development of children in their first few

[1] Frankwood Williams. *Adolescence—Studies in Mental Hygiene* (New York: Farrar and Rinehart, 1930)

[2] Peter Blos, *The Adolescent Personality* (New York: Appleton-Century, 1941) p. 275.

years. Using a biological analogy of the unique time and place for the development of the various organs in the human fetus, he suggested that there were equally crucial times for certain aspects of personality development in the first few years of life.[3] A time for leaving off sucking and commencing to eat solid food; a time for becoming interested in one's genitals and a time for resolving one's jealousy of one's parent of the same sex by identifying with him or her. Dr. Erikson was a consultant to the Adolescent Study Staff, and he made them familiar with these ideas of his.

Meanwhile, there was a controversy among educators over the use of the term "need" in stating the objectives of general education. The Progressive Education Association's Commission on Secondary School Curriculum had led off with a statement of the purpose of general education as "to meet the needs of individuals . . . in such ways as to promote the fullest possible realization of personal potentialities and the most effective participation in a democratic society." [4] Some thought this statement too child-centered, too much open to the interpretation that education was to take its directions from the whims of children, in spite of the PEA Commission's definition of a "need" as "personal-social" in character, rising out of the interaction of the individual and his society. Professor Boyd Bode abandoned his membership on the Commission on Secondary School Curriculum and blasted the "needs approach" in an article in the journal *Progressive Education*.[5]

Meanwhile, the concept of "developmental task" was being used occasionally in Workshops of the Progressive Education Association, and Daniel Prescott, Director of the Division of Child Study of the Commission on Teacher Education of the American Council on Education, began to use it frequently and to introduce it to his collaborators at the University of Chicago.

When I joined the faculty of the University of Chicago in 1941,

[3] Erik Homburger Erikson, "Problems of Infancy and Early Childhood," *Cyclopedia of Medicine, Surgery and Specialties* (Philadelphia: F. A. Davis Company, 1940), pp. 714–30.

[4] Commission on Secondary School Curriculum, *Science in General Education* (New York: Appleton-Century, 1937), p. 23.

[5] Boyd H. Bode, "The Concept of Needs in General Education," *Progressive Education*, 15 (1938), pp. 7–9.

the term was being used quite frequently in discussions of Prescott's group. At that time I began to teach a course in the psychology of adolescence, and I had to decide what terms to use in discussing the purposes of education in relation to adolescent development. Because I had seen so much misunderstanding result from the use of the equivocal term "needs" as a central concept in such discussions, I was determined to try out the term "developmental task" instead. I defined the purpose of education as to help the young person achieve his developmental tasks in a personally and socially satisfactory way, and I organized the lectures of the course around a series of *developmental tasks* of adolescence.

Prescott was using the concept increasingly in his writing during 1941 and 1942, and during the same years he and Fritz Redl and I collaborated on a chapter for the North Central Association's book, *General Education in the American High School*.[6] This was the first publication to give the concept a central role.

In the summer of 1941, the University of Chicago Workshop in Human Development and Education had as the topic of one of its seminar groups, "Developmental Tasks of Adolescents" under the leadership of Dr. Caroline Tryon. This topic immediately became a very popular one, especially for teachers who were beginning the serious study of child development as part of their in-service training. No workshop could be held in the human development field without one or more groups studying "developmental tasks."

Dr. Tryon, a member of the staff of the Division of Child Development of the Commission on Teacher Education, and formerly a staff member of the Adolescent Study of the University of California, also made effective use of the concept in her chapter in the yearbook on *Adolescence* of the National Society for the Study of Education.[7]

In the autumn of 1943, I was at Harvard University serving as a consultant to the Harvard Committee on the Objectives of Edu-

---

[6] B. L. Johnson, Ed., *General Education in the American High School* (Chicago: Scott, Foresman, 1942), Chapter 4.

[7] National Society for the Study of Education, 43rd Yearbook, Part I. *Adolescence*. (Chicago: Department of Education, University of Chicago, 1944), Chapter 12.

cation in a Free Society. For the use of that committee I wrote a thirty-five-page report entitled "Developmental Tasks and General Education." When copies of this report were distributed to my class in adolescent psychology the class members found them interesting and told so many of their friends, who asked for copies, that my supply was soon exhausted. Then a staff member of the U.S. Department of Agriculture saw a copy and asked permission to mimeograph copies for the use of 4-H Club leaders.

Stephen M. Corey wrote a very useful chapter for the John Dewey Society Yearbook of 1946,[8] discussing the high-school program in relation to developmental tasks of adolescents.

Then, in 1947–48, I worked with others on a sequence of three courses in the field of human development, to trace the development of the human individual from the womb to the grave. Here I found the developmental task concept surprisingly useful in organizing material on human development in adulthood and old age.

Quite extensive use of the developmental task concept was made in the National Conference on Family Life, of 1948, by the Committee on Dynamics of Family Interaction with Evelyn Millis Duvall and Reuben Hill as co-chairmen. In the report of this committee, the career of the family is followed from its beginning in marriage to its end in the death of husband or wife, by describing the "developmental tasks, goals, and responsibilities" of the various family members and the ways by which society might aid people to achieve their developmental tasks better. This committee made a step forward in the use of the concept by showing how each member of the younger, middle, and older generations in the family has his own developmental tasks, and how the successful achievements of one person's tasks is dependent on and contributory to the successful achievement by others in the family of their appropriate tasks.

An interesting and important development of the concept was made by Caroline Tryon and Jesse Lilienthal in 1949 when they identified *ten areas of growth* and defined the developmental tasks of each area at five stages of growth from infancy to late adoles-

[8] H. Caswell, ed., *The American High School* (New York: Harpers, 1946), Chapter 5.

cence.[9] They made clear the idea that developmental tasks come in coherent series within areas of growth.

The developmental task concept occupies middle ground between the two opposed theories of education: the theory of freedom—that the child will develop best if left as free as possible, and the theory of constraint—that the child must learn to become a worthy responsible adult through restraints imposed by his society. A developmental task is midway between an individual need and a societal demand. It partakes of the nature of both. Accordingly, it is a useful concept for students who would relate human behavior to the problems of education—useful without, I hope, obscuring important issues in educational theory.

[9] National Education Association: Association for Supervision and Curriculum Development. *Fostering Mental Health in Our Schools.* Chapters 6 and 7, by Caroline Tryon and Jesse W. Lilienthal, III (Washington, D. C.: National Education Association, 1950).

Acknowledgments

IN THE EPILOGUE I have expressed my indebtedness to a number of colleagues with whom I have been associated in the use and development of the developmental task concept—Lawrence K. Frank, Caroline Zachry, Erik Erikson, Peter Blos, Daniel Prescott, Fritz Redl, Stephen Corey, Caroline Tryon, Evelyn Duvall, and Reuben Hill. To Caroline Tryon I owe a special debt. She and her students were making specially significant adaptations of the concept, and if it had not been for her untimely death she would have added some important new writings on the subject.

In the preparation of this book I have had the pleasure of drawing on the work of three younger colleagues. Dr. Aileen Schoeppe made excellent use of our data on the achievement of developmental tasks by Prairie City boys and girls in writing her doctoral dissertation, from which I have drawn the substance of Chapters 19 and 20. Ruth Nedelsky worked with me for almost a year on problems of middle childhood, and she wrote three sensitive and thoughtful papers on the peer group and on intellectual development during middle childhood. These papers are being published by her, and I have drawn freely on them for Chapters 5, 6, and 7. Dr. Douglas More and I worked together on a memorandum for the Educational Testing Service describing the educational outcomes of elementary education in terms of developmental tasks. A good deal of this memorandum is reproduced in Chapter 8. I am indebted to the Educational Testing Service for the stimulation and opportunity to do this work.

The empirical study of developmental tasks, reported in Part Five, was done as part of our Study of Moral Character, in which a number of colleagues and students have worked. I am especially indebted to the Clinical Conference Group, whose ratings on Prairie City children were used in the empirical study. Members of the Clinical Conference Group were: James Abegglen, Clara Berghofer, Ruth Cooper, Gerald Handel, Walter Hartmann, Jesse Lilienthal, Wilma Lux, Douglas More, Robert Peck, Jeremy Sarchet, and Stuart Wright. Bettie Belk assisted me in organizing the data on the intellectual development of the group, and Dr. Robert DeHaan worked up the material on the "Case of Elsie."

The case studies and the illustrations used in this book have come from a variety of sources, and no one case study represents a particular individual. Any resemblance to any individual, living or dead, is coincidental.

R. J. H.

Index